Translating Chinese Cultu

Translating Chinese Culture is an innovative and comprehensive coursebook that addresses the issue of translating concepts of culture. Based on the framework of schema building, the course offers helpful guidance on how to get inside the mind of the Chinese author, how to understand what he or she is telling the Chinese-speaking audience, and how to convey this to an English-speaking audience.

A wide range of authentic texts relating to different aspects of Chinese culture and aesthetics is presented throughout, followed by close reading discussions of how these practices are executed and how the aesthetics are perceived among Chinese artists, writers and readers. Also taken into consideration are the mode, audience and destination of the texts. Ideas are applied from linguistics and translation studies and each discussion is reinforced with a wide variety of practical and engaging exercises.

Thought-provoking yet highly accessible, *Translating Chinese Culture* is essential reading for advanced undergraduates and postgraduate students of translation and Chinese studies. It will also appeal to a wide range of language students and tutors through its stimulating discussion of the principles and purposes of translation.

Valerie Pellatt, Eric T. Liu and **Yalta Ya-Yun Chen** are all based at Newcastle University, UK. Valerie Pellatt and Yalta Ya-Yun Chen are both Lecturers in Chinese Translation and Interpreting Studies and Eric T. Liu is Senior Lecturer and Head of Translation and Interpreting Studies.

'This is a wonderfully conceived book which I cannot wait to have on my bookshelf and use in my advanced-level translation classes. As in their previous works, the authors have a knack for selecting the most relevant and theoretically interesting topics in Chinese–English translation, this time exploring the issues of literary translation, artistic translation, translation of irony and humour, translation for the stage, and others – all pertinent issues that are not only relevant for Chinese–English translation, but also shine a light on the general theory of translation.

Through a work like this, the student of Chinese–English translation will better appreciate issues in translation theory, the canonical works of which often do not give examples from Chinese. The furnishing of examples (authentic texts and translations) from different fields to illustrate each theoretical point is also immensely useful. The authors provide wonderful close readings of each text that provide context and aid in the thinking process for translation, staying true to the book's subtitle "The Process of Chinese–English Translation" – this, to me, is the most attractive, most useful, and the best written part of this book.'

Chris Wen-Chao Li, *San Francisco State University, USA*

Translating Chinese Culture

The Process of Chinese–English Translation

**Valerie Pellatt, Eric T. Liu and
Yalta Ya-Yun Chen**

LONDON AND NEW YORK

First published 2014
by Routledge
2 Park Square, Milton Park, Abingdon, Oxon OX14 4RN

and by Routledge
711 Third Avenue, New York, NY 10017

Routledge is an imprint of the Taylor & Francis Group, an informa business

© 2014 Valerie Pellatt, Eric T. Liu and Yalta Ya-Yun Chen

The right of Valerie Pellatt, Eric T. Liu and Yalta Ya-Yun Chen to be identified as the authors of this work has been asserted by them in accordance with sections 77 and 78 of the Copyright, Designs and Patents Act 1988.

British Library Cataloguing in Publication Data
A catalogue record for this book is available from the British Library

Library of Congress Cataloging in Publication Data
Pellatt, Valerie.
Translating Chinese culture : the process of Chinese–English translation /
Valerie Pellatt, Eric T. Liu, Yalta Ya-Yun Chen.
pages cm.
1. Chinese language--Translating into English. 2. Language and culture--
China. 3. China--Languages. I. Liu, Eric., author. II. Chen, Yalta Ya-Yun.,
author. III. Title.
PL1277.P47 2014
495.18'0221--dc23
2013023251

ISBN: 978-0-415-69312-7 (hbk)
ISBN: 978-0-415-69313-4 (pbk)
ISBN: 978-1-315-85702-2 (ebk)

Typeset in Times New Roman
by Taylor & Francis Books

MIX
Paper from
responsible sources
FSC
www.fsc.org   FSC® C013604

Printed and bound by CPI Group (UK) Ltd, Croydon, CR0 4YY

Contents

Acknowledgements

The authors and publishers would like to thank the following people and institutions for permission to reproduce copyright material. Every effort has been made to trace copyright holders, but in a few cases this has not been possible. Any omissions brought to our attention will be remedied in future. Awakening Foundation (婦女新知基金會出版部) for extracts from *Women's Writing* (女書); Birgit Hopfener for extracts from her essay on Lin Tianmao in Grosenick and Schübbe; Chen Xuan for use of her blog 'Lost Values' (失落的价值); Hsin Pei and his team of translators for extracts from *How to Copy Sutras and Enjoy it*; Jonathan Stalling and Counterpath for extracts from *Yingelishi*; Liao Jielian and MCCM for material from *Chinese Font Designers after 1949* (一九四九年後中國字體設計人); Pul'ka for her previously unpublished rap-style version of *Peach Blossom Spring*; Wan Fang for allowing us to translate 有一种毒药.

Introduction

Chinese, translatability, and the problem of linguistic determinism

In *Thinking Chinese Translation* we emphasised schema development: that is deep understanding of the source text and the re-structuring of its formal and content schema in the target text. We organised the book on the basis of text type: tackling texts that ranged from very simple, formulaic texts to complex, abstract texts – and in so doing, covered a range of areas of expertise, such as law, science and technology, medicine, literature. In this book we will address the challenges of translation of what also might be termed areas of expertise, but with an emphasis on the culture and the arts of China. We will look at texts that relate to indigenous Chinese practices and aesthetics, discussing how these practices are executed and how the aesthetics are perceived among Chinese artists, writers and readers, taking into consideration the mode, audience and destination of the translated texts. Alongside discussion of these areas of interest, we will apply ideas from linguistics and translation studies that may be of use to the practising translator.

In *Thinking Chinese Translation*, we adumbrated the notion of understanding the text in a way that goes beyond the words. The debate over 'sense for sense' and 'word for word' translation has exercised the minds of linguists in Europe since the time of Cicero, in the first century BC (Munday 2001: 19–20). It is also evident that in China, translators went through phases of differing approaches (Hung and Pollard 1998: 368). It goes without saying that in many cases a word for word rendition may also supply sense for sense. Sense implies meaning, rather than the superficiality of the words. We can go further, and use the same word 'sense' to apply to the five senses: every text comes from the writer and appeals to the reader physically as well as intellectually. Thinking is not necessarily verbal, though language is a powerful vehicle of thought, and, as we pointed out in *Thinking Chinese Translation*, thoughts expressed in language are often thoughts about non-linguistic processes. An undergraduate student recently writing from China remarked that 'the Chinese think differently', and Chinese students frequently tell us that this is so. Is this really the case and, if so, differently from what or from whom? Is it really the case that superficial differences in language and behaviour give the impression that 'Chinese think differently'? We would certainly admit to cultural differences between, for example, the British and the Chinese, but are those differences greater than those between the French and the British, or the Chinese and the Indians? To what extent is a cultural difference symptomatic of a difference in cognitive processes? Is an ideological difference actually just a variation based on meteorological or climatic difference? The Chinese language is distinctive, but shares many of its characteristics (topic-dominant sentences, absence of grammatical gender, number and tense, and so on) with other languages around the world.

The notion of untranslatability, and the conviction of many native Chinese speakers that Chinese concepts are unique, different, or have an 'inner logic' begs the question of linguistic determinism. This is the notion that language determines or structures, to a greater or lesser degree, the way humans think. A similar, but weaker theory, that language influences thought, is known as linguistic relativity, and is often attributed to Benjamin Whorf (Carroll 1956).

There is no firm evidence that either linguistic determinism or linguistic relativity are workable theories, though there may be more than a germ of truth in both, since much thought is channelled through language and vice versa. There exists a perception that the 'visual' nature of Chinese characters makes the meaning directly accessible visually. Yet researchers claim that between two-thirds (de Francis 1984) and 80 per cent (Gong 2001) of Chinese characters are based on sound rather than visual image and that reading is processed via phonological codes (Tzeng and Hung 1981). Rayner and Pollatsek (1989: 99) propose that reading is a 'culture-free cognitive activity'. Ash shows how problematic the Sapir-Whorf hypothesis may be: if linguistic determinism were a workable theory, concepts would be untranslatable (Ash 1999). Yet translators deal with difficult concepts on a daily basis, and untranslatability happens in only rare cases.

Patterns of language in Chinese text necessarily differ from those of other languages, and there are both recognised, conventional ways of dealing with the discrepancies, and creative ways of dealing with them. If patterns of thought in Chinese texts are truly different from 'other' or 'Western' patterns of thought, should the translator take the differences into consideration? Is this a case for awareness, rather than overt action?

Nord observes that 'translating means comparing cultures'. She goes further, saying that 'everything we observe as being different from our own culture is, for us, specific to the other culture' (Nord 1997/2001: 34). What is omitted from this generalisation is that comparison does not entail contrast, and at the same time, culture may entail convention or habit, but it does not entail rigidity and regulation. If we set out to contrast, and seek for unwavering consistency in 'culture-specificity', we may be setting up false barriers. Nord's example of coffee drinking is a case in point (ibid.: 34): the drinking of coffee is common, but the time and circumstance differ between, for example, the British Isles, Spain and Germany. A more detailed investigation would reveal not only cultural differences in the time and perhaps the accompaniments of coffee within nations and among classes, but also similarities between nations. Coffee drinking is cultural, and also economic, and the habits associated with it change with world markets: in China 40 years ago, it was virtually impossible to buy coffee, but now Chinese cities boast locally run and multi-national coffee shops where trendy business people and intellectuals gather. Taiwan, which has a Chinese-speaking culture and, as might be expected, a strong tradition of tea drinking, also has a long tradition of coffee shops owed to a multiplicity of foreign and colonial influences. Would the translation of coffee drinking as a cultural phenomenon be problematic? Probably not, for it is as universal as it is diverse, and readers will be capable of adjusting their schemata as required.

There has been much discussion among Chinese translatologists since the 1980s about the nature of Chinese thought and language, as scholars first espoused 'Western' theories of and approaches to translation, then either worked to develop new and appropriate theories, or reacted against the 'Western' theories. There is a consciousness among a significant number of translation scholars in the People's Republic of China that 'Western' theories are not fit for the purpose of Chinese translation. Various reasons are given, but these may be summed up in the notion of 'uniqueness': the belief that Chinese language, history and culture, and thus the way of thinking, are unlike any other, and that theory and practice must be carried out in an exclusively Chinese way. Tan, an advocate of ethnoconvergence, shows how problematic this notion is, for 'Chineseness' is a vague and multi-faceted notion (2009: 291). But he identifies five distinctive features of Chinese translation approaches (2009: 294): pragmatism (which he notes is also a characteristic of other traditions); reliance on cultural heritage; preoccupation with 信 *xin* ('fidelity': itself a very vague term); intuitive thinking (as opposed to analytical discussion) and terseness, a common feature of Chinese discourse, which may entail polysemy, and thus vagueness and even ambiguity (Tan 2009: 292–95). There is a school of thought that emphasises that 'Chinese translation ... is a unique system which must be protected from outside influences' (Tan 2009: 295). To many outsiders the 'protectionist' attitude that Tan describes would look like an extension of stereotypical Chinese attitudes of a bygone age. This type of thinking on translation studies could be motivated by political concerns and may have developed in line with the 'China can say no' phenomenon of the 1990s (Song and Qiao 1996). Guo believes that it is necessary to 'understand Chinese translation from a political point of view' (Guo 2009: 249). Mao Sihui maintains that 'Maoist thought shapes and continues to shape many Chinese as ideological consumers rather than critical thinkers' (Mao 2009: 266). She suggests that Chinese scholars should engage more actively with scholars from other countries in discussions and reflections on translation.

While it may not be useful or appropriate to subscribe to Sapir-Whorfian approaches to Chinese thought and language, it is certainly the case that a culture is expressed and discussed through the medium of language, and that language reflects the historical, geographical, social and ideological moulding of a people. Well-educated Chinese are deeply aware of certain foundations of their culture: of thousands of years of apparently uninterrupted recorded history, of the implicitness of their marvellously succinct classical written language, of China's historical excellence in invention and technology and the ability of its youth in areas such as mathematics (Pellatt 2007: 31). Characteristic Chinese cultural phenomena, such as the writing system and medical lore, sometimes lead to a belief that China 'is unique' and that its language and cultural practices are 'unique'. Notions of 'Western thought' as explicit, logical, analytical, patterned, even symmetrical, contrasting with notions of Chinese thought and language as implicit, intuitive, emotional and having 'inner logic', appear frequently in meta-China discourses, both among well-known, knowledgeable writers, and among students.

The notion, sense or claim of China's uniqueness may, by some scholars, be ascribed to Orientalist, or to Occidentalist attitudes. One of Said's definitions of Orientalism is 'a way of coming to terms with the Orient that is based on the Orient's special place in European Western experience' (Said 1978/2003). Chen suggests that Occidentalism may be 'a counter-discourse, a counter-memory and a counter-Other to Said's Orientalism' (1995/2002: 6). These are quite mild definitions of the way in which we see the Other. Buruma's and Margalit's definition of Occidentalism is much less restrained: it is a 'dehumanising picture of the west painted by its enemies ... [a] cluster of prejudices' (2005: 3). Said shows in his writing that Orientalist attitudes on the part of colonisers, merchants and explorers were far more, and far more sinister than simply 'coming to terms'. In effect, Europeans who visited and wrote about anywhere east of Istanbul re-structured and re-wrote those places, cultures and people within their own schemata of what life should be like. For some of them 'the East' spelled romance and beauty, for others it connoted a hotbed of flies, disease and corruption. The counter-discourse saw the West as urban, modern, and glamorous, or conversely as soulless and materialistic (Buruma and Margalit 2005: 22). There is always a temptation, or perhaps an intuition, to regard our ethnocentric selves as not only different, but unique.

This idea of uniqueness leads in turn to the idea of inaccessibility; inexperienced Chinese student translators on the one hand and champions of literature on the other often claim that certain items are 'untranslatable' or that 'foreigners would not understand'. What is it that foreigners would not understand – the words, the ideas, or the customary attitudes and behaviours? Much of what human beings do and say is common, though couched in culture-specific guise. One of the greatest intangible problems for a translator is knowing how much or how little the target audience has in common with the source audience, and how much they know about the source culture. Given that we do not always know who our audience is, judging the degree to which we do or do not explicitate the thoughts of the author is a high-risk business. We run two risks: one is that we do not give enough information, and leave our audience in the dark; the other is that we give too much information, and our audience feels deprived of the pleasure of working out the message, and possibly even in some measure patronised. In our global world, ethnoconvergence has been on the agenda for some time. We can no longer assume that the source culture is totally foreign to target readers, but we must be aware that they are not fully conversant with all the idiomaticity of the source culture and language.

While it is possible to look at the theory of translation from a 'generalist', non-language-specific point of view, the reality is that all translation, even of aspects such as paratext, is inextricably linked to at least two languages, two cultures, two political systems and probably multiple ways of thinking. When translating into Chinese, the demands of the target audience, the client and monitoring or censoring bodies may be paramount, and require a character-istically Chinese approach. In the case of translation out of Chinese, these demands are parallel, but specifically targeted towards the needs of the 'foreign' reader or client. Jin says: 'loyalty to the author is meaningless if it does not co-exist with a loyalty to the receptor' (Jin 1989: 163), a standpoint that is supported by many, including Leppihalme, who states 'It is no excuse that a text is "correctly" translated, if the target readers cannot understand it' (1997: ix), in other words, comprehensibility of a translated text is of paramount importance.

A text in Chinese will have been written by a writer who, to a greater or lesser extent, will be steeped in Chinese climate, Chinese culture, Chinese attitudes, Chinese ways of doing things. While a British chef serving fish may do so with a fish-slice or spatula, a Chinese chef will perform the same task with chopsticks. Both chefs are thinking while they carry out the operation: their brain cells are directing their hands in the manipulation of the serving implements and the fish. They are doing exactly the same thing in a super-ficially different way. The fish has been caught, cooked and presented in very similar fashion, but is served up to its consumers somewhat differently. Kingsolver tells an interesting cross-cultural parable in *The Poisonwood Bible*. An American missionary in the Congo insists on sowing his seeds in flat seedbeds, ignoring the advice of his housekeeper to use raised seedbeds. Inevitably, the seedlings are washed away in the rains (Kingsolver 1999/2007: 47). This is a telling account of a fundamental, universal, human activity, which must be implemented according to varying climatic conditions, and thus becomes, on the surface, a 'culture-specific' activity. Deep down, it is driven by the universal of common sense. Lakoff and Johnson remind us that the metaphors on which we construct our conceptual system 'emerge from our constant spatial experience, that is our interaction with the physical environment' (Lakoff and Johnson 1980: 57).

It is well known that apparently universal sensual or motor experiences can differ widely in the way they are reported, in speech and writing, by members of different cultural groups. This includes those who speak a different lan-guage. For example, in Chinese, 黄 may express the colour of a river in spate (a kind of rich cappuccino), the colour of a European's hair (anything from blonde to brunette) or the colour of a person's skin (flesh colour). Yet it may also be lemon, cadmium, gold, or shades of orange. A glance at a British or American paint merchant's catalogue will show a colour spectrum that is rich, refined and foreign to the non-expert native-speaker user, demonstrating that colours have a different spectrum and range for users of distinct areas of expertise within the same language culture. Numbers are also an area of language in which there are cultural differences: some peoples, such as the Munduruku in South America count '1, 2, 3, 4, handful' – they have no need in their hunter-gatherer society for any measure beyond that. They know their children and animals individually and intimately and therefore do not need to count them. It has been shown, by Bellos for example, that languages that lack numbers tend to assess and express relationships (greater than or less than) rather than specific amounts (Bellos 2010: 34). These are culturally specific ways of seeing, that is, thinking. A group of five great Russian composers is known as 'the mighty handful': Balakirev, Cui, Mussorgsky, Rimsky-Korsakov and Borodin. In China such a group would almost certainly be 'the mighty five'. Yet number culture changes across generations: maths is taught in new ways and new tools are introduced as time goes by. The Chinese character numbers common in business names, for example 'Third Sister Hair Salon' (三姐理髮店) are gradually giving way to Arabic numerals in names such as '85° Coffee' (85° 咖啡), or '888 Spectacles' (888 眼镜), a visual pun indicating a shop that offers three pairs of spectacles for the price of two.

It is not only visual image that has a wide range of interpretation. Fragrances, tactile sensations, sounds, including music, and, perhaps most 'ethnocentric' of all, the taste of each culture's exclusive and special food, are of infinite variety. Language is a wonderful currency. When it cannot be understood it becomes its own tool of understanding: it defines, and explains. Most ideas and most words are translatable. Most of what we do, feel and think as human beings is common to us all, differing in the details of communication, but having a common core. It is instructive to note that Chiang Yee, who was one of the most important, popular and reader-friendly twentieth-century interpreters of Chinese culture to the West, 'playfully undermined' arbitrary barriers to understanding, and was able to 'draw out differences in similarities – and similarities in differences – between the East and the West' (Zheng in Introduction to Chiang 2004: xvi).

A note on the reader

By using the perceived similarities to undermine perceived differences, the translator can help the reader towards an informed understanding of the text. In the study and discussion of translation, the reader has not gone unnoticed, and deservedly is becoming more important to translatologists. Readers of translations span a spectrum, from those who do not read any foreign language, and urgently need a translation for instrumental purposes, such as a manual, to those who, in spite of their proficiency in the target language, choose to read a translation in order to exercise their powers of critical analysis. The 'target audience', as we so aggressively label them, is potentially far more varied and interesting, and has far more complex needs and wants than the source text author or the go-between translator. Some scholars take sides and debate in terms of extremes, particularly it seems, those who prefer author-oriented, foreignised approaches, such as Nabokov and Venuti. In practical terms, however, the translator working towards a deadline will be looking for balance, creating a work that is not necessarily easy to read: no reader has a right to expect that from any author, and no author has a responsibility to write 'easy reading'. Rather, the translator will be working towards a text that is coherent, unambiguous (unless required to be ambiguous) and holds the readers' interest. Burgess's *Clockwork Orange* is not an easy read: it depicts violence, it requires a modest knowledge of Slavic languages for a reader to understand the argot, but it is fascinating. Joyce's *Ulysses,* similarly, is in parts elegant, in parts rude and crude and in parts full of linguistic conundrums, but rarely easy to read. The work of Gao Xingjian, for example, *Soul Mountain* (灵山), readily conjures images for the reader, but may present linguistic challenges. A reader would not necessarily expect elegance or ease of reading in either the source text or the translation of these works, and a translator would not be expected to produce an 'easy' text.

Chan cites Barthes's notion that texts within a culture are 'pleasurable' and 'comfortable': 'readers are supposed to participate in the imagined text-world', and 'the reader is also the writer of the text that he or she reads' (Chan 2010: 28–29). Pleasure and comfort are not the requirements of every reader, or of every text, but participation and stimulation are.

Talking on BBC Radio Four about the inclusion of culture-specific items and terms in her fiction, Arundhati Roy said that she had never been pressurised [by publishers] to explain or delete material in her work. She believes that a writer can explain without doing so obviously, by means of their skills, and that readers will 'walk that extra mile' to understand (Roy 2011).

Roy knows that the magic of reading lies in the reader's ability to infer, and that this comes from the reader's existing schema, the schema developed during the course of the text, and the formal schema that the text provides in terms of context. If we read the words 'he wore a *magua* over his *changpao,* which had become muddied from contact with his shoes' we can infer the following: both italicised items are obviously garments, and probably garments for men; a *changpao* must be long, if in contact with his shoes, and a *magua* probably shorter, since it is not said to be muddied. This inference can be made from the text. We add another layer of inference from our general knowledge, this time visual, of Chinese gentlemen of a certain period wearing long, plain gowns, with a shortish jacket on top. The reader would understand without explanation, but might be interested to know exactly what the Chinese words mean. Alternatively, the use of the English words 'jacket' and 'gown', in conjunction with the schema of Chinese male clothing, would also trigger an accurate image.

There may be contexts in which the reader does need help. Information contained in data analysis in a scientific paper, or mechanical processes in a patent application, for example, must be as full as possible. Leppihalme states: 'The conception of a reasonably well-informed or competent readership who are to be "let in" to share the experience may well fail to apply in an intercultural situation, with secondary receivers' (Leppihalme 1997: 23). But on the whole, readers read because they want to know more, and they are prepared for novelty, and prepared to put some effort into solving the puzzles that reading necessarily brings with it. In some fields, such as fiction, articles, essays and poems, it can be quite insulting for the reader to be given too much information. Leppihalme acknowledges the pro-active role of the reader:

> In literary studies there has been a 'return of the reader' (Freund, 1987), which sees the reader (even the reader of translations) not just as a passive receiver of instruction and education but as a participator, a co-author almost, or even the 'real author' (Genette, 1980: 262) without whose interpretation a text does not exist.
>
> (Leppihalme 1997: 21)

Nord observes that 'different receivers (or even the same receiver at different times) find different meanings in the same linguistic material offered by the text' (Nord 1997/2001: 31). Chan is at pains to argue that readers need greater assistance when reading a translated novel, because even if the translation manages to bridge the linguistic boundaries, the cultural barrier remains (Chan 2010: 40). There is a growing feeling among some translators that a preface or introduction that explains the translator's choices should be provided as part of the paratext of a translated work (McRae 2012). Yet we must be careful not to go too far in the assumption that a reader needs help. Every reading experience is a potential learning experience: this is why we read. We are looking for more than we find in our own lives, and we are therefore prepared for novelty and for challenge in our reading.

Reiss and Vermeer (1984) coined the useful term 'skopos' or purpose. A text is always written for a purpose, and that purpose involves the reader and his or her requirements. Nord explained this as follows:

> Every text is made meaningful by its receiver and for its receiver. Different receivers (or even the same receiver at different times) find different meanings in the same linguistic material offered by the text. We might even say that a text is as many texts as there are receivers.
>
> (Nord 1997/2001: 31)

This is borne out in translation versions: if a text is translated by 100 translators, whatever the language pair, there will be 100 widely varying, correct versions.

Clients, as Nord points out, do not always give an explicit or correct brief: an agent may not know for sure the purpose or 'skopos' of the translation required (Nord 1997/2001: 30). We do not know for certain who the reader is. We can target a certain kind of reader, but there is no guarantee that that kind of reader will be the actual recipient, or that they will react in the way we expect. Readers change books. The history of the children's book in Europe is an excellent example of this. Until quite late in the nineteenth century, children in Europe learned to read from alphabets and 'primers', and would go straight on to adult books. The great Chinese classics aimed at teaching children to read, the *Three Character Classic* (三字经), the *Hundred Family Names* (百家姓) and the *Thousand Character Classic* (千字文) contain highly esoteric, inaccessible language. The three texts, collectively known as 'three, hundred, thousand' are still available in bookshops today and apparently popular. Students nowadays will often say that they learned excerpts from these classics, but often admit that they did not understand them until they grew up.

Structure and rationale of the book

This volume tackles some creative and artistic areas of Chinese life not addressed in *Thinking Chinese Translation*. Each chapter begins with a general introduction to the subject matter. Our readers, no doubt, are well versed in Chinese culture, but it is sometimes useful for us as translators to step back and be reminded of the world beyond the words, and the significance and impact of the source text in its broad cultural context. Each chapter contains examples for which suggested or possible translations are provided. Each chapter is rounded off with one or two practical exercises. These are not necessarily translations per se, but tasks designed to get the novice translator thinking about ways, means, ends, and not least, subject matter. In cases where the practical exercises are translation tasks, a suggested solution is provided in the Appendix.

We go first to matters that represent the very roots of Chinese national and individual identity. Chapter 1 deals with the discourse of the visual arts in China over the last century. It is not by chance that in China, the traditional styles of painting are known as 国画 (national painting). The twin apogees of Chinese culture – calligraphy (书法) and painting – are areas that are well known and researched in the West. While remaining traditional, and maintaining a status of almost sacred significance, they continue to develop and to be adapted to contemporary life. The discourse surrounding calligraphy and painting goes on, and we will attempt to unravel some of the more traditional and the newer skeins of painterly ideology and the ways in which the meta-discourse of art may be comprehensibly translated. The traditional approach to painting is explored through the words of two of the best-known creators of modern Chinese traditional painting, Qi Baishi and Wu Guanzhong. These two artists represent the modern face of a long Chinese tradition. We take as our starting point the autobiography of Qi Baishi, whose larger than life insects and plants are known around the world. Rooted in Chinese tradition, his life and work reflect a different idiom from that of Wu Guanzhong, born half a century later. Wu's creative spirit encompasses the shared genius of East and West, offering the audience new insights and a new language of artistic expression. We complete the chapter with a discussion of an artist working in the twenty-first century. The nature of contemporary art is global, and calls for the use of global terminology. Translation of Chinese discussion of art may well involve using terms that derive from other languages. We may find ourselves translating back, but not simply 'back-translating'. Lin Tianmao, an installation artist, works with conventional, representational forms that symbolise and question family and gender relationships in China. The practical exercise draws on a description of the skill of another great Chinese artist, Zhang Daqian.

Chapter 2 explores the language of writing and calligraphy. Calligraphy (书法) is regarded as the apex of Chinese culture, and we explore the relationship of the script to national, personal and cultural identity. To be able to write accurately and elegantly is a sign of refinement and education, and a passport to power. When examinations for Imperial office were held (from 605 to 1905), handwriting was an examinable skill. Gifted handwriters could achieve high office on the basis of that skill (Yen 2005). Writing not only has instrumental power, but also ritual power. Endorsements and inscriptions are highly valued. Even today, celebrities will be sought after to write the masthead of a newspaper, the name of a business, the logo of an institution, or a motto. The continuity of Chinese writing imbues Chinese history and culture with permanence and might; the characters used in inscriptions on bronzes dating from 1,000 BC are recognisable and even comprehensible to the expert modern reader. Writing is not only a vehicle of information and an instrument of power. It is also an art form, and is considered the most important of the art forms. Traditional paintings always include or are part of a piece of text, which may be a poem, an essay, or a dedication. Calligraphy epitomises Chinese culture. As translators, we take Chinese characters for granted: they are the material we work with on a daily basis, yet they open doors to the weighty subjects of nation, ideology and culture. The chapter opens with an exploration of the ideological debate surrounding simplified and traditional characters and the strong sense of national and cultural identity associated with the writing of Chinese characters. This is followed by a discussion of the metalanguage surrounding 'women's writing' (女书), a historic, specialist variety of written Chinese whose cultural identity is gender specific. The chapter concludes with a discussion of font design. The creation of fonts, though not recognised as a calligraphic skill by the general public, has been at the heart of printed publication and creativity, and now, in a digital world in which each of us types on a daily, even hourly, basis, is an unseen force in blogs, essays and articles all over the world. Modern fonts that are grounded in Chinese calligraphy are a core part of cultural identity today.

Chapter 3 explores the mechanics of calligraphy, including manual operations and tools and the spiritual and psychological implications of calligraphic practice. Liu Gongquan, a calligrapher of the Tang dynasty, is well-known as a model of skill and virtue. The techniques of his style, still taught nowadays, are echoed in the 1960s 'New Wei Style' calligraphy, aimed at young people and encouraging them to write with oil paint and household brushes; even in the radical, unconventional world of the 1970s, physical technique was fundamental in forming good Chinese characters. We conclude the chapter with an example of the Buddhist practice of copying scriptures. The physical practice of writing can be a deeply spiritual activity, instilling discipline, calm and aesthetic appreciation in the student.

In Chapter 4 the translation of texts relating to clothing and costume in ancient and modern contexts is addressed. Clothes and fabrics are an extension of the Chinese 'self' in which the rest of the world is very interested. The identity of a nation or culture may be emblazoned in its dress. Now, in the twenty-first century, China clothes the world, and its history of decoration and décor cannot be ignored. We see how centuries of writers have written about the power and identity of costume, and how the language of costume crosses cultures. Fashion and costume, like other visual arts, lend themselves to a language-free graphic discourse, but inevitably, experts and lay people use sometimes quite eccentric and complex language to convey notions of dress. We look at the intricacies involved in translating dress in ancient, modern and contemporary contexts.

Chapter 5 presents Chinese nursery rhymes as a literary genre that contains rich information about the social and historical situation of the family in China, but hitherto has not often been translated. The rhymes share many features with traditional Chinese poetry for adults, and in many cases there is overlap. As poems, the rhymes require thoughtful treatment if they are to succeed, either as rhymes for children, or as social and historical documentation in the target language. In all cultures, nursery rhymes provide a comical means of representing the awful truth of the adult world to young children. Until now, the somewhat rare examples of published translations of Chinese nursery rhymes and children's poems have focused on the sweet romantic type. We have attempted to break free of Orientalist romanticism in order to find ways of translating the rhymes honestly and accessibly.

Chapter 6 discusses some of the theoretical approaches to adaptation and transcreation of poetry, and reviews the work of two innovative translators. Both examples may at first seem extreme, for both attempt to break stereotypes. We look at Pul'ka's expansive, explicatory rap-style version of Wang Wei's well-known *Peach Blossom Spring*, which is recognised as a core work of the Chinese classical canon. In its length and prolixity, Pul'ka's version contrasts with Jonathan Stalling's economical sinophonic technique, as seen in his *Yingelishi* (吟歌丽诗), which draws on 'found' poetry. Since 'fidelity' and 'accuracy' are, in any case, highly problematic notions when applied to translation of poetry, transcreation or creative adaptation may not be considered a step too far.

Chapter 7 looks at irony and absurdity, the curious combination of comedy and tragedy by means of which we criticise individuals and institutions. This is an area of human interest that may be highly culture-specific and will certainly challenge the translator, yet, in its intent, is common to many cultures. The most powerful literary genre of the twenty-first century is the blog, a medium that, owing to its brevity and immediacy, is ideal for wicked observation of the human condition. Many blogs are translated for the world-wide web audience. Well-known writers are still publishing books and short stories in hard copy, and we take a look between the covers of the writing of two best-selling Chinese writers of the comedic and the absurd: Wang Meng, whose writing reveals the contradictions of Chinese society in the mid-twentieth century, and Yan Lianke, who makes astute observations of twenty-first century academia.

Chapter 8 is a case study of drama translation. Chinese drama, either traditional or modern, is relatively rarely translated into any other language. Yet this is an area that informs us of the way life is lived, and the way people think in the source culture. Drama is an overt and covert vehicle for establishment and dissenting views. Translation of traditional 'opera' is often limited to awkwardly rendered surtitles dimly projected above or beside the stage: the foreign audience is left to guess a great deal, and may be left bemused. At a performance of Hamlet adapted as Peking Opera (京劇), a neighbour in the audience asked 'are the surtitles meant to be funny?' Unfortunately, many a tragedy is unwittingly turned into comedy by translators who work at a superficial level, without fully immersing themselves in the thoughts and behaviour of the characters represented on stage or screen. This type of approach leaves the audience with reinforced perceptions of Chinese culture as inaccessible. At the time of writing, the number of Chinese dramas staged in the United Kingdom is growing, but theatre companies are often reliant on adaptations made from 'literal' translations. Here we take a more in-depth approach to the translation of contemporary Chinese drama, in an effort to bring non-stereotypical Chinese drama to a wider audience. The chapter is based on a pilot study and a later, planned case study of collaborative translation. We use the term 'collaborative translation' in its original sense of 'working together', and not specifically to apply to computer-aided translation or work done on virtual platforms, though virtual working is now popular, and sometimes required by agencies.

Chapter 9 deals with the complex task of translating film. The linguistic differences between Chinese and English place severe constraints on the translator of film. In this chapter different approaches to film translation are compared, and through two brief examples and a longer case study, we see how subtitles are made to fit, and how they can best convey the information implicit and explicit in the filmic images.

Throughout the course of this book, we aim to demonstrate, like Chiang Yee, above, that arbitrary barriers to understanding can be undermined, and that the difference often found in similarity and the similarity frequently found in difference can facilitate and enrich the work of translation. Our readers may not agree with our ideas, or approve of our translations, but we aim to stimulate novice translators to explore and reflect upon a source text and the reality of its reception in the target culture. Translation studies moves fast, and inevitably, there will be some omissions.

A practical note: in the case of individual words and phrases quoted in the body of the text, we have in most cases given an English version or equivalent followed by the Chinese, for the sake of smooth reading. In cases where coherence requires it, the Chinese version is given first. The use of simplified characters and traditional characters depends on the source texts quoted. We have not provided pinyin versions, as it is assumed that readers have a reading knowledge of Chinese. The exception to this is in the case of terms that are commonly used in transliteration, rather than translation, such as *qipao*. Where transliterated terms are quoted from older works or works from Taiwan which use Wade-Giles romanisation, we have kept the Wade-Giles spelling. All the translation solutions provided by the authors of this book ('Authors' translation') are suggested solutions only, rather than definitive translations. Other translators' work is acknowledged. We welcome readers' suggestions for improvement.

1 Translating modern and contemporary Chinese art and artists
Art and artists as culture-specific entities

In this chapter we will explore the way in which discussion of the visual arts, or at least some of them, is expressed in Chinese, and how it might best be rendered into English. Human beings have been making images for thousands of years, in two dimensions and in three dimensions. Our culture of art must cross not only geo-political boundaries, but also generational boundaries. What our grandparents saw as tasteful and chic may now seem outmoded and vulgar to us, and what they would once have seen as indecent may, to us, be ravishingly beautiful. The differences are compounded when we work between languages and cultures, but on the other hand, we may be attracted by what is exotic, and identify with novelty.

In the following sections we see how artists describe their own motivations, ways of working and inner processes. Most artists are accustomed to working in visual, audio or tactile media, making their art communicate what writers would put into verbal media. This is something of an over-simplification, since some visual artists work with words, and in China painting is integrated with calligraphy and poetry. Yet even when the message of a painting or graphic is clear, a forest of discourse grows up around it, as artists and critics defend, deconstruct and debate. In this chapter we will look at translation of the meta-discourse of art: that is how artists and their critics or commentators talk about their work, how they fit into the cultural milieu, how they see their ways of working and how they use their art as a vehicle for change. We see how post-liberalisation artists have adapted and adopted from Western forms and techniques in order to shock and challenge

Traditional Chinese painting

The Chinese paint on paper, as do artists in many other cultures, and other supports, which are made from all sorts of materials, as in other cultures. In creating a 'national', or Chinese painting (国画), they use brushes, which are a universal tool of the painter, and they use water-based inks and colour paints on highly absorbent paper, ideally handmade. The tools of any artist range from the highly specialised to the mundane, and differ in detail between cultures. They may be regarded as culture-specific items, but as concrete items that can be described in terms of material, form and function, they present relatively few problems in translation. On a more abstract level, the styles of painting, the nature and appellation of the artists and the language of criticism and appreciation are also culture-specific items, but may present a greater degree of abstraction and a wider range of choices for the translator, inviting translators' exploration of nuance and rhetoric.

While the brush is a universal tool for a painter, the way it is held and handled may be specific to the culture. As we will see in the following sections, the display and storage of a work of art may differ between cultures, but what drives an artist to create may be universal. The artists whose work is covered here 'dovetail' historically, covering a century of change. Wu Guanzhong was maturing as Qi Baishi reached old age, and our younger subject, Lin Tianmao, was maturing at about the time that Wu was reaching old age.

What it means to be an artist in the Chinese tradition: Qi Baishi

Qi Baishi (1863–1957) is one of the best-known Chinese painters of the twentieth century. Spanning two half-centuries in which China underwent major political and cultural changes, his work is still greatly admired today. While he was evidently a master of the traditional, he took the *xieyi* or impressionistic (写意) style to new heights of freedom, expanding the range of subjects in ever looser and bolder brushwork. Significantly, he rose from artisan, to craftsman, to painter, following a path that probably gave him greater insights into life than if he had been 'born into' the literati world of painting. The following excerpt is from He Huaishuo's introduction to Qi's autobiography 白石老人自述 (*Old Baishi's Autobiography*). He reflects on why Qi is held in such great esteem, given that he was just one in a long line of superb painters and calligraphers. He Huaishuo first summarises the essence of a Chinese artist as traditionally and conventionally perceived:

Example 1a

> 齊白石繼承了文人畫傳統的精華。'何謂文人畫？ 即畫中帶有文人之性質，含有文人之趣味。'而以 '思想、學問、才情、人品' 為特質 。這是陳衡恪（師曾）對文人畫的看法。 '文人畫' 原來也被稱爲 '士大夫寫意畫'。具體而言，包括了幾個特色：寫意的技巧，以水墨爲主或淡設色，書畫同源（在用筆方面常以書法用筆為依據），詩（文）、書法與畫合一，加上篆刻，成爲 '三絕' 或 '四絕' 的綜合体。
>
> (He Huaishuo in Qi 2001/2003: 19)

Qi Baishi continued the refinement of traditional literati painting. In the view of Chen Hengke (also known as Shi Zeng), literati painting has all the qualities and taste of the scholar artist. It embodies ideology, scholarship, talent and personality. 'Literati painting' was originally known as 'the impressionistic style of the scholar'. In concrete terms, it had certain specific characteristics: the technique is chiefly ink painting, with some light colour, and the calligraphy and painting spring from the same source. The brush technique of the painting relies on calligraphy technique; the poetry and the calligraphy are integrated into the painting – a combination known as the three perfections. The addition of seal carving gives us the four perfections.

(Authors' translation)

This short passage tells us a great deal about the veneration in which scholar-artists were held in China and the kind of person they were expected to be. The first challenge for the translator here is how to label the concept, well known in China, of *wen ren* – the literary person (文人). The concept distils, in the briefest possible way, the ideas of culture, refinement, education, talent in painting, skill in calligraphy, ability to carve seals, knowledge of poetry, intimacy with nature and landscape and rapport with other 文人. The dictionary gives us 'man of letters' (from a gender point of view this is largely correct, as traditionally, prior to 1911, few Chinese women would be poets and artists), 'scholar' and 'literati'. We cannot possibly say that this broad notion of the artist does not exist in European or British culture, for it does: many of the great artists, from Leonardo to Lear, from Ruskin to Paolozzi, have been polymaths, people of broad and deep understanding of literature, art and artifice. The traditional Chinese perception of the artist may be more aesthetic, perhaps even tending towards the feminine or effete. There is a contrast in Chinese culture between the ideal literary male, whose qualities embodied *wen*, that is culture and refinement (文), and the ideal military *wu* male (武), who embodied physicality, roughness and aggression. The terms *wen* and *wu* are not confined to discussion of male character types: they are found, for example, in the preparation of Chinese medicine: 文火 (gentle heat) and 武火 (fierce or strong heat). The Chinese artist was not, generally speaking, an engineer or architect, though he might have considerable skill in garden design. He would not necessarily be a craftsman, though he would be able to carve the all-important seal that signed off his work. Prior to the twentieth century, he would almost certainly have been a civil servant, since all educated men aspired to recruitment to the Imperial civil service through the examination system. The examinations would have tested his knowledge of the Chinese classic works of literature, philosophy and history, and his ability to write the conventional essay and poetic genres.

So what do we call a 文人 in English? It may be the case here that we need a hyphenated solution such as 'scholar-artist' or 'poet-artist'. Reverting to Latin is another option, in the choice of 'literatus', but most often this is used in the plural in English (literati) to denote a class of people. In Foster and Hartman's English translation of Gernet, the term 'lettered person' is used, and expanded as 'the man of culture and taste, qualified to exercise political

functions' (Gernet 1972/1999: 33). 士大夫 *shi daifu,* the term He cites above
as an earlier label of the Chinese artist, is a synonym of 文人, but what is
the difference? How are the terms distinguished in Chinese, and if there is a
distinction, how can we reflect this distinction in English?

The expressions 'the three perfections' (三絕) and 'the four perfections' (四絕)
can be said to be culture-specific, for they are characteristic of Chinese definition
and categorisation in their use of numbers in the service of abbreviation and
memorisation, creating a quasi-jargon. Number expressions are used in English,
but less frequently than in Chinese. What the respective three and four perfections are is clear from the context, so it is unnecessary for the translator to provide footnotes or lengthy parentheses, but 絕 has to be integrated coherently into
the English text. 絕 is to cut off, in other words to define; it also implies excellence, in other words a cutting off from the ordinary. 三絕 and 四絕 are
what define a true artist, and conventionally are called 'perfections' (Von Spee
2012: 17). We have become accustomed to Chinglish slogans such as the 'four
modernisations', the 'three represents' and so on, but they do not always read
comfortably in their grammatical micro-context. Does a twenty-first century
translator need to adhere to conventions established many decades ago? It would
be possible to translate as follows:

> The definitive mastery of literati painting lies in the consummate skills of
> painting, calligraphy and poetry, rounded off by the fourth skill of seal
> carving.

This slightly adaptive approach avoids the clumsiness of slogans and the
reduction to hyperbole of these very high-level skills. If the editor wished to
keep the Chinese terms, especially for the purposes of an index, they could be
added in brackets.

Qi Baishi rose to prominence as a painter over his long life not only by
means of pure talent, but by 'turning art around':

Example 1b

> 齊白石的畫風既然是由八大、八怪、趙之謙、吳昌碩而來，繼承在野文
> 人畫的傳統，而且其風格面目，尤其與八大、金農、老缶如此相近，
> 爲什麼仍享有最高的評價？我認爲主要在於齊白石的創造性，表現在
> 將傳統文人畫的美感情趣轉向移位，開闢了一個平民化、世俗化的繪
> 畫天地，注入了生機活潑的世俗人情。

> (He 2003: 18)

Qi Baishi's style continued the 'outsider' tradition of Ba Da, the Eight
Eccentrics, Zhao Zhiqian and Wu Changshuo, yet, whereas his style was,
on the surface, similar to that of Ba Da, Jin Nong and Lao Ji, why does
he enjoy so much greater critical acclaim? My belief is that his creativity
lies in the way he has changed the direction of aesthetic appreciation,

opening it up for ordinary people; he has universalised the universe of painting, filling it with the vigour and vitality of human emotion.

(Authors' translation)

This explanation of Qi's success appears to be a string of clichés, and perhaps that is what is required for a man who was and is a household name. His achievement is compared to that of his predecessors, including the 'eight eccentrics' or 'mad monks', working during the late years of the Ming dynasty and the early years of the Qing. They included Bada Shanren and Jin Nong. As artists who, by choice or by force of circumstance, did not hold positions as officials, they were outsiders (在野文人) (Hejzlar 1980: 24). A note on these earlier artists may be desirable, depending on the destination of the text.

   Qi was creative. He took the image of the eccentric scholar-artist and turned it around, he made it accessible to everyone, he universalised it. This is where his achievement breaks the mould. In his autobiography he tells the story of his rise from cowherd to carpenter, and from carpenter to carver to painter. As in many cultures, the 'art' of Chinese painting and calligraphy are considered to be more elevated, and indeed, elitist, than the craftsman's skills of carving, potting, weaving, lacquering etc. Qi tells how people would buy his paintings, but ask him not to sign them: they considered him of too lowly a social class to be publicly acknowledged. In the following excerpt we see the link between Qi's artisan skills and his art, when he learns the traditional techniques of mounting pictures. The passage is a simple narrative, but is full of 'the tools of the trade': paper, fabric, timber and gadgets. It is also full of conventional Chinese third person reference and terms of address, which must be sensitively but readably rendered in English.

Example 1c

我們家鄉，向來是沒有裱畫鋪的，只有幾個會裱畫的人，在四鄉各處，來來往往，應活做工，蕭薌陔師傅就是其中的一人。我在沁園師家讀書的時候，沁園師曾把蕭師傅請到家裏，一方面叫他裱畫，一方面叫大公子仙逋，跟他學做這門手藝。特地勻出了三間大廳，屋内中間，放著一張尺碼很長很大的紅漆桌子，四壁牆上釘著平整乾淨的木板格子，所有軸幹、軸頭、別子、綾絹、絲條、宣紙以及排筆、漿糊之類置備得齊齊備備，應有盡有。沁園師對我說：“瀕生，你也可以學學！你是一個畫家，學會了，裝裱自己的東西，就透著方便些。給人家做做活，也可以作爲副業謀生。”沁園師處處為我打算，真是無微不至。我也覺得他的話，很有道理，就同仙逋，跟著蕭師傅，從托紙到上軸，一層一層的手續，都學會了。

(Qi 2001: 77)

There had never been a picture mounting shop in my home town, just a few people who could do the job, who travelled about from place to place, taking jobs as and when. Master Xiao Xianggai was one of them. When I was studying at the home of Master Qin Yuan, Master Qin invited Master Xiao to his house to mount some pictures, and at the same time teach this craft to Master Qin's eldest son Xian Bu. He had set aside three big rooms. In the centre stood an enormous red-lacquered table, and on the walls were hung wooden boards, all very neat and clean. There were dowels, knobs, clips, silk gauze, silk strips, *xuan* paper, paste brushes and paste – all the materials needed for mounting pictures. Master Qin Yuan said to me: 'Pinsheng, you can learn too. You are a painter, and if you can learn to do mounting, you can do your own things, and that will be much more convenient. You could do it for other people too, as a sideline.' Qin Yuan always had a thought for me; he was very considerate. He was absolutely right. I joined Xian Bu and together we learned from Xiao Xianggai every step of the procedure, from making the paper support to fixing on the roller.

(Authors' translation)

A good English version would need some re-structuring within the sentences, as Qi Baishi's narrative contains a number of typical Chinese 'paratactic' sentences, strings of co-ordinating clauses, or short sentences (短句), divided by commas. These might be replaced in English by full stops, and they might need to be re-ordered. Often, explicit linking words are needed to indicate co-ordinating, causal, conditional and temporal links.

Titles and terms of address are important culture-specific items. English is miserly in its use of titles and endearments in the second person, for courtesy in English dialogue is much more likely to be expressed through complex verb forms, and respectful titles are not repeated unduly in narration, but are expressed as pronouns. Throughout the passage, Qi refers to his seniors in the trade as Master (師傅), the usual term in Chinese for a craftsman who is senior in age or in experience and skill. It is an honorific, used to this day to address older men in a professional or working context. In this short passage two characteristics of Chinese writing are shown: respectful reference to seniors, and repetition of the full noun phrase (Master Xiao Xianggai). This means of expression should probably be kept, rather than exchanged for 'Mr,' as the events are taking place at the end of the nineteenth century. In order to preserve the cultural feel of an earlier time, the slightly archaic form is appropriate. In English, the general term 'master craftsman' is still used, and many crafts and skills have official qualifications or designations of 'master': there are master classes, masters' degrees, masters of colleges and of hunts. It is a term of deep respect for a highly skilled professional. The use of the titles in this passage would help to avoid the ambiguity of an English pronoun-heavy approach, since all the characters referred to in the passage are male.

While referring courteously to his seniors, Qi narrates in a matter-of-fact, reader-friendly register: he is telling his story as an ordinary man who rose gradually and coincidently to fame. There would be no reason to translate in a more formal or literary register. It should be noted that the reference to the three big rooms (特地匀出了三間大廳，屋內中間，放著一張尺碼很長很大的紅漆桌子. ...) is not entirely clear, but we have assumed that the three rooms had been knocked together, and are used as one.

Tools and techniques

At the time when Qi was active, the motivations and attitudes surrounding art were governed to a great extent by conventions. When Qi talks about the processes of his work, he is mainly interested in tools and techniques, rather than any high-minded or rebellious intellectual motivation. In Example 1c above, we see the relationships of the generations of artists, and we also see how the techniques were passed on. Qi expands his professional skills by learning the techniques of display and preservation of paintings. One of the terms the translator needs to think about is 裱畫: Chinese pictures are pre-pared for display in a very different way from traditional European pictures, mainly owing to distinct methods of storage and display. In earlier times, Chinese paintings would not necessarily be hung on a wall, but stored rolled in a mothproof chest and taken out from time to time to be enjoyed. Do we translate 裱畫 as 'mounting' or 'framing'? 'Mounting' in English is only one stage on the way to the framing of a picture, so is it adequate for the Chinese procedure? The translator needs to think about what the reader will infer from the use of either term, and also consider whether a footnote should be used. An observant reader of our English translation would notice the boards hung on the walls and might question their purpose. A brief explicitation in the text would provide the information that when Chinese paintings are pasted onto their backing paper, ready for mounting, they are dried on vertical boards, and held in place by the wet paste.

The list of materials provides information on the process. 'Axle tree', 'roller', or 'dowelling' (軸幹) and 'axle tree ends', or 'knobs' (軸頭) tell us that this is not 'framing' as is known in the West. But we need the English terms that would be used for these types of materials. 排筆 might need a footnote or parenthetical note: it is a Chinese brush, but made from a row (排) of brushes joined together, so that it is very wide, like pan pipes, and used for large-scale painting, and for brushing paste onto paper or silk.

When the themes are the arts, especially poetry and painting, there is undoubtedly a tendency among some translators to over-romanticise in translation from Chinese. In his autobiography, Qi calls a spade a spade: he does not romanticise his life and art, and while the expressions he uses may be new to the foreign reader of Chinese, the concepts of making a living and finding rice to put in the pot are universal. Here is an excerpt that deals with Qi's incipient success as a painter.

Example 1d

> 我三十歲以後，畫像畫了幾年，附近百來里地的範圍以內，我差不多跑
> 遍了東西南北。　鄉里的人，都知道藝術匠改行做了畫匠，　說我畫的
> 畫，比雕的花還好。生意越做越多，收入也越來越豐，家裏靠我這門手
> 藝。光景就有了轉機，母親緊皺了半輩子的眉毛，到這時才慢慢地放開
> 了。祖母也笑著對我說：‘阿芝！你倒沒有虧負了這支筆，從前我說
> 過，哪見文章鍋裏煮，現在我看見你的畫，卻在鍋裏煮了！’我知道祖
> 母是說得高興話，就畫了幾幅畫，又寫了一張橫幅，題了‘甑屋’
> 兩個大字，意思是：可以吃得飽啦，不致於像以前鍋裏空空的了。

> (Qi 2001: 76)

By the time I was thirty, I had been painting portraits for several years, and I had travelled all over the locality, covering an area of about a hundred *li*. Everyone in this rural area knew that I had turned my hand to painting, and said that the pictures that I painted were better than the flowers that I carved. Business steadily improved, my income grew, and the family came to rely on my art. With time came opportunities, and at last I saw my mother's forehead, wrinkled from a lifetime of worry, gradually relax. My grandmother smiled, and said to me 'A-Zhi! You have made good use of your brush. I used to say that you couldn't cook and eat an essay, but now I see that we can live on your paintings!' When I saw how happy my grandmother was I painted several pictures. I also painted a vertical scroll with the words 'A pot for the house', signifying that we could eat – we would no longer have an empty pot.

> (Authors' translation)

This extract illustrates idiomatic wordplay, the humour of a household, and the symbolic use of the pun. When Qi Baishi was a young man, writing was still done with a brush, as was painting. The pivot of Qi's grandmother's remark is the brush that once wrote useless essays, but now produces profitable paintings. The Chinese, 你的畫，卻在鍋裏煮了 could be literally translated as 'your paintings can be cooked in the pot'. While this would not make perfect sense in English, it would be understood. It could alternatively be translated as 'live on' which can mean either 'eat', or 'support life financially'. Qi's reaction to his grandmother's compliment was to create a symbolic artwork that would continue to bring good fortune to the family: in writing 甑屋 on a scroll, he was using a pun. 甑 means 'pot' but is a homophone of 贈 – to give a gift (to the home – 屋). Qi's grandmother addresses him with a family calling name, or pet name, with familiar 'a' prefix – 'A-Zhi'. Many non-Chinese readers will know that this is a name, a term of address, but for the artist reader, who may not know about Chinese culture, perhaps some indication that it is a name would be helpful. It does not need to be a footnote, but we could add the kind of phrase a grandmother might use, such as 'my boy': 'A-Zhi, my boy … '. Hyphenating the two syllables of the name will reduce the chance of ambiguous interpretation of 'a' as an article.

These homely anecdotes appear to contrast strongly with the abstractions and metaphors used by the successor generations of painters who practised after the 1940s, when Chinese artists, like their nation, had begun to modernise and westernise.

Ambiguity and sensitivity in source text and target text: Translating an interview with Wu Guanzhong

Artists generally express themselves via the work that they do: in the case of painters, the messages are mainly visual, but the celebrity opportunities of modern media have enabled many artists to express themselves verbally, and talk about their work to a mass audience. As visual art has moved away from the purely representational, some explanation or justification on the part of the artist is sometimes necessary. It may be by means of a self-authored essay or article, or more often, using the vehicle of the interview.

The interview is an interesting, powerful tool. It allows freedom for the interviewee to talk, yet at the same time imposes control and structure. It is at least partially prepared, by the interviewer, and on the part of the interviewee is at least partially spontaneous. As a spoken medium the interview can be aired undoctored on radio or television, or it can be edited and disseminated in writing on the internet and in the traditional press. For the audience, it is often a way into celebrity minds, an opportunity to see and hear them as 'real people' and a way of understanding what they do, what drives them and the challenges they meet in their science or art. The translation of an interview transcript, like drama or dialogue in fiction, presents a multiple crossing of boundaries, between transcript, translation, interpreting and drama. The transcript (speech recorded in writing) must be rendered as writing that looks and sounds like speech. It must be grammatical, coherent and accessible, but retain the conversational tone of the original recording.

Wu Guanzhong (1919–2010) was one of the greats of the twentieth century, his life and work overlapping that of his older peer Qi Baishi, and that of his Spanish counterpart Picasso. Unlike Qi Baishi, whose formation was in China, Wu's training took him to Paris, where he experienced the explosive movements of twentieth-century art in Europe. Like Qi, Wu paints in the national, or Chinese tradition (国画), but has embraced styles and techniques of the European tradition. In the extracts that follow, we examine Wu's explanation of the process of artistic creation and how we can sensibly translate it.

In December 2006, an exhibition of all the new works Wu had done during the course of the year was held at the Tsinghua University Academy of Arts and Design in Beijing, and he was interviewed about his creative process. The interview was published in transcript on the internet. The tone is set for the interview by a quotation from Wu's own introduction to the exhibition, in which he states that, as an older artist, aged 87 at the time, losing the urge to create would be tantamount to losing hope. Wu's responses to the interviewer are about painting as an inner, cerebral, spiritual and emotional process.

In the following exchange, the interviewer guides Wu towards discussion of this inner process, stating that Wu has often used the word 'pregnancy' (怀孕) in relation to art:

Example 1e

> 记者：您是这么形容的，比妇女生孩子还要痛苦，对，我就经常看到您的文章里出现怀孕两个字。
>
> 吴：是，确实是这样的。但我们讲了，怀孕是最困难了，这个画家一般是不容易怀孕，他能怀孕了，他能够成长了，他将来分娩的问题，这个不是很大的问题，关键是不能怀孕，我们很多画，都是叫无孕分娩，没有怀孕，他就画画了，实际上他没有感情，没有真感情，是这样的。所以这个文艺作品，不完全是哪一行的，是文学的，美术的，他必须有真感情。

(Wu 2007)

Interviewer: You have described [art] as being more painful than giving birth is for a woman – indeed, I've often seen the word 'pregnancy' in articles you've written.

Wu: Yes, that's exactly how it is. But, as we've said before, pregnancy is hard. It is hard for an artist to be pregnant. He can 'conceive', he can 'grow' the baby, and eventually he'll give birth. That is not a problem, but the key problem is that if we cannot conceive, there'll be many paintings, but they will be works that are born without being conceived, without being gestated. It's just painting, with no feeling, no real feeling. That's how it is. It doesn't matter whether it's literature or art, a work of art has to have true feeling.

(Authors' translation)

The interviewer introduces the idea of a woman giving birth (妇女生孩子). It will not, however, have escaped the reader that the pronouns used by Wu and the journalist are transcribed as the masculine 他, which might equally have been transcribed as feminine 她 or even neuter 它. The Chinese transcriber (who we may, perhaps, regard as the initial translator) is forced to impose a gender on this innocent little word, and the translator working from the transcript must find a sensible solution. In this written version of the interview, the 'artist' is undoubtedly male, a logical decision, since Wu is obviously speaking from his own point of view. In this context, however, the masculine pronoun leaves us with a slight conundrum.

Wu is pointing out that the difficulty of artistic creation is not so much in the 'giving birth' (the 'delivery' or implementation of the work of art) as in what we might label 'inspiration' or 'conception' of the artwork. His point is that in any artistic creation, true feeling is needed for the work. For the translator, the key term is 怀孕. In English translation, that can be 'pregnancy/pregnant' or it may be 'conceive/conception', two very different concepts. Wu claims that many paintings are 'delivered without pregnancy' (无孕分娩), for the work is able to develop, the artist is able to go through the pregnancy and deliver the work, but 'cannot be pregnant' or 'cannot conceive' (不能怀孕). We have to bear in mind that this was probably a spontaneous response, so we cannot expect the coherence we would see in an article written by the artist, and in addition, we have to take into account the ambiguity and the figurative nature of the term 怀孕. If, in our English rendition, we do not vary the translation of 怀孕, we end up with an apparently contradictory statement. What Wu appears to be saying is that some artists' completed work is superficial: it is not inspired at the conception stage, and it does not develop in the foetal stage, because there is no feeling – it is 'just painting' (就画画了). We also need to consider the nature and meaning of 'pregnancy' (怀孕): why has Wu chosen this term rather than a more abstract term such as 'development'? 怀孕 carries with it notions of love, humanity, innerness, physicality: it is a metaphor for the sensations and motivations of a committed artist. It could also be associated with the Chinese term to brew or ferment (酝酿). It is a deliberate choice on Wu's part. The translator could opt for a scientific, formal term, such as 'gestation' but it lacks the personal and emotional force that Wu probably has in mind. It is perfectly possible to talk about conceiving a work of art, but less feasible (though not now impossible) to say that a male artist is 'pregnant'. Converting the idiom to a simile ('it is like being pregnant') would solve a number of problems of sense, register and plausibility, while retaining the thrust of the meaning. One obvious solution is to use 'the artist' as grammatical subject throughout: by avoiding anaphoric pronouns, we would avoid specifying a gender, but this could sound a little awkward. Another solution is to translate directly, but use inverted commas around 'conceive', 'pregnant' etc., so that the metaphor is retained, but does not sound surreal.

The interviewer asks Wu about his style, which has absorbed elements of both 'western' art and Chinese traditional painting:

Example 1f

> 记者：您在您的这个国画里引入西洋画派的，像这个"面"，还有在西洋画派里引入国画里面的"线条"这样，我觉得在不同的时期，您一定也遭受过一些争议，比如说吴冠中的画，中不中，西不西。

(Wu 2007)

Journalist: You adopt the methods of the 'Western school' in your traditional Chinese painting, like planes, and when you are painting Western-style, you introduce the Chinese technique of line. I think there are times when you have been criticised for this – people have said that Wu Guanzhong's painting is neither Western nor Chinese.

(Authors' translation)

The concept of 线条 is clearly and unambiguously 'line', but what should we do about 面, which the interviewer takes to be a characteristic of 'Western' art? Is it 'face' or 'surface'? Could it possibly be 'mask' or 'covering'? It is obviously opposite or complementary to 'line', so the translator has to take an artist's perspective and investigate what that might be in this particular context. There are two major features of Chinese traditional painting that distinguish it from the European tradition. From fairly early on, European artists attempted to re-create the three-dimensional in their paintings, by means of the use of shade (tonality) and the use of single-point perspective. Gombrich notes that in Persian painting, there is 'no foreshortening and no attempt to show light and shade or the structure of the body' (Gombrich 1993: 103). Similarly, in Chinese landscape painting, which developed far earlier than it did in other parts of the world, perspective was differently executed, as multiple-point perspective. Hughes notes that 'perspective is a generalization about experience', schematising, rather than representing, the way things are seen (Hughes 1991: 17). In Chinese traditional painting it is the multiple points of view and staggering of different planes that give the viewer the sense of near and far (Gernet 1972/1999: 207). Wu Yangmu notes that in Chinese painting 'it is not easy to distinguish between what is near and what is far and what should be dark and what light' (Wu 1990: 46). In the European tradition of painting, the various surfaces of a three-dimensional object would be depicted by means of light and shade, while a Chinese artist would use texturing. This is what the interviewer means by 面: changing representations of surface that create the illusion of three dimensions, by contrast with line (线条), which creates the reality of the shape or outline of a person or object. In practical terms, these are very long explanations that may or may not have a place in the translation of an interview. The interviewer does not explain the concepts, for his art-world jargon is shared by the artist he is talking to, and he expects the interested audience to share the relevant knowledge. If the translation of the interview is to be rendered as subtitles or a voice-over, there is simply no chance of a footnote. It is therefore imperative that we find a succinct equivalent, and in English art terms, it is 'plane', the surface of an object that faces towards or away from the light. Wu's final analysis, however, is that in spite of cultural differences, the aesthetic of European and Chinese art is not entirely different.

Icons and concepts in post-liberalisation China

Qi was grounded firmly in his Chinese locality and practice, Wu trained abroad, becoming Chinese yet not Chinese, Western, yet not Western (中不中，西不西). He and his contemporaries were bound by social and political constraints. Artists who have trained since 1979 have had the benefit of modern methods, motivations and approaches available since China's liberalisation, and pursue ground-breaking practice in multi-media, abstraction, performance and conceptual art. Grosenick and Schübbe (2007) describe this as 'image spaces which oscillate between tradition and super-innovation', and note the unprecedented growth of the art market. 'Market' is significant, for commercial concerns as much as, if not more than, artistic or conceptual motivations, drive contemporary (当代) Chinese art. Ai Weiwei, a driving force in post-1989 art, is scathing about this; commenting on a 2012 exhibition in London, he asked 'How can you have a show of "contemporary Chinese art" that doesn't address a single one of the country's most pressing contemporary issues?' (2012: 10–11). 'Art needs to stand for something' he says (ibid.). The photos accompanying his article illustrate his point that the art sanctioned by the leadership for international consumption is derivative and bland.

Since 1979, artists have enjoyed somewhat greater freedom to smash the icons of the past. New forms, methods and techniques have been exuberantly adopted from practice in other parts of the world and moulded in characteristic, but contemporary Chinese fashion. How does the world of art critics and commentators talk about artwork which in the last century has departed so widely from the Chinese norm, and how are the comments translated? For the twenty-first century translator, the language of contemporary Chinese art could be less problematic than dealing with traditional Chinese forms and techniques. Ideas and techniques have been borrowed from the West, along with appropriate technical and specialist terms. Individual artists and critics, however, will use abstract and sometimes quite idiosyncratic epithets to describe and evaluate the work.

We have drawn the example in this section from Grosenick and Schübbe's *China Art Book* (2007). This encyclopaedic work exemplifies the importance of translation in global markets. The text that accompanies illustrations of artists' work consists of Chinese, English and German parallel commentaries. The commentaries are contributed by individual critics, and in some cases we can only guess which of the three languages is the source language of the commentary. It appears that in most cases it is English or German, but we cannot say for certain. In many cases, it is highly likely that the specialist terms used to describe contemporary Chinese art are of Western origin, but the reader might not know whether the Chinese artists reviewed have themselves used Chinese or foreign language terms to describe, label and classify their work. Whatever the provenance and process of the commentaries in the work, the parallel use of terms could be of great benefit to the practising translator.

Installation: The work of Lin Tianmao

Chinese artists have enthusiastically adopted the installation, and with it the term installation (装置) or installation work (装置作品). In her installations, Lin Tianmao uses the radical media of the twentieth century to discover the etiquette of social relationships (社会礼俗关系) of China. Lin's work, while neither gory nor shocking, provokes. She uses motifs such as the winding of thread to connote the complexity of relationships. Her processes include 缠绕、盘绕和包装 (Hopfener in Grosenick and Schübbe 2007: 195). The English equivalent used by Hopfener for these highly iconic techniques is 'winding, coiling and wrapping'. The German parallel version (ibid.: 195) is somehow much more expressive: 'Wickeln, Aufwickeln und Einwickeln': the repetition of 'wickeln' echoes and emphasises the binding element, just as the Chinese repeats 绕. To achieve this effect in English, 'binding' and 'winding' could be used. 'Coiling' is the winding of a yarn of some sort on and in itself, but Lin's work is really about binding other things with yarns.

Often the clue to interpretation of a work of art lies in its title. A title is a verbal translation of a visual product. So, for example, Lin's model of a woman, whose metres-long veil-like hair is being lifted by a giant frog, is called 'Initiator' (创始人) (Grosenick and Schübbe 2007: 197). 创始人 may also be translated as 'founder' or 'originator', both of which carry rather different connotations from 'initiator'. Should we be thinking here about the role of reptiles in evolution? The resonances in this piece are multiple, from the allusion to the frog-prince story to the binding possibilities of the long hair. The title guides viewers some way towards the perspective the artist has in mind: something is or was about to start: who starts it, or started it, the frog or the woman? The suggestive brevity on the one hand, or overwhelming length of a title on the other, can command the attention of the viewer.

As Chinese art evolves, it absorbs terminology and techniques from the West and simultaneously draws on traditional practice and history. Translators need to involve themselves in the language of art, which derives from both East and West.

Practical 1.1 Talking about art

The excerpt below is taken from *Zhang Daqian* (张大千) by Chen Zhulong (陈洙龙), an illustrated volume that discusses the work of Zhang Daqian (1899–1983). Zhang was a near contemporary of Qi Baishi and is revered as a great twentieth-century exponent of traditional yet powerfully innovative depictions of the natural world, including landscape and bird and flower paintings. Translate the text, bearing the following in mind:

i   The excerpt uses literary grammatical structures and expressions. Why would it be appropriate for the source text author/editor to use this style? Should it be reflected in the target text? If so, how would it be rendered?
ii Repetition of grammatical linking words provides the cohesion for the whole paragraph. To what extent should this repetition be reflected in the target text? If repetition is not used, what techniques could be used to provide an adaptive translation that conveys closely the writer's ideas?
iii How important is the punctuation to the structure of the text? Should the inverted commas be kept? Is it likely that new sets of inverted commas would be introduced in the target text?

iv The text includes culture-specific art terms and proper names. Would footnotes be imperative, and if so, what contribution might they make to the translation?

v The tone is laudatory. Should the unalloyed praise be fully reflected in the translation, or should it be toned down?

大千先生实为大师也。 他的山水、人物、花鸟、要工就工，要写就写，要泼就泼，要大就大，要小就小；花鸟画也就花鸟画吧，还特擅画那出污泥而不染的荷花，凡工凡写凡泼均极尽荷花之净、之致、之意、之情、之态。读也、看也、观止也、有人评他之画荷曰： "兼取古今各家画荷之长，于石涛取 '气'，与八大取 '毅'，于宋人得体察物情之理，乃集古今画荷之大成。居士画荷，无论工笔、没骨、写意、设色、水墨皆精绝当世，更创泼墨泼彩法为之，气势撼人，不但超越了花卉的属性，更将文人花卉的笔墨范围，拓展至另一境地。"

(Chen 2003: 164)

2 Chinese characters

National, cultural and personal identity

Closely integrated with traditional Chinese art is the art of writing. Chinese characters are considered the core of Chinese civilisation, and the ability to write them is the sign of a civilised person. Of the 'three perfections' (三绝: poetry, calligraphy and painting), calligraphy (书法), the writing of Chinese characters, is considered the chief. As a modern nation state, China draws heavily on the authority of its history, which unlike that of other great civilisations, is claimed to have continued unbroken for around five millennia. This continuity is largely due to its writing. Chinese characters are not always considered convenient or accessible, and over much of history have excluded, rather than included, the great mass of the people. The characters are, however, old, accessible to those who have the privilege of learning them, and, above all, are greatly loved and treasured by Chinese-speaking peoples. Traditionally, paper that had been written on was burned so as to avoid any desecration such as trampling (Taylor and Taylor 1995: 75; Chiang 1973: 5). This may well have been partly due to a desire for security and confidentiality on the part of the writers, but nevertheless it illustrates the regard in which writing was held. Ancient paper burners can still be seen in Taiwan, where Hakka people still burn waste paper, out of respect for the written word.

The umbilical hold that Chinese characters have on literate Chinese-speaking people is explored by Yen (2005). She shows how Chinese characters are a sign of power, personality and national belonging. They are used to express authority and glamour, to endorse business, and as a traditional and persistent route to personal advancement (2005: 15–32). In June 2012, one hundred well-known writers and artists were invited to copy by hand the record of the *Talks at the Yanan Forum on Literature and Art*. In these talks, in Yanan in 1942, Mao emphasised to revolutionary intellectuals and artists the importance of connecting with the masses, and using art and literature for social (and socialist) purposes (Spence 1990: 473). The 2012 appeal was no doubt intended, on the one hand, to restore some semblance of socialist ideology in an ever more capitalist and materialist society, and on the other to give the talks, which are now at worst reviled and at best ignored as irrelevant, some authority (Ifeng 2012; Link 2012). Most importantly, the appeal drew on the writing of Chinese characters by hand as an activity that is at the heart of Chinese culture and Chinese nation.

In this chapter we will look briefly at the meta-discourse of Chinese writing, and how the source texts impact on translations: some aspects of Chinese characters are arcane and culture-specific, yet other aspects are common to other cultures and easily understood. We will look first at the political and cultural significance of Chinese characters and the way writing relates to personal and national identity. The focus of identity then shifts to women, as in the next section we look at a traditional and formerly secret handwriting system. Like many endangered or extinct languages, 女书, the women's writing of Jiangyong County in Hunan Province, has fallen into disuse. In the third section we move on to a discussion of the language of modern font design. Once the arcane, yet artisanal and unrecognised preserve of the typesetter and publisher, fonts are now an integral part of daily life for every literate person, as we choose a means of electronic expression.

The nomenclature of the system and the way it is used are key to the significance of 'writing' in China. The script is known to the Chinese people as 汉字, 'Chinese characters'; simply 'writing characters' is 写字; those who practise and excel in writing characters practise 书法, the art or method of writing. The character 书 has come to have broad extended meanings of books and literature, much like the English 'writing'. In the following sections, 汉字 and 书法 are discussed as deeply culture-specific manifestations of social, political and personal identity in China.

Chinese characters: 'Handwriting of inordinate importance'

Over the 5,000 years of the existence of Chinese characters, billions of people have learned to read and write and understand through this medium, not only in China, but also in Korea and Japan. Herbert Read, in his preface to Chiang Yee's *Chinese Calligraphy* (Chiang 1938/1973: vii) declared that 'the Chinese attached what seemed to be an inordinate importance to their handwriting'; he goes on to praise the clarity with which Chiang describes the aesthetic principles of Chinese calligraphy, which are 'the aesthetic principles of all genuine art' (Read in Chiang 1973: vii–viii). Barras, writing much more recently, notes that Chinese calligraphy 'has re-emerged with a new vitality ... attracting the interest of a much wider international circle of people, most of whom are unable to read Chinese' (2002: 11). This would indicate that the artistic expression of Chinese calligraphy has a universal appeal, quite apart from its meaning for the literate. The characters are primarily a medium of communication and they are intricately bound to the world of art and poetry. They are ancient, yet appear in ever-changing modern forms and styles. They have been used for thousands of years to express contemporary, cutting edge ideas; they have at various times expressed new, foreign ideologies such as Buddhism and evolution, fashionable material imports from opium to iPads and the political impositions of foreign rulers; they have served to incite revolution; they now express the thoughts of Chinese youth on the internet and mobile phones. The UNESCO website for Cultural Heritage points out that Chinese calligraphy 'is still valued in an age of ballpoint pens and computers' (UNESCO 2003). While the number of characters has not substantially increased over the millennia, creative new combinations are appearing on a daily basis as the language is adapted for use in the internet age. The widely used term for computer (电脑) has become well established, and colloquial terms such as 'cool' (酷) and the latest equivalent of 'impressive' (给力), denoting and connoting more abstract notions, emerge and flourish or fade. Chinese characters have expressed every emotion from the loneliness of the frontier soldier in Tang dynasty poetry to Gao Xingjian's stream of consciousness novels and Han Han's rebellious, quirky essays. Chiang notes that he does not know of any other country that approaches writing in the way that China does (1973: 1); Yen adds support to this notion, arguing that a Chinese person's 'culture' (文化), that is, becoming civilised or being changed by writing, gives him or her 'the deep meaning of written characters' and keeps them in touch with history, an argument we will see later. For Yen it is central to the definition of Chinese-ness (2005: 50). Artistic uses of Arabic script and mediaeval illumination of Western European languages are examples of the way in which all cultures use writing in aesthetic and spiritual ways. The magic of literacy and literature and the beauty of writing are not absent in other parts of the world, but perhaps Chinese is approached in this aesthetic way on a daily, rather than an occasional basis, and with a more conscious linking to identity and nationality.

Whatever the cognitive processes of reading and writing, and whatever the ideological stance we take, the creation of characters by hand and in print and digital media is necessarily largely visual. Translation of writing-related matters will inevitably involve visual and spatial awareness and description. This will link with the jargon of painting, drawing and image-making, but to it we must add considerations of standardisation: writing is carried out within certain constraints in order that it may be readable. At the same time, invariably, discussions of Chinese calligraphy, characters and literacy are emotionally charged.

Chiang claims that Chinese characters 'express in a peculiar way the beauty of the thought' and that Chinese calligraphy is mysterious and perplexing to Westerners (1973: 1). Many scholars would dispute the claim that Chinese is mysterious or perplexing: the Chinese writing system is accessed both visually and phonologically (de Francis 1984) and can express trivial, evil and ugly thoughts, as well as beautiful thoughts. While handwriting is still valued more than print as an artistic expression, seal carving and now font design are approached with equal commitment and creativity. In the following sections, we discuss the expression of the meta-discourse of Chinese characters.

Simplified or traditional: The deixis of cultural and personal identity

Chinese characters certainly stimulate fierce and emotional discussion, not least because they unify otherwise linguistically and politically distinct groups. While all the characters in use today have evolved from the early marks on oracle bones and Neolithic painted pottery (Taylor and Taylor 1995: 43–48), two distinct 'systems' are used in different geo-political areas. Simplified characters (简体字) have been designed, published and promoted in largish batches since 1956, and are in use in the People's Republic of China and in Singapore. In Hong Kong and Taiwan, and in the Chinese diaspora, traditional characters (繁體字), that is, those current prior to 1956, are still used. 'System' may be the most convenient term, but neither traditional nor simplified characters can be said to be truly 'systematic'. The distinction is fuzzy, for many simplified forms have been popular in all Chinese-speaking areas for hundreds of years, and many traditional forms are still in use alongside the simplified forms. Some characters do not need to be simplified, and many would be difficult to simplify without losing their distinct meanings. Now that Hong Kong and Macau are once more part of China, and as Taiwan grows closer to China, users of simplified and traditional characters are conscious of the difference and openly discuss the pros and cons.

Since liberalisation in the People's Republic of China in the early 1980s, there has been something of a revival of the traditional forms in formal, literary or aesthetic contexts: on, for instance, name cards, menus, shop fronts and book jackets. Yet, the deep division remains. Blogs and media articles reveal the major political schism represented by traditional and simplified characters. Terminology differs between Taiwan and mainland China, and even the term for traditional characters is significant in this respect. From a Taiwan point of view, the full-form characters handed down over thousands of years are upright, correct or orthodox (正), whereas in mainland China they are complex or complicated (繁). In American and British terminology, a 'complex' character is one that has many strokes. Of course this is simply terminology, but it is determined by deixis, that is, the point of view of the speaker (Pellatt and Liu 2010: 114–15) and, however neutrally reported, demonstrates the geo-political distinctions, and demands sensitive decision making on the part of the translator.

The terms for 'traditional' and 'simplified' themselves give rise to antagonistic discussion. An article in *Epoch Times,* a journal overtly critical of the People's Republic of China, cites the apparently erudite evidence of a linguist based in America:

Example 2a

有一群人對於自己所使用的文字被稱為繁體字心生不悅，為了自明
[sic] 為文化正統便找出一個較令人寬慰的詞 － 正體字。正者正統

也；統者傳統也。然而自稱為正統者又無膽說出『正』的相對語詞是什麼。相對於簡者繁，相對於正者歪。因此，稱自己的文字為正體字的人應稱另一方為歪體字才是？非也。正的『對文』是邪。」「因此，稱傳統漢字為正體字的人應稱另一方為邪體字。因為有『簡』才有『繁』，既稱此為『正』，應稱彼為『邪』。既有漢賊之別，為何無正邪之分？」

(Shao 2009)

This excerpt reveals the depth of feeling in the debate. The string of rhetorical questions, and the use of the traditional *wenyanwen* (文言文) style to argue the point are crucial to the thrust of the argument, but very challenging to render in good English translation. One of the key issues in translation of this excerpt would be whether or not to render the *wenyanwen* style. It may be better to summarise to a certain extent, retaining the slight implied by the elegant definitions. The next key issue for the translator is that the writer's argument revolves around an elegant play on words involving the Chinese term 正, a common epithet, with multiple positive interpretations in English, and its counterparts or opposites 歪 and 邪. While 歪 is simply 'not right' or 'not straight', 邪 could be variously rendered as 'evil', 'irregular', 'abnormal' 'fallacious', 'devious', 'perverse' and so on, and in all cases the thrust is decidedly negative. The problem in rendering this text in English is that of finding actual linguistic opposites that present a logical dichotomy within a coherent argument:

> There are those who are not happy that the characters that they use are dubbed 'complicated', and for the sake of their self-acclaimed main-stream cultural tradition, have adopted the rather more comforting term 'orthodox or correct'. However, they might not dare to state openly the opposite of 'orthodox', if applied to the corresponding simplified characters.
>
> The opposite of 'simplified' is 'complex', and the opposite of 'correct' is 'incorrect' or 'wrong', so should the people who use the term 'correct' for the traditional characters they use, use the term 'wrong' for the characters other people use? No.
>
> The opposite of 'correct', or 'orthodox' is also 'unorthodox' or 'perverse', so those who refer to traditional characters as 'correct or good' should call simplified characters 'wrong' or 'perverse'. If the opposite of 'simplified' is 'complex', then the opposite of 'correct' must be 'incorrect'. Since we distinguish between what is genuinely Chinese and what is not, should we not distinguish between correct characters and incorrect characters?
>
> (Authors' translation)

One point of interest for outside observers in these debates is the use of political pro-forms for the agencies involved. It is noticeable that the term

'Taiwan authorities' (台當局) is used, a nicely neutral term for the government of Taiwan, which in China, of course, is not regarded as a nation, but as part of China. At the time of writing, the KMT (the Kuomintang nationalist party, of which the original raison d'être was to be considered the government of China, operating from Taiwan) was in power. The term 'mainland' (大陸) rather than 'China' (中國), is on the one hand, geographically correct and, on the other, strategically diplomatic, implying that Taiwan and China are part of the same geographical entity. Retaining this terminology in English preserves the desired nuance of an argument that is mired in the contradictions of cultural belonging and political schism. The term 'mainland' in English is unproblematic, but may imply a nationalist point of view. Some translators might prefer to use the term People's Republic of China. For readers who are not well acquainted with the situation of Taiwan (though ignorance on this point is decreasing), the terms 兩岸 'two banks or coasts' and 對岸, 'the opposite bank or coast' may not be familiar. Used adjectively, this regular shorthand denoting physical and political China–Taiwan relations is often rendered as 'cross-strait'. In translation it may be necessary to explicitate to some extent.

In recent years, efforts have been made to recognise Chinese traditional characters as World Heritage. On 20 December 2008, Ma Yingjiu, then President of Taiwan, called for traditional (rather than simplified) Chinese characters to be given World Heritage status (Phoenixtv 2012). The internet debate surrounding this proposal revealed divided and sometimes extreme positions on the topic, in English and in Chinese (e.g. Turton 2008). The terms used to render the notion of listing as cultural heritage (列為世界文化遺產) are straightforward in translation, and it is important that the conventional international terms are respected, not least for the sake of international understanding. The terms used in the UNESCO literature are 'list as' and 'cultural heritage'. In this case, as in the case of Chinese calligraphy, which was listed in 2009, it is 'intangible cultural heritage' (非物質文化遺产).

Discussion of the proposal appeared on numerous websites, in both simplified and traditional characters. The bloggers criticised mainland and Taiwan leaders over attitudes towards the two systems of writing, showing strong political motivations and a tendency to allude to history to support their arguments.

Example 2b

In a sina.com blog, Ovid Tseng, Minister without portfolio, is quoted:

> 對于台灣民眾能突破時空限制，使用現存的文字跟兩千多年前的古人交流，很多人都覺得不可思議。

(Phoenixtv 2012)

For many, the notion that the people of Taiwan are able to use the current writing system to break down the barriers of time and connect with the people of 2,000 years ago may be inconceivable.

(Authors' translation)

As it is reported, Tseng's statement centres the traditional characters in Taiwan, using the authority of history and the emotional thrall of the ancestors. Tseng perhaps exaggerates the communicative power of traditional characters: he uses the verb 'to communicate or exchange' (交流). To translate it this way would be to imply some kind of time travel, but if we say 'connect with', we stay within the bounds of simple understanding, rather than any closer contact. This centring implies that this is something mainland China does not have.

As China and Taiwan draw closer politically, socially and culturally, the gulfs in linguistic and cultural practice become more apparent. Businesspeople and academics work together, young people study together, and they are realising that they have to learn one another's idiom and script. In the fierce debate over the desirability, necessity and responsibility of knowledge of both systems, each side has characteristically coined its own abbreviated terms to use as slogans:

- 識正書簡/识正书简 (read, or recognise traditional and write simplified);
- 用簡識繁/用简识繁 (use simplified and read traditional);
- 識簡書正/识简书正 (read simplified and write traditional);
- 由簡識繁/由简识繁 (from simplified recognise traditional).

There are, however, still discrepancies and political axes grinding quietly in the background. China and Taiwan seem to be wanting the same thing, that all readers should be able to access both traditional and simplified characters (繁簡體字都通), yet some pundits are using a stubbornly distinct terminology.

As long as we tackle the slogans coherently, they should not present a problem for the reader. The Chinese slogan style uses the simplest possible Verb + Object form 'know traditional write simple' (識正書簡). It cannot be conveyed fluently in English without some grammatical adjustment. The verbs, at least, must have a usable form that can be integrated into a sentence. Using a gerund (e.g. knowing/reading) helps to make this clear. It is also advisable to find a suitable synonym for the lexical items. 識 in this context only makes sense as 'reading' or perhaps 'recognising'; 正 (as discussed above) will only be understood in this context as 'traditional' (the term 'full' was common some years ago, but seems to have fallen out of use); 'to write' (書) is the term used in 'calligraphy' (the term used in the mainland slogan is 寫), and in this context 'writing' is appropriate; 簡 is the adjective 'simple' but is a reduction of the phrase '简体字' simple-form characters, or simplified characters. In a context in which reference is made to a policy, we might talk about 'the policy of reading traditional and writing simplified characters'. In a context in which the phrase is a slogan, we might use an unadorned imperative: 'read traditional and write simplified'. It is evident that in the case of this type of Chinese 'portmanteau' phrase, simplicity, clarity and adjustment to the context are required. As the debate develops, the rest of the world must be involved, and the translation must be clear. Any translation of the debate must be fully informed and sympathetic to the attitudes and sensitivities of the protagonists.

Women's writing

Like the English expression 'women's writing', the term 女书 conjures not only the realm of literary creativity, but also the notion of a woman's handwriting. In a certain small area of China, women's handwriting has been an identifiable, distinct script, marked out from that of men. It was practised mainly in Jiangyong County in Hunan Province, in an area that in recent decades has been an autonomous county of the Yao ethnic minority (瑶族). As Gong notes, prior to the Han dynasty, it was an area of uncertain political identity, passing from one state or ruler to another, and was reckoned to be 'a place full of barbarians' (蛮夷之地) (Gong 1991: 15). It was a remote area, economically and culturally backward (地理偏僻、經濟文化落後的山區) (ibid.: 15). By the 1980s, when scholars first began to research what they now knew was a dying cultural phenomenon, the area was a mixed community of Han and Yao peoples, but it was mainly Han women who used the script. Women's writing had always been a script kept secret from men, though, as See suggests in her fictional account (2006), it could not have been kept entirely secret – 'men just considered our writing beneath them' (ibid.: 201). During the 1960s and 1970s the diminishing band of women who maintained the skill imposed a self-censorship (自我噤声), only, on their deathbed, asking their descendants to preserve the tradition (Zheng Introduction to Gong 1991: 7). Anything secret would have been suspect during those years of the Cultural Revolution, let alone a script that only a minority of the population could read, and See (2006: 335) gives anecdotal evidence of this. It is noteworthy that Gong's introduction to women's writing repeatedly locates women's writing activities 'before 1949'. The very nature of this female-only code meant that samples were rarely preserved. The skill was passed from person to person, and the documents of women's writing, such as letters, fans, embroideries and third day books, were burned during funeral rites. It has now fallen into disuse.

The meta-discourse of women's writing is necessarily retrospective, and veers towards a feminist tendency, although two of the major researchers involved in the rediscovery of women's writing have been men, Zhou Shuoyi and Gong Zhebing. Stories about how women's writing was 'rediscovered', documented and researched vary. Zhou was forced to destroy his collection of women's writing during the Cultural Revolution. Gong was fortunate to make the acquaintance of the last practitioner of the script, Gao Yinxian, who, in her final years, was able to explain and demonstrate the technique. It was possible to gather fragments, on paper, on fans and incorporated in embroidery, which a group of volunteers copied by hand so as to render the samples printable (Gong 1991).

How is women's writing described? What identifies it as 'women's' and how is it different from 'men's' writing? Zheng is clear about the function of women's writing: 内容多在訴説婦女的苦情 (ibid.: 7). The barest translation of this statement would be 'the content is mainly complaints about women's bitter feelings', a frank statement that reflects the role of the script as an accompaniment to discontent. The style of the statement could be polished, for the term 'content' (内容), when it appears in a Chinese text, is not always translated into English: it gives a slightly Chinglish feel to the rendering. Should we keep 'complaints'? The writers of the script used it because they could not complain to their menfolk: they could only talk about their diffi-culties among their female companions. 苦情 could be variously interpreted: 苦 was a term commonly used during and after liberation, as in the common expression to suffer or 'eat bitterness' (吃苦), and 'speak bitterness', a com-plex activity of remembering and often accusing (说苦): it evokes the bitter-ness, the hardship and misery of workers' and peasants' lives; it carries undertones of exploitation and oppression. 'Bitter feelings' might not be quite sufficient in the context. In an English-speaking context, we might say that women's writing was a channel or outlet for all the pent-up misery of a woman's life. The Baidu entry for 女书 describes this function as 'recording the experience of their troubles' (为了把自己的苦难经历记下来). The com-plaints included accusation, sarcasm and scolding, according to Gong (1991: 29). Women's writing was, however, not entirely negative, for it also carried rou-tine information and expressions of joy: for example, the third day letter (三朝书), or book (See 2006: 46), presented to a young woman on the third day after her marriage, when she would return to visit her parents. There were also song fans (歌扇), inscribed with the words of songs sung by groups of women as they did their women's handicraft work (女红), which included all the delicate crafts such as sewing, embroidery and paper cutting. Women could use the secret writing to convey their own, or other women's stories, and their prayers to a goddess (ibid.: 30). The structure of a composition in women's writing was often a seven character poem (七言诗), in other words, a poem composed in lines of seven characters, a common metre in China.

Sisterhood and writing

An important social factor in the phenomenon of women's writing was sister-hood. Betrothals were often made while children were still in the womb, but if both babies in the proposed match turned out to be girls, they would become sworn sisters, and writing to one another would be a core part of their relationship:

Example 2c

> 一九四九年以前，上江墟鄉　的女子喜歡結拜姐妹，結拜時，雙方互送禮物，比如，毛巾、手帕、女書之類，並且各請對方吃一餐。一旦結爲姊妹，關係就非常密切，甚至賽過親姊妹。

(Gong 1991: 20)

Prior to 1949, the women of Xu County in Upper Jiangsu liked to become sworn sisters. When they swore allegiance to one another, they would present reciprocal gifts, such as towels and handkerchiefs inscribed with 'women's writing' and would invite one another to a meal. Once they had become sworn sisters, the relationship was as close as, if not closer than, that of biological sisters.

(Authors' translation)

This excerpt, which is very typically structured with many short sentences (短句) and commas, does not present challenges, except perhaps the contrast of 結拜姐妹 and 親姊妹. The accepted translation of 結拜姐妹 is sworn sisters, but 親姊妹 could be 'real sisters', 'natural sisters' or 'blood sisters'. There are complications with the term 'blood sisters', as 'blood brothers' (in English) are not natural brothers, but sworn brothers, so 'blood sisters' may not be the most useful term. 'Natural' in descriptions of family relations carries implications of illegitimacy, and different parents. Using a more familiar register, we could say 'their own sisters', or a more formal register 'biological sisters', which is simple and clear. See, who distinguishes the closer relationship of 'old sames' (老同) as more special than sworn sister, uses the useful term 'natal' to refer to a woman's own maternal family (2006: passim).

Describing linguistic and aesthetic qualities

Women's writing differs from standard Chinese characters in a number of ways. The major difference is that there is a very limited stock of characters. Gong (1991: 7) suggests around 600, and some estimates give as many as 1,700 (Baidu n.d.). The flexibility of the system lies in its phonetic qualities. Like Chinese characters, each character corresponds to a spoken syllable, but each character of women's writing can have many more meanings, according to context. According to Baidu, it is a phonosyllabic script (音节文字). A term used for other scripts of this nature is 'syllabary': Japanese hiragana and katakana and Tibetan are examples of syllabaries.

The characters of women's writing have a slanted form, and are sometimes nicknamed 长脚蚊 or 长脚文, an obvious pun, and even in official documents were called 蚊形字. A literal translation of these terms would be 'long-legged mosquitoes', or 'long-legged writing' and 'mosquito-shaped characters', all of which are expressions very close to the English expression 'spidery writing', a slightly disparaging epithet we apply to idiosyncratic, irregular writing. Cody described it as 'wispy and elongated' (2004: 29). But women's writing is not irregular: in all the extant cases it is regular, neat and legible.

Zheng describes opening a 'booklet' (裝訂冊頁成書) of women's writing. The epithets she uses, in contrast to the stereotypical terms quoted above, are descriptive and objective:

Example 2d

> 翻開來是泛黃的粗軟紙張，像用蘸墨不多的禿筆寫著柴瘦而不柔弱的字，疏朗有致，右高左低的筆畫使每一個字基本上呈斜菱形，筆畫相接之處多形成尖細的銳角，犀利帶英氣。
>
> (Gong 1991: 10)

> [The booklet] opened to reveal fragile, yellowing paper, covered with fine, yet not weak, characters that appeared to have been written with a dry, sparsely-bristled brush. The characters were neat lozenge shapes, the strokes of each character extending obliquely from high on the right to low on the left, with the intersections of the strokes creating sharp, strong angles.
>
> (Authors' translation)

We all know the experience of opening an old book: the mustiness, the yellowing of the pages. The characters contained in the booklet are described partly in terms of the writing instrument: a 'bald' brush with sparse ink, something that might imply bad writing skills. Here, it reinforces the idea of thinness and delicacy of the characters. We would probably not use the term 'stick thin', which is more often used to refer to the sick or to supermodels. The strokes, which are 'high on the right and low on the left' contribute to the diamond or lozenge shape of the characters, and give an overall effect of sharp corners. The description of these rather delicate characters is balanced by the subjective evaluation: they are 犀利帶英 – not simply 'sharp', but incisive or trenchant and heroic, even noble, and the very use of the term 犀利 carries a hint of the masculine. Adhering too closely to the Chinese in a rendering of this excerpt might produce contradictory statements.

Standard Chinese characters (汉字 or 男字) are associated with men: they are considered conventional, acceptable and powerful. Comparing the system of women's writing with Chinese characters, Gong (1991: 34) notes that Chinese characters are 方方正正, 橫平豎直, 上下左右力求對稱, 很像男性敦厚的體形、穩重的風格, while the characters of women's writing are 修長輕盈, 舒展秀麗, 不拘一格, 像少女苗條的體形、飄逸的品格. While this comparison of 'squareness', 'balance', 'honesty' and 'stability' with 'slenderness', 'grace' and 'unblemished beauty' can in no way be regarded as negative, it could be regarded as somewhat subjective. In an English rendering, the excerpt is also highly redundant, as, without risking verbosity, it may be hard to find a wide range of synonyms for 'slender' and 'graceful'. Translation of the 'masculine' attributes of standard Chinese characters into English notably gives us a wider range of lexical choice. No doubt in years to come women's writing will be the subject of an ever-broadening range of research, and perhaps a gradually more objective description.

Font design and cultural identity

China has printed its characters for hundreds of years, and printing is as much a part of writing as handwriting. For the last two or three decades, well-educated Chinese have realised their thoughts digitally, as well as manually, and are dependent on font design, not only in the books and documents that they read, but also in the fonts they choose to type on their computers. At the time of going to print, a debate is raging among UK Chinese language educators as to whether to teach Chinese word processing skills pro-actively, and to what extent to allow word processing in examinations, or even assess the skill. If we read and write Chinese, we cannot ignore the printed word, and that inevitably compels us to consider font design.

Font designers and critics are deeply aware of the significance of fonts. Simon Garfield quotes Steve Jobs's perceptions of typography as 'beautiful, historical' and 'artistically subtle' (2011: 11). Garfield notes that there are 100,000 fonts in the world (ibid.: 14): he does not state whether this includes non-alphabetic scripts, but either way, it is a vast number, and demonstrates the weight of privilege and responsibility the designers bear in creating fonts for the discerning reader and writer.

Fonts have associations. We cannot state objectively that fonts have aesthetic qualities, but they are seen, by designers and users, as having attributes that affect communication beyond language (ibid.: 25–26). They may be described as funny, threatening, friendly, graceful, or authoritative. Like Chinese characters and the women's writing we discussed above, they can be assigned gender (ibid.: 33), depending on the solidity or fragility of their form. The anthropomorphism of English type is extended right into the terminology of the typesetter, who uses terms like 'body', 'beard', 'shoulder' and the term we all use, 'face' (ibid.: 46), terminology very reminiscent of the way Chinese characters are sometimes described. Types have all the characteristics we attribute to handwriting, with one addition, that is, their permanence and consistency. Garfield shows how type exists in a world of convention: publishers and companies prefer and even prescribe certain types (ibid.: 31). Fonts evolve and vary with great rapidity, as they are always a product and a tool of advancing technology. The technology imposes constraints, particularly on size, since not only must the letter fit its font in the press, but must also be marshalled and managed to fit into tightly regimented patterns of lines on a paper or digital page. Given the apparent uniformity required by a mechanised or digitised system, the naming and description of fonts, in both Chinese and English, is surprisingly subjective.

In a finely printed volume, Liao (2009) evaluates the evolution of font design from 1949 to 2009, and the importance of the largely unsung heroes who have worked at the designs. The title of the introduction reveals the significance of print: 'One Chinese character, one story, passed on from generation to generation; one printed character, one paragraph of life' (一個漢字一個故事。家傳戶誦。一個印刷字一段人生). Prior to 1949, the traditional character fonts were 'totally random' or literally 'scattered, chaotic and not standard' (散亂不齊), in size and shape, limited in variety and partly imported from Japan (ibid.: 14). This was not an ideal situation for a nation that had supposedly just thrown off the shackles of imperialism. During the 1950s, the People's Republic of China undertook a major language reform (文字改革) during which the forms and strokes of printed characters were standardised and simplified (ibid.: 14). According to Liao, the big private printing presses of the period co-operated with the government, releasing their type free of charge for use in government publications (ibid.: 14). At that time, there was no such profession as a font designer, but calligraphers, seal carvers, commercial artists and book designers were enlisted to work on the huge task of font design. In 1965, a list of standard designs for 6,196 characters was published, the design of which was based on the idea of the Song style with elements of the Kai style (宋體楷化) (ibid.: 14).

Like everything else in China's economy, font design was subject to five-year plans, a measure intended to produce variety and creativity (百花齊放), and which included national and international competitions (ibid.: 15). It was at this point that font design became a recognised profession (ibid.: 16). Liao notes that the labour of producing type was lightened considerably by the advent of computers in the 1980s (ibid.: 15).

With Liao's book, we return to the interview format we explored in Chapter 1: like the interviewer who questioned Wu Guanzhong, the editor/interviewer here is eliciting deeply rooted convictions and emotions from the interviewees. In the opening interview with Zhu Zhiwei, Liao notes how, in 38 years of design career, Zhu has expanded his vision from that of individual artist to encompass his reader (Liao 2009: 62). Zhu's first response might come as a slight shock to some literate Chinese:

Example 2e

大多數中國人都知道中國字體有輝煌的歷史，但可能不知道中國字體很落後。。。與日本的相比，有很大的差距 ...

(Zhu in Liao 2009: 65)

Most Chinese people know that Chinese characters have a glorious history, but perhaps they don't realise that the character font forms are backward ... they fall far short of those of Japan ...

(Authors' translation)

He goes on to explain (like Garfield above) that it is the font designer's pride and responsibility to create comfort for the reader. Words like backward (落後), dignity or pride in oneself (自豪), and pride (驕傲) carry a somewhat negative tone. There may appear to be a one-to-one correspondence between the Chinese and the English, but the translator might wish to question whether the dictionary equivalents are suitable in the context. What does Zhu mean by 'backward?' It is a word that is regarded as rather politically incorrect, carrying, as it does, connotations of the days when countries of the southern hemisphere were labelled 'third world'. China is certainly not third world, and during the millennia of development of Chinese characters, has been one of the most advanced civilisations. Do we really want to say that Chinese character fonts are backward? Do we want to shock, or in the case of Western readers, possibly reinforce stereotypes? Could we opt for a term such as 'outdated', or, at the risk of being accused of infidelity, produce a more nuanced effect, such as: 'Most Chinese people know that Chinese characters have a glorious history, but perhaps they don't realise that, compared with those of Japan, they are less well-suited to the modern reader'? On the other hand, perhaps Zhu would prefer the translator to retain his candour.

Like European language fonts, and like the handwriting styles they emulate, Chinese fonts have names and individual identities. Zhu talks about some of the prize-winning fonts he has designed:

Example 2f

> ‘鐵筋隸書’吧，　這是九九年的，得的是評審員獎。‘北魏楷書’是九
> 六年的，　得的是銅獎。‘亮點’也是九九年創作的。當時這三個都是
> 為參加比賽設計的，這個‘鐵筋隸書’用了一個月的時間，意境最高，
> 就是平淡。人們寫隸書都是強調它的蠶頭燕尾，我恰恰是削弱這個。
> 歷史上也是有這樣寫的，但是形狀不是這樣。這一個‘蘭’我也很喜
> 歡，用了三個多月，下了很大功夫，這個很很難。

(Zhu in Liao 2009: 68)

Tiejin Lishu or 'Iron Sinew Li' is a design I created in 1999, which was awarded a judge's prize. *Liangdian* 'Bright Spot' was also 1999. *Bei Wei Kaishu* or 'Northern Wei Kai' dates from 1996, and was awarded a bronze medal. I designed all three especially for competitions. I spent a month working on 'Iron Sinew Li' and its significance lies in its understatement. When people write Kai style, they emphasize the flourishes – what we call 'the silkworms' heads and swallows' tails', but I downplay these features. There are historical precedents, but the form is not quite the same. I am very fond of this style too: *Lan* or 'The Orchid'. It took three months of enormous effort.

(Authors' translation)

As we noted above, fonts exist in their thousands, yet for designers and users, each is distinctly characterised and named. The non-Chinese-speaking reader of our translation is likely to be an expert in the field, and will need to know the names of the fonts, for the purposes of research and discussion. We are therefore duty bound to give the fonts their proper Chinese names: *Tiejin Lishu, Liangdian* and *Lan*. But is this enough? The transliteration solution without support is very often the reason why meaning is 'lost in translation'. Zhu has told the interviewer how much effort and time these designs cost him, and we know from elsewhere in the interview that he is a highly creative person. The names he gives to his fonts indicate their provenance in the history of Chinese calligraphy, their inspiration, their nature and their place in modern Chinese culture. If we add the meaning of these names to the transliteration, we furnish that information for the reader, and we are not guilty of reducing the designer's role.

The first font name mentioned in this excerpt, *Tiejin Lishu* (鐵筋隸書), carries a wealth of historical and stylistic implication. It has been developed on the basis of 'Li Style', also known as 'official' or 'clerical' style, one of the five great styles of Chinese handwriting (see page 46). Its 'iron sinews' or 'iron bars' tell us that it is bold and black, and perhaps, to some readers, rather masculine. This impression may be intensified when we read on and discover that, in order to achieve sophistication, Zhu reduced the traditional flourishes, or 'silkworms' heads and swallows' tails' (蠶頭燕尾), associated with the style. The two other font names, 亮點 *Liangdian* and 蘭 *Lan* are equally redolent and at the same time contrast strongly in the aesthetic schema that they trigger. The reader knows intuitively that *Liangdian* ('bright spot' or 'sparkle') is certain to be a bright, modern style, and *Lan* ('orchid') is likely to be a more natural, sweeping style. The concise nomenclature tells the target reader as much as a paragraph of descriptive detail.

Later in the interview, Zhu claims that for him, font design has no depth (沒有深度), but perhaps this is because his deep foundations of seal carving and calligraphy have become so much a part of the design process that he takes them for granted. He says that the 'depth' of font design is not for the designer to decide, but exists objectively (是客觀存在的) (Zhu in Liao 2009: 74). This observation might mean simply 'objective' but might mean that the beauty is in the eye of the beholder and certainly reflects the characteristics of the fonts, in their execution and in their names.

An interest in the cultural and political properties and implications of Chinese characters is no longer exclusive to China. UN diplomats, collectors of international art, publishers and learners of Chinese and many others all depend on translations of the discourse surrounding China's handwritten and printed scripts.

Practical 2.1 Cultural identity and calligraphy

Find examples, descriptions and discussions of calligraphy from cultures other than China. These might include, for example, mediaeval illuminated texts from Europe, such as *The Book of Kells*, or examples of Arabic calligraphy.

i   Compare the way in which descriptions and discussions of other scripts are expressed.
ii How does the specialised lexis differ between cultures?
iii How does the expression of aesthetic values compare and contrast?
iv Do the scholars describing and discussing the scripts write from a nationalistic, patriotic or ethnocentric point of view? If so, what kinds of deictic or subjective language do they use?

Practical 2.2 Avoiding subjectivity in description

Read the following comparison of Chinese characters and women's writing. To what extent should the translator reduce any redundancy, or re-structure using different parts of speech in English? Do you see this description as subjective? If so, would it make sense to adapt it, for example for a female readership?

> 漢字方方正正，橫平豎直，上下左右力求對稱，很像男性敦厚的體形、穩重的風格。女書修長輕盈，舒展秀麗，不拘一格，像少女苗條的體形、飄逸的品格。　女性一般比男性富於幻想、更有浪漫氣質，因此，女書的形體佈局不像漢字那樣莊嚴、規範，而是根據筆畫走向，不太嚴格地組成單體、上下、左右、雙合、夾心、包圍等各種組合，其中隱含著一種對稱，如右上與左下均衡，雖傾斜卻不失中心，給人一種特殊的美感。
>
> (Gong 1991: 34)

Practical 2.3 Aesthetic description

The font designer is asked why he gave *Liangdian* ('bright spot' or 'sparkle') its name. Translate his response, below:

> 古人說：　‘一成一字之規’，意思是筆一落到紙上便是點，其他筆劃都是這一點的延伸，筆鋒向右運行，　是橫，向下運行，是豎。　‘亮點’就是根據這個論點創作的，撇和提的起筆　處可以明顯地看到點的形狀；左豎則一點來造型，像日、品、內、國等字；　豎勾頓挫出鋒後留下點的痕跡，橫劃輕入重出，從中能體會到速度與重量的有機結合；豎的起筆輕捷委婉，一帶而過，　平添了幾分輕鬆和靈動；點劃間顧盼呼應，使字生動活潑，結構端莊均勻。字體貼近人，閱讀就感到親切。
>
> (Liao 2009: 71)

3 Calligraphy

Physical and spiritual aspects of writing

The socio-cultural significance of Chinese characters is evident in the passages we have discussed above, and every Chinese child internalises the ideology of writing. From a very early age every educated Chinese native reader-writer learns how to hold a brush and how to move the hands to achieve the right stroke. The highly tactile sensory-motor activity of writing helps to instil the memory of the character and its phonological, visual and semantic components. Ignoring the rules may result in characters that offend the eye and hamper reading. To this end, innumerable manuals and copy books are available. It makes sense to translate the manuals and copy books, for foreign learners, like Chinese children, start to learn to write long before they are able to read fluently. Chiang Yee notes that the 'delectable' hobby of calligraphy is the most popular of the arts (1938/1973: 17). This could be due to the fact that everyone who is educated possesses a greater or lesser extent of skill in the medium. The language of the manuals, while predictably ideological and emotional, necessarily focuses on the tactile aspects of processes and technique and the visual aspects of style.

Yen speaks of 'becoming a person through *wen*' (文), that is the whole process of becoming literate, refined and civilised in a Chinese context (2005: 46). To be uncivilised (沒文化) is to be ignorant, and is associated in the Chinese mind with negative attitudes towards the less well educated, and in particular rural people (ibid.: 34). Writing Chinese characters represents a profound integration of mind, body and spirit. The terms of calligraphy draw on the physical terminology of bones, sinews and flesh (骨、筋、肉) and the practice of writing is literally embodied in the writer's stance and actions, a phenomenon that Yen calls 'technique of the body' or 'body engineering' (2005: 81).

Learning to write: Studying the great masters

The teaching and learning of calligraphy are deeply embedded in history. The five standard styles originated hundreds of years ago, and are literally 'set in stone'. The craft of the eminent calligraphers of the past was reproduced on the great memorial tablets that may still be visited today, and from which amateur and professional calligraphers still take rubbings, to enhance their skill by emulating the great masters. Texts like the 'Kaicheng classics' were

carved on large stone tablets (often human height or even taller) as perma-
nent models to prevent copying errors (Travel China Guide n.d.). It is reported
that Mao Zedong, an avid calligrapher, collected examples of inscriptions on
stone (Barras 2002: 109).

Calligraphy education starts with copying the great historical styles or
'hands'. The five principal styles of calligraphy are seal script or *Zhuanshu* (篆
书); official or clerical script said to have been invented in the second century
BC or *Lishu* (隶书); a regular, much-used style called *Kaishu* (楷书); the freer
'running' style or *Xingshu* (行书) and 'grass script' or *Caoshu* (草书) a free-
hand script named for its speed or roughness, yet still considered elegant
(Chiang 1973: 41–105). Of these, *Kaishu* is considered the most accessible, and
it is mainly from this style that beginners are taught, or teach themselves. All
these styles include variants, and in the following paragraphs we will look at
an older variant and a more modern variant, exploring the language used in
description and instruction. In the twenty-first century, the many non-Chinese
learners of the language need to access the sophisticated language of instruction long before their Chinese vocabulary is adequate to the task. It is with
the learner of Chinese in mind that we approach the translation of physical
and spiritual aspects of the mechanics of writing.

Our first example is that of a historically renowned calligrapher, Liu
Gongquan (柳公權), as described and taught in Huang Yaoshu's (n.d.)
manual *Liu Gongquan's Calligraphy Style: Getting Started* (書法入門). This is
a very typical manual that assumes a knowledge of basic writing technique,
and is suitable for teaching from the fourth year of primary school to the
early years of secondary school. The manual contains a set of instructions,
dealing with all aspects of writing, from tools and posture through to brush
strokes and stroke order. It provides perforated detachable pages with exem-
plars, and a fold-out model of 'nine palace square' grid paper (九宮格紙).
Between these practical sections is a brief biography of Liu Gongquan, the
master on whose style the book is modelled. This is an all-important section,
investing the instruction with authority and providing a context of veneration
and of aesthetic and moral quality.

The story of Liu's life is a microcosm of the spirit and practice of calligraphy. Liu was a Tang dynasty official and lived from 778 to 865 AD, under a
fairly stable regime. This relative stability, the editor points out, enabled him
to develop his art of calligraphy. The following examples show how the editor
of the manual depicts the calligrapher's life as an implicit model for children
to follow, what we would nowadays call a role model. An English translation
might be aimed at children beginning to learn Chinese in the upper stages of
primary and early stages of secondary education, or at older learners.

Translating register and lexis: The specialist terms of history

The style of the writing is quasi-classical, reflecting, though not aping, a fairly
high literary register, as compared with the calligraphy instructions, which are

in a more practical register. Instructions have their own special style, which we will discuss in the next section. In cases where instructions are enhanced by historical or biographical details of, for instance, artists, athletes and calligraphers, the writing needs to be appropriate to the reader, not only in terms of register, but also in interest and appeal. Here is an excerpt from the potted biography of Liu Gongquan:

Example 3a

柳公權生平
　柳公權是唐代的大書法家。生於唐朝代宗大歷十三年，即公元七七八年。距離現在一千二百年了。他科舉進士出身，在朝任官四十多年，官至太子太師。仕途總算平穩。他雖曾一度因牛李黨爭失去了權勢，只任閒缺，但還沒有貶離京師。也正因爲這樣，反可以專心鑽研，成就了他的超人書法藝術。

(Huang n.d.: 14)

Liu Gongquan was a master calligrapher of the Tang dynasty. He was born twelve hundred years ago, in 778 AD, the thirteenth year of the reign of Dai Zong. He passed the provincial degree examination and the metropolitan degree examination, and served as an imperial official for over forty years, reaching the rank of Grand Tutor to the Heir Apparent. His career path was generally stable. Although he was briefly appointed to a position without responsibility, owing to the Niu-Li factional struggles, he was never exiled from the capital. It was this, however, that enabled him to focus and perfect his sublime artistry.

(Authors' translation)

This small excerpt is very typical of Chinese writing on historical matters: it necessarily refers concisely to periods, people and phenomena which have precise labelling. The labels have to be integrated coherently into the grammar and discourse of the target text.

Dates in texts present issues of arithmetical and political correctness. Here the writer gives two dates, the reign name and year, and the date in the international calendar. A quick check reveals that the Dai Zong accession took place in 763 AD, which would mean that Liu was born in the fifteenth year of the reign, or that he was born in 776 AD. Wrong information will leave the translator and the publisher open to criticism. In the case of a discrepancy like this, it might be preferable to omit the international calendar equivalent, and provide a footnote that indicates the accession year of the Dai Zong reign. If we decide to keep the international date, we can opt for 'AD' (anno domini – the year of the Lord), which is widely used, but is not always considered politically correct, since it has obvious references to Christianity. The alternative is to use 'CE', the abbreviation of 'common era'. In the case of pre-AD/CE dates, the respective choices are BC, the acronym for 'before

Christ' or BCE, 'before the common era'. Both options have their champions and detractors, and whatever our personal beliefs and preferences, we should be guided by our editor. Do we need to say that this was twelve hundred years ago? If editors are pressing for fewer words, this rather obvious fact could be omitted. On the other hand, in both source text and target text, it serves to emphasise to young people the historical authority of the calligrapher.

Reference to the imperial examination system is made in the text. Liu passed the imperial examinations at *keju* level (科舉) and at *jinshi* level (進士). Given the overwhelming importance of the examination system in pre-republican China, it is only fair to do justice to Liu's achievement in our translation. The *keju* degree was a not inconsiderable achievement, taking place at provincial level. The *jinshi* degree, while not the apogee of the system, was the dream of most Chinese scholars. It was held at metropolitan level, and gave the graduate the opportunity to serve in the Imperial Court (Reischauer, Fairbank and Craig 1965: 84–86). This brief information about Liu's qualifications, contained in four characters, confirms his status as a man of letters. The contextual information that follows, that he served in the Imperial Court, to some extent obviates the need for full explanations. The key to a succinct, but informative translation would be the connector 'and', which connects the notions of *jinshi* degree and court service:

> 他科舉進士出身，在朝任官四十多年，官至太子太師。He held the provincial level *keju* degree, as well as the metropolitan level *jinshi* degree, *and* served in the Imperial Court for over forty years, rising to the rank of Grand Tutor to the Heir Apparent.

Some translators might prefer to provide notes on 太子太師, but a succinct English rendering, which gives the conventional names of the rank and the person served, gives high-density information and can be retained in the body of the text.

The source text writer moves smoothly and succinctly from dates to career, to the story of the master calligrapher. In the last two lines of this small extract, we find a crucial discoursal link of the kind that is sometimes mistranslated:

> 他雖曾一度因牛李黨爭失去了權勢，只任閒缺，但還沒有貶離京師。也正因爲這樣，反可以專心鑽研，成就了他的超人書法藝術。At one point he lost power because of the Niu-Li factional struggles and occupied a post without responsibility, but was never exiled from the capital. It was precisely because of this that he was able to focus on calligraphy and develop his sublime artistry.

反 is an important link in the discourse. It indicates a contrary meaning, but in this context it provides additive rather than contrastive or negative meaning, and some translators might prefer to emphasise the point with the word 'ironically' rather than 'precisely'. 牛李党争 presents obvious issues: in how much detail should the 'Niu-Li factional struggles' be translated? In the later period of the Tang dynasty, there were factional struggles among court officials. The '*Niu dang*', or 'Niu party' was headed by Niu Sengru and Li Zongwen, while the '*Li dang*' or 'Li party' was led by Li Deyu. The so-called Niu-Li factional struggle went on for forty years (Hudong n.d.). Is it important for the target reader to know the detail? Will it enhance their writing skill or their appreciation of Chinese calligraphy? There is no reason why an explanation in the body of the text or a footnote should not be provided, but it is worth considering how useful it would be.

Mind and matter in calligraphy

The writer develops the theme of Liu's gift. In Liu's own words '用笔在心, 心正则笔正'. This aphorism encapsulates the essence of good calligraphy, and is now ubiquitously quoted in books on calligraphy as a motto for all aspiring calligraphers. In English, the two clauses, or short sentences (短句) may require some kind of linking: either temporal or conditional. The use of 正 could be regarded as a play on words (as seen in the text on traditional and simplified characters quoted in Chapter 2): when writing, the brush must be in the 'right' position, that is, straight. A wide range of translation solutions is possible, for example:

> Writing is in the heart: when the heart is right, the brush is right/ straight.

A longer, closer translation would not go amiss:

> Wielding the brush is a matter of the heart: if the heart is right, the brush is right.

Alternatively, the somewhat redundant 用笔在心 can be dispensed with in an English version, for it is at least implied, if not entailed by the following clause. 'If the heart is right, the brush is straight' is possible, and if this is really used as a motto, 'right heart straight brush' will trip off the tongue and be easily remembered. To make the motto fluently English-sounding, a freer version may be better: 'Writing comes from the heart: a steadfast heart means a steady hand'.

   Not only is calligraphy a matter of emotion for the calligrapher, it also touches the hearts of those who read or commission work. A mark of standing for a calligrapher was having his work reproduced on tombstones or ancestral tablets, reflecting the glory of the famous calligrapher, in much the same way as a famous painter's signature would enhance a painting (see Chapter 1).

Example 3b

The writer of Liu's biography notes that:

公卿大臣的墓碑，如果不是出自他的手筆，別人就會認爲不孝 …

(Huang n.d.: 14)

The three clauses (短句) here are in a paratactic relationship characteristic of Chinese grammar. To create a coherent English sentence, some re-ordering should be done, but the double negative ought to be respected, in order to lend weight to the significance of the statement:

> People would regard it as unfilial if the calligraphy on the tombstones of aristocrats and high officials did not originate from his brush.

(Authors' translation)

The mechanics of writing

Understandably, emulating Liu's unsurpassable artistry is not easy, and necessitates strict adherence to Huang's guidelines, including use of the correct posture and the correct tools. The learner is advised to sit quietly with feet firmly on the floor and in accordance with the motto of 'right heart straight brush', must maintain 'a straight back and waist' (腰背正值) and 'head held erect' (頭要端正). In contrast to Chiang Yee's recommendation (Chiang 1938/1973: 136) that grinding the ink will have a calming effect, Huang suggests that the learner can save time by using good quality ready-mixed ink (好的機制墨汁) – a practical measure in these busy times!

The tools recommended in this manual are standard. Chinese writing brushes come in a range of animal hair, each perfectly suited to a different style of script. A 寸楷羊毫 筆 'a one inch goat hair brush' is recommended for writing Liu Gongquan's style of *Kaishu*.

Master calligraphers throughout the ages have inspired and instructed learners of all ages, and latterly of all nations. The translator may be a pivotal figure in the transmission of the art.

Translating visual and tactile aspects of calligraphy

The manuals produced in the People's Republic of China at around the same period, the 1970s, differed in ideological orientation from the manual discussed above, but preserved the messages of correct posture, correct handling of the brush and the right tools. At this time, young people were encouraged to write slogans and 'big character posters' (大字報) on walls, on doors, on banners, or anywhere that would attract attention. At a time when television viewing was minimal and there was no internet, the main means of written public communication were posters, slogans on walls and wall news-papers. It was a period when 'old' things were discredited and destroyed: the 'four olds', old customs, old habits, old culture and old thinking, were viciously attacked and destroyed (Spence 1990: 606). Calligraphy, however, survived and blossomed, due in part to the power of endorsement (Yen 2005) and Mao Zedong's own attachment to the art. Calligraphy became huge, red and brutal. China was not a wealthy nation, and public calligraphy and poster art, core political genres, were executed by hand, if necessary with the help of bamboo scaffolding. The giant brushes and commercial paints used in this kind of work were a far cry from the delicate brushes of the calligrapher's studio.

How to Write in New Wei Style (怎样写新魏书) is a manual produced in 1974, typically for the time authored by a group identified only as 'the editing team' (编写组). The team is described on the frontispiece as 'an editing team led by workers, peasants and soldiers' (以工农兵为主的编写组). For the sake of convenience, we will abbreviate references as 'New Wei 1974'. The New Wei editorial team has borrowed Mao's dictum 'the ancient in the service of the modern' or 'use the old to serve the new' (古为今用) to validate the choice of style. New Wei Style evolved from the Wei tablet inscriptions of the Northern Wei (386–534), and was developed during the Qing dynasty. It is square, bold and distinct in execution. It was probably these characteristics, the 'strong square brush strokes and compact, rugged structure' (笔画方正有力, 结构严谨险峻) (New Wei 1974: 1), which made it a suitable medium for Cultural Revolution propaganda. Not only goat hair brushes, but also large, flat, wide brushes made up of a row of small ones *paibi* (排笔), and household brushes are recommended, along with oil-based paints. The authors of the manual describe the style as similar to standard *Kaishu*, but rather more 'robust' (粗壮) and 'heavy' (重). In twenty-first century idiom, we would say it is 'chunky'.

In spite of the chunkiness, New Wei Style requires a certain finesse in handling the brush, as recommended below:

Example 3c

> 新魏书的执笔方法，一般是用食指和中指的第一节弯凹处钩住笔杆（普通执笔，笔杆在食指和中指的第一节弯凹处略向外一些），食指与中指相距约一寸左右（写普通楷书可不分离或稍许分离），用大拇指抵住笔杆，要抵在食指与中指之间，这样可以更好地掌握毛笔的重心，使转笔时保持稳健。再用无名指第一节背处上端向外方顶住笔杆（普通执笔法用无名指指甲与肉相接处）。

(New Wei 1974: 5)

This excerpt gives extraordinary visual detail in the positioning of the fingers and finger joints. Manuals usually provide line drawings to aid the learner in finding the configuration of fingers, but even so, the reader must be able to match the words and the pictures successfully, and in addition, there are some people who prefer verbal to visual instructions. The translator must therefore enable the target reader to feel the way the hand grasps the brush. Correct names for the digits are the first priority here: English speakers have a name for every finger, so the 无名指 is named the fourth finger or ring finger. The little finger is also sometimes called the pinkie, the 食指 can be the first finger, the forefinger or the index finger, while the middle finger has an exact equivalent in English and Chinese.

The 笔杆 'shaft' or 'handle' of the brush is sometimes called brush or pen 'holder' in English, but this could be misconstrued as a pot or stand for brushes. While we are studiously manipulating our fingers around the handle of the brush, and simultaneously trying to hold it firmly, we would prefer not to be distracted by wandering grammar. Both sentences in this extract are long, containing not only multiple clauses, but also parentheses. One of the reasons for the length and complexity of the instruction is that, at each step, a contrast with the conventional method is given in brackets. A division of the long Chinese sentence would result in a coherent English reading, and the parenthesis could be transposed as a contrastive clause:

> In the New Wei Style, the first joints of the forefinger and middle finger are bent and hooked firmly around the shaft of the brush, in contrast to other styles, where these joints are bent slightly outwards, away from the shaft of the brush. The forefinger and middle finger should be about an inch apart, as compared with usual *Kaishu* styles, in which the two fingers are close together or only slightly separated. Use the thumb, positioned between the forefinger and middle finger, to support the shaft. This will enable you to hold it steady as you manipulate it. The upper part of the back of the first joint of the fourth finger turns out slightly to hold the brush shaft steady, in contrast to other styles, in which the fourth finger supports the brush at the point of the cuticle.
>
> (Authors' translation)

These are minute differences, but they are crucial to the execution of good calligraphic style. It should be noted that we have sometimes used imperatives in this version, sometimes not. The Chinese text uses the topic-comment structure, positioning 新魏书的执笔方法 (method of holding the brush in the New Wei style) at the very beginning of the paragraph and not repeating it. This allows great variation in the target text. We have made the fingers the subject of the English sentences at the beginning of the paragraph, then switched to an imperative. In instructions, positive imperatives are polite and acceptable.

It is instructive to see how Chiang Yee, a great expert, writing in English, gives instructions for holding the brush:

> The thumb and three fingers should grasp the handle on four sides, with the little finger in support. The upper phalange of the thumb presses on

the left side of the handle, the top of the second finger on the right side; part of the handle lies on the middle phalange of the second finger. The top of the middle finger hooks round the anterior side of the brush, and the finger nail and some of the flesh of the fourth finger backs on to the posterior side. The little finger is held close behind the fourth finger, supporting it and giving firmness to the stroke.

(Chiang 1938/1973: 138–39)

Chiang's instructions, written in the 1930s, are elegant and precise, but his terminology of 'phalange', 'anterior' and 'posterior' might be associated with medicine or anatomy, rather than writing, and might not be immediately accessible to children.

Negative instructions must be couched in sensitive terms, as we see in the example below, which deals with the use of larger brushes:

Example 3d

> 油画笔油漆刷子等握执方法，可根据自己的习惯，以能灵活运转为原则。一般和钢笔执法基本相同，以大拇指和食指为主进行运转。但不宜握得过紧或过松，要使之能灵活转动。必要时，也可转动手腕来运转刷子。这种方法也适宜于刷墙头大标语和蹲在地上写巨幅标语。底纹笔的执笔法和油漆刷子基本相同。

(New Wei 1974: 6–7)

When using an oil painting brush or a household brush, hold the brush in your usual way, so that you can manipulate it flexibly. This is similar to the way a fountain pen is held, and allows the thumb and index finger to lead the movement of the brush. So as to move the brush flexibly, avoid holding it too tightly or too loosely. If necessary, you can move the wrist in order to move the brush. This method is suitable for painting big slogans on walls and for squatting down on the floor to write giant characters. A wash brush is held in the same way as a household brush.

(Authors' translation)

Here we see the differences in technique employed in the use of bigger brushes: the tools and medium are different and the intended audience in this case will probably be driven by revolutionary zeal, and will write with vigour rather than refinement. It is noticeable that the phrase, literally 'not suitable' (不宜) is used frequently in these instructions, as in '但不宜握得过紧或过松'. In an English manual, 'don't' might be used to translate 但不宜, but it could be phrased as delicately as the Chinese: 'it is better not to' or 'it is better to avoid' or simply 'avoid holding the brush too tightly or too loosely'. It is noticeable also that 可 is used frequently in the source text. In a manual like this, designed for ordinary people who want to put up posters, rather than for fastidious scholars in their studio, an active verb ('you can hold' or 'hold') would be much more natural and appropriate than the more formal passive voice, as we can see in the following example:

> 油画笔油漆刷子等握执方法，可根据自己的习惯，以能灵活运转为原则。
>
> (New Wei 1974: 6–7)

This could be translated as:

> The method of holding the brush when using an oil painting brush or a household brush may be according to one's own habit, on the principle of dexterous movement.

But this is very pompous-sounding. A more natural version might be as follows:

> Hold oil painting brushes and household brushes in your usual way, for ease of movement.

The instructions provide a good example of a prepositional phrase that must be properly positioned in English in order to avoid ambiguity, and, contrary to received notions of Chinese translation, is better occupying the same position in the English sentence as in the Chinese sentence. 蹲在地上写巨幅标语 is better translated as 'squatting on the floor to write giant characters', than as 'squatting to write giant characters on the floor': the latter would be correct in the case of a calligrapher writing 'water' characters on a pavement. Chiang notes 'when writing very large characters we lay the whole sheet upon the floor and write there, kneeling down or bending over' (1938/1973: 137).

The terms used for materials

As we noted above, the writers of this manual are writing for people who are far from wealthy. Like Huang, above, they recommend the use of ready-mixed ink, and they note that as far as possible, scrap paper (废纸) should be used. They go so far as to say that any kind of paper can be used for practice: calligraphy paper (元书纸), rough-edged paper (毛边纸), shiny paper (油光纸) and newsprint (白报纸) can all be used, but not too rough (粗糙) or too shiny (光滑) (New Wei 1974: 7).

Making the brush strokes

Attitude, posture, materials and manipulation of the brush are all crucial elements in the making of Chinese characters, but brush strokes are the core of technique and the way to excellence. Even using a household brush and a tin of emulsion or gloss paint, the calligrapher can achieve good results by means of good brush strokes. Chiang gives two technical terms: 用笔, which he translates as 'brush treatment', and 运笔, which he translates as 'brush movement' (1938/1973: 144). The movement results in the mark on the paper, which we call a 'stroke' or a 'brush stroke'.

As might be expected for its time, the New Wei Style instruction manual is slightly dismissive of some of the more aesthetic or refined terminology, while to a greater degree espousing it. There are four epithets usually applied to brush technique: 虚、玄、直、紧, which Chiang translates as 'empty, suspended, upright and tight' (1938/1973: 144).

Example 3e

The New Wei editors remark that:

> 写字的落笔，行笔和收笔等运笔方法，前人总结了不少经验，其中除了一些 故弄玄虚之外，确实还有好多合理，宝贵的部分。 新魏书吸收了前人关于落笔 "逆入平出"， "欲左先右，欲右先左"， "欲下先上"， "横画竖下， 竖画横下" 以及 "中锋行笔" 等含有辩证关系的经验，再加上恰当地运用边锋，从而形成了自己独特的风格。

> (New Wei Style 1974: 8–9)

Our predecessors had a great deal of experience in applying the brush to the paper and withdrawing it at the end of the stroke. Apart from some deliberate mystification, there is a lot of logic and good sense in their practice. The New Wei Style has absorbed various traditional approaches based on dialectical experience: go in against the flow, come out with the flow; to move left, first move right; to move right, first move left; to make a horizontal, come down vertically; to make a vertical, come down horizontally, manoeuvring the brush from the centre of the tip, and manoeuvring the side of the tip. This is what gives New Wei Style its individuality.

> (Authors' translation)

Like the terms 'empty' and 'suspended', these descriptions of the way the stroke is created are tricky. The essence of the instruction is complementarity rather than opposition: whatever the direction of the stroke, there is a just a hint of going in the opposite direction. The movements named in this paragraph are not dissimilar to other physical activities, like martial arts, throwing a ball, wielding a racquet: they involve a slight withdrawal that aids the forward impetus. At the end of the excerpt is the frequently encountered problem of 自己 – whose individuality is it? The predecessors (themselves), the writers of the instructions (ourselves), the intended audience (ourselves, yourselves, themselves) or the New Wei Style (itself)?

The names of the eight strokes are unproblematic: 点 dot, 横 horizontal, 竖 vertical, 提 lift, 钩 hook, 折 bend, 撇 left sweep, 捺 right sweep. The names of the movements, or components, however, which were first classified by Wang

Xizhi in the fourth century, are not universally agreed by translators: 側、勒、努、趯、策、掠、啄、磔. Qu (2004: 9) renders these terms as 'shove', 'rein in', 'incise', 'kick', 'whip', 'sweep', 'peck' and 'slash', most of which sound rather violent. Chiang Yee, in spite of his long stay in America and his fluent, expert English, prefers not to translate them at all, but use transliteration: *tse, le, nu, yo, ts'e, liao* [sic], *cho, and chieh* [sic] (1938/1973: 151). Nowadays, we would use pinyin: *ce, lei, nu, yue, ce, lüe, zhuo* and *zhe*. The great advantage of using transliteration would be that calligraphy enthusiasts of different language backgrounds would have common calligraphy terms, but the transliterated terms in themselves do not convey much meaning to the non-Chinese speaker or learner. It is hard to believe that on this occasion Chiang was lost for words: it is more likely that he felt that one could only understand these terms through practice and through feeling the impetus of the brush in the hand.

Painting and calligraphy in all cultures are at the same time intellectual and physical pursuits. They are executed through the five senses, and they are perceived and appreciated through the five senses. It is the translator's business to convey this fully in the target text.

Writing as spiritual practice: Copying the sutras – A case study

Chinese writing and Buddhism have had a strong interdependence and mutual influence. The written word was key in disseminating Buddhism in its early stages in China, and the foreign concepts of the new way of thought infused the Chinese language with new words and ideas. Meditation is a core practice of Buddhist spirituality, and its methods often involve a repetitive physical activity such as chanting, spinning a prayer wheel and, germane to our discussion, copying the sutras by hand. Buddhism is a worldwide philosophy, attractive to many people beyond the confines of India for its messages of non-violence and peaceful spirituality. The very term 书法 (calligraphy, literally 'writing method') resonates with Buddhism, in that 法 is the term used to translate 'sutra'. A great deal is now written to aid Buddhists in their daily routines of faith, some of which is in Chinese, and some of which will require translation. This kind of text is exemplified in a small book entitled *How to Copy Sutras and Enjoy it* (歡喜抄經), by the Monk Hsin Pei (心培和尚) (2008).

Translations of the Chinese language of Buddhism are vulnerable to the twee romanticism to which Chinese classical poetry often falls prey. The need to speak to a modern international community of believers calls for language that inspires, but at the same time is lucid. Texts that deal with devotional matters do not need to be posh or archaic. Hsin Pei's book is published as a parallel text, with Chinese and English versions, some small facsimiles of sutra fragments, and cartoon illustrations. It is evident from its presentation that it is not intended to be a dull book, but a lively, inspirational and instructive text. The first thing to note is that the translation has been done by a team of three; collaborative translation being a concept closely identified with Buddhist texts. The reader might then notice that the style, starting with the title of the book, is refreshingly direct, simple and colloquial.

Like the calligraphy manuals, this book is an instruction manual. The illocutionary force of an instruction is basically 'do this, don't do that'. As we noted above, however, the writer of instructions in English who wants to keep the reader on side, while not avoiding naked imperatives, which can be perfectly polite and appropriate, might wish to avoid any hint of bossiness. A common conception among Chinese linguists is that Chinese is 'verby' and that English is 'nouny'. Some writers of English like to use many Latinate abstract nouns, but this style is not appropriate to every genre. Some examples from the English version of Hsin Pei's text show what can be done to vary parts of speech, but retain appropriate terminology and coherence of style. A glance at the English version reveals a distinct tendency towards 'verbiness'.

Example 3f

In the introduction, Meng Hua notes:

佛法在恭敬中求，　　我們應以恭敬心來書寫經文。心存恭敬，內心就容易清淨，對於經文義趣則容易了解，道業即能增進。

(Hsin Pei 2008: 16)

The parallel English version runs as follows:

Buddhism should be learned with respect; we should also copy sutras with respect. This allows us to purify our minds, understand the essence of the sutras and advance our way to Buddhahood.

(Hsin Pei 2008: 17)

This coherent, reader-friendly text is instructive in a number of ways, quite apart from its overt message. The Chinese source text shows how succinct instructions can be, and also illustrates the flexible status of what may loosely be termed verbs, adjectives and nouns in Chinese, and how they may be flexibly translated as verbs, nouns, adjectives or adverbs in English. 恭敬 (respect) appears in the Chinese text in the role of noun and adjective, and has been translated as 'with respect' – a prepositional phrase acting as an adverb. A possible alternative would be 'respectfully', but the two shorter words may be more reader friendly. 清淨 similarly appears here as an adjective or possibly verb (according to Chao (1968: 663 ff.), any word which can be modified by 不). The string 內心就容易清淨 may be rendered as 'the mind is easily (made) pure' or 'the mind is easily purified'. The translators have sustained the use of the first person pronoun ('this allows us'), rendering the text simply, and personally, thus appealing very directly to the reader. It is noticeable that the translators avoid translating the word 心 explicitly: after all, if something is done with respect, it necessarily comes from the heart – there is no need for an explicit translation. While Chinese 心 and English 'heart' overlap to some extent, 心 carries more connotations of the cognitive and psychological than 'heart', which tends to focus on the emotional.

Metaphor, simile and parables in spiritual instruction

Parables, fables and allegories are common to many cultures, and abound in the great religious and philosophical teachings of Confucianism, Taoism, Buddhism, Islam and the Judeo-Christian tradition. One of the reasons they are used in this kind of teaching is that they offer ordinary, less well-educated people a way into moral and philosophical concepts. They are, in effect, elaborate metaphors. Lakoff and Johnson have demonstrated how deeply metaphors are embedded in language, to such an extent that often we are not aware that we are using them. They show how human conceptual systems may be metaphorical, in that the expression of abstraction is based on the physical and cultural world in which we live, 'understanding and experiencing one kind of thing in terms of another' (Lakoff and Johnson 1980: 5). The language we use on a daily basis is stuffed with metaphor, dead and alive, covert and overt, because, as Pinker observes, 'the mind couches abstract concepts in concrete terms' (1998: 353). This may be taken a step further: subconscious metaphors may produce mental models (Aitchison 1994: 70). This could have some bearing on the Whorfian notion (explained in the Introduction) that language shapes thought. Chinese students tell us frequently that Chinese people think differently. When we investigate more deeply, however, we find that a 'way of thinking' or metaphor that is regarded as typically or even uniquely Chinese, may be a metaphor held in common with other cultures. Conversely, the abstract notions that human minds from different cultures share may be couched in concrete terms that are not shared, or only partially shared.

Parables often begin with the formula 'like' and are technically similes. Once the likeness is established, it is not necessary to state 'like' and the simile becomes a metaphor. Once a story and a moral are added, the metaphor or simile becomes a parable. In this regard, metaphors, similes, parables, fables and allegories may or may not be culture-specific, and it is up to the translator to decide whether readers may require explanation.

The translation of Hsin Pei's text is aimed at a group who are simultaneously an 'in-group' and an 'out-group'. Leppihalme implies that 'secondary receivers', that is, the target audience of a translation, 'may not be in a position to be "let in" to share the experience' (Leppihalme 1997: 23): there is an out-group, and also an in-group of readers (Leppihalme 1997: 33). The non-Chinese-speaking Buddhists who read this text are out-group readers in their inability to read Chinese, but in-group readers in their knowledge of Buddhism. They will be accustomed to interpreting ideas through the medium of parables, similes and metaphors. We can assume that they are an international group, since they will read the English version of the book.

The main section of the book deals with the spiritual and emotional benefits of copying sutras, one of which is delving deep into Buddhist teachings (ibid.: 40–41). Here, the story of Ananda and the knots is a simile, formulated as a story about a certain disciple, becoming in form a mini-parable. It explains the vexations, or defilements (煩惱) of the human mind. It is a traditional story, with hints of the succinct literary language (书面语), which root it in the philosophical tradition, but is told in a mainly modern and colloquial style. In reply to troubled Ananda's question about the nature of defilements, the Buddha created a physical illustration of a mental model by tying knots in a towel.

Example 3g

> 阿難聞佛所問，的確感受到心有千千結打不開，好比長頭髮很久沒有清洗梳理，一根根盤錯成結繩一樣。所以，應以般若慧將它打開。如果能打開結，煩惱即菩提，不就解脫了嗎？
>
> (Hsin Pei 2008: 40)

> When Ananda listened to the Buddha's teachings, he felt that his mind was so uncomfortable as if thousands of knots were tied to it. It is also like a person who has not washed his or her long hair for a very long time and every single strand of hair was tangled up. So we should untie the knots with prajna wisdom to liberate ourselves from defilements.
>
> (Hsin Pei English version 2008: 43)

The demonstration used by the Buddha to help Ananda is in itself an explanation in concrete terms of an abstract problem. Here the translators have chosen to explicate on several levels. First, they have described Ananda as 'uncomfortable'. In addition, they have intensified the adjective with 'so', and they have introduced two aspects of the knots: discomfort and tangling. They have emphasised the degree of tangling ('every single strand of hair'). This strategy of explicitation leaves the reader in no doubt as to how Ananda felt. It would, however, be possible in this case not to add to the bare bones of the parable, for unwashed, tangled hair is a universal human experience: it is a subconscious metaphor that produces the mental model 'knotty problem'. A native English-speaking translator would probably write 'knots in it' rather than 'knots tied to it'. The simile could be intensified by adding a word like 'matted', which is associated or synonymous with 'tangled' and 'dirty' when applied to animal and human hair. The options are wide open, for the translator is re-telling a story that is re-told by the author of the book, who in turn took it from countless previous re-tellings. The important thing is that we help the non-Chinese-reading Buddhist to understand how 煩惱 feels, and how the exercise of calligraphic copying of sutras calms the spirit and unties the knots.

Practical instruction

The physicality of calligraphy, meditation and sutra-copying is evident throughout Hsin Pei's instructional book and is echoed in the calligraphy manuals discussed above. Inevitably, there is spiritual instruction of a more overt nature:

> 2 抄經前，靜坐片刻，調整呼吸，讓心沉靜下來，亦可三稱佛號，誦念《開經偈》。
> 3 抄經時，姿勢要端正，最重要的是手到、心到、眼到。
>
> (Hsin Pei 2008: 126)

English version:

> 2 Meditate for a short time, adjust breathing, and calm down the mind. Recite the name of the Buddha three times or recite the verse for opening a sutra.
> 3 Sit properly and concentrate on the three points: the mind, the eyes, and the hand.
>
> (Hsin Pei 2008: 129)

These are two instructions from a full list of six. Where the Chinese instruction states 'when', or 'before', the English version does not necessarily include the time adverbial, because the reader is fully aware that these instructions refer to preparation or execution of the activity. The English uses brief imperatives, just like the Chinese. The explicit phrase 'the three points', added by the translators, strictly speaking is unnecessary, but is useful in two respects. Apart from helping the reader to remember the three points, it overcomes the problem of 到, (as in 手到、心到、眼到). It would also be possible to render the sentence as 'The most important thing is to focus on mind, eyes and hands.'

The motivations and methods of Chinese calligraphy are many, varied and rapidly becoming globalised. The concentration of mind, manual dexterity and sensory-motor co-ordination central to writing Chinese characters are described in centuries-old terminology. Yet it is a terminology that lives and evolves, and is now being carried to all the corners of the world. Translators will play a key role in bringing the body and soul of calligraphy to an international audience of sinophiles, artists and believers.

Practical 3.1 Putting brush to paper

i   Compare the Chinese source text in Example 3e with similar instructional texts in English or other European languages.
ii Words like 'empty' and 'suspended' have been used for decades, without much consideration of their appropriateness. Think about possible improvements on these received translations.

iii Make your own translation of Example 3e, giving full consideration to the movements required for the brush strokes.

Practical 3.2 *A workman and his tools*

Wei Dan (179–253) was a native of Jingzhao, now Xi'an in Shanxi Province, during the Three Kingdoms period, a philosopher of the Mohist School, and a court official. His name lives on today as one of the great calligraphers of history, and his characters were said to be like coiling dragons and prowling tigers, or like brandished swords and taut bows (Baidu, Wei Dan 2013).

Wei was said to have coined the following motto:

工欲善其事，必先利其器

Translate this into English for the frontispiece of a book on calligraphy.

Practical 3.3 *Building a glossary of materials*

Go to your nearest art shop or calligraphy shop.

i   Make an inventory of different kinds of brushes, paint and paper, or other supports and tools used for Western-style painting.
ii Make an inventory of similar materials for Chinese painting and calligraphy.
iii Using existing books, internet sources, reference works and artist informants, create a bilingual glossary of calligraphers' materials.

4 The meaning of clothes
Cultural, political and historical significance

Clothing and body decoration have always served to distinguish, identify and protect members of the human race. Like language, music and art, the clothes we wear mark ethnic, national and geographical distinctions. Colonisation and now globalisation have removed some of the distinctions in daily dress and use of fabrics, but all cultures talk about and write about dress. In the creation of the latest catwalk marvel, the exploitation of technology which offers better, cheaper and more beautiful garments, and in the reproduction and re-use of traditional garments and fabrics, designers, manufacturers and conservators are using language. Like many other facets of life, costume is an area that appears to have been almost destroyed by globalisation yet, unusually but not uniquely, has also been revived by globalisation. As societies become aware of the uniformity brought about by international commerce, they may find some way to exploit and emphasise the characteristics that mark them out from others. The top Chinese designers make unashamed use of stereotypically Chinese motifs, to the delight of their international customers. In most parts of the world traditional costume is no longer worn on a day-to-day basis, but lives on in drama, re-enactments, museum displays, cultural and religious ritual, working uniforms and, at its most sublime and vigorous, on the catwalk. Costume and fabric have always been a core element of Chinese society and culture, and it is a field that is written and talked about extensively in business, industry and the arts. Translating clothes requires understanding that spans centuries and encompasses a wide range of specialist vocabulary, from engineering, through design and aesthetics to economics. 'A dress is a dress is a dress' some people would say, and add proudly that they are not 'interested in' clothes. But who cannot be interested in clothes as protection, warmth and a means of identity?

The comfortable, washable synthetic fabrics that billions of people wear have an evolutionary and aesthetic history that mirrors and complements the history of art and of industry. Historic clothes, not only those worn hundreds of years ago, but also those worn quite recently, such as Marilyn Monroe's dresses and Michael Jackson's stage costumes, are conserved, catalogued and displayed as important historic artefacts. In greater China it is Zhang Ailing

(Eileen Chang) who has become a focus of attention for her love and analysis of fashion, documented in her novels and articles.

Nation, dominance and dress

Chinese fashion is now on the academic agenda, and is a core interest of business and economics. Fashion is an indicator of a nation's sophistication and of its status among other nations; the great fashion houses have traditionally been based in Paris, Milan, London and New York. Now, however, fashion shows take place in Beijing and Shanghai (Chen and Zamperini 2003: 267), and showcase Chinese designs among the great names of the West. At the same time, it is a bone of commercial contention. On 13 December 2007, Peter Mandelson, then Trade Commissioner to the European Union, criticised China openly and frankly for erecting barriers to the European textile and clothing industries. The ensuing arguments between China and the EU became known as the 'bra wars' (This is Money.co.uk 2007). Centuries ago, the silk that travelled between China and Rome was in effect gold, a form of currency that crossed continents (Rossabi in Watt and Wardell 1997: 7). It was used as a standard, as gold is now, was paid as wages and as tax (Mayer Thurman 2000: 13). Now fabrics and ready-made garments cross continents on factory ships.

Clothes distinguish humans from animals, and mark out people who are considered civilised from those who are considered 'barbarian' (Zamperini 2003: 303). Fictional and non-fictional writing in China shows the extreme care and confusion surrounding changes in fashion decreed by political change and technological innovation (ibid.). The symbolism of dominance may be as important as sex appeal and glamour in fashion. Vestimentary or sumptuary laws have decreed overtly for many centuries the clothing that is worn as an outward sign of rank. From the emperor's yellow robes and five clawed dragon motifs to the 'white working clothes' of Mao's China (Chen 2003), dress has distinguished rank and power.

Translation of clothing terms works, or does not work, at the most basic level: Finnane notes the 'profound ignorance' of some European and American writers on fashion (2007: 8), but they should not be 'judged too harshly'. She notes that these Western writers, who were very often missionaries, may not have had the means of describing the Chinese garments they saw. This may have been a case of true ignorance: outside observers may not have seen the glories of clothes hidden in sedan chairs and behind doors, and if they had seen them may not have had the linguistic equipment to describe or analyse them (ibid.: 9); they had to fall back on describing what they were not, by contrast with the Western dress that was familiar to them (ibid.: 12). Inability to translate was a question of attitude as well as language. Harrison shows how the Chinese themselves expressed dominance through their attitudes to dress, which were to some extent bound by ignorance of local climate, customs and beliefs, particularly in the case of indigenous peoples

(Harrison 2003). Orientalism in fashion scholarship seems to have been rampant, but has only recently been noticed (by, for example Garrett 1987, 1994; Wilson 2001; Finnane 2007), perhaps because clothes have not always been considered a dignified subject for academic study. Great Chinese thinkers like Lu Xun wrote about clothes, because they were, and still are, a manifestation of political beliefs, indices of health and welfare, and symbols of gender roles and status.

Like other empires and monarchies, Chinese regimes had rules and conventions on what should be worn by whom. Dress was an explicit sign of rank and statement of power in Imperial China. Even after 1911, when modernisation and education had induced the wealthy to exchange their long gowns for more practical '西裝' (Western suits) the 'Sun Yatsen jacket' (中山裝) gave a man modern, yet Chinese identity; the *qipao* (旗袍), the fashionable adaptation of what was thought to be a Manchu traditional garment, gave women a very distinctive 'ethnic' glamour. Even during the bleak years of Mao's regime, when colour and comfort were low on the agenda, there were fashions, though of a harsh, ideological nature. Elegance and sex appeal became marks of decadence, and the simple clothing of the proletariat became both the norm and the ideal. The white lab coat of the scientist, the overalls and white shirt of the worker, and the head cloth and loose jacket of the peasant became the 'discourse of proletarian dress' (Chen 2003). A negative reaction to these uniform, masculinised fashions may well have provided the impetus to the glamour bounce-back in the 1990s.

Over the twentieth century in China daily dress has undergone the same revolutions and changes that Chinese people have experienced. Finnane points out that 'a series of political regimes through the century was matched by a parallel series of vestimentary regimes' (2007: 15). Zamperini shows how the fashions of Shanghai at the end of the Qing dynasty revealed the 'chaos' that reigned in Chinese society at that time (2003: 311). Traditional Confucian approaches to appropriate clothing that reflected the status of the wearer are paralleled in Mao's China, in rigid distinctions between the theoretically united workers, peasants and soldiers, and Party bureaucrats (Chen 2003). The iconic 'Sun Yatsen' jacket in effect replaced the imperial robes of the Qing dynasty, its simple decoration of pockets and buttons symbolising a new set of principles on which the Republic would be ordered (Carroll 2003: 468). In the early days of the Republic it differentiated the revolutionary from the decadent wearers of Western suits and the reactionary wearers of old style *changpao* (Finnane 2007: 184) and gradually became the uniform of the leadership classes. Often known as a 'Mao suit' among non-Chinese, the Sun Yatsen jacket seemed to symbolise and stereotype Communist China.

Clothes are visual insignia indicating a gamut of identities: rank, wealth, ethnicity, occupation, nationality, region, person and gender. High fashion, or haute couture, holds a place among the aesthetic arts and can only be implemented by highly skilled tailors and dressmakers. The visual and textural properties of costume require a complex language that reflects the impact those properties have on the spectator in terms of understanding the wearer's status, role and message. This language is complicated further by structure: every garment, from steel-toed safety boots to pointe ballet shoes, from straw rain-capes to acrylic bikinis, is designed to fit a shape that moves in a certain way. Collars, cuffs, sleeve insets, button holes, and all the other minute details of human apparel require a language that is close to that of engineering in its expression of weight, movement, support and co-ordination.

In this chapter we will explore how the notion of the semantic field can engage the translator in the complexities of fashion and tailoring. In the second part we discuss the visual messages that clothing carries about its social, sexual, political and psychological impact, and how the power relationships of clothes are put into words.

Transliteration, contextualisation and coining

In the preceding paragraphs, we used a number of different words to refer to the fabric we use to cover our nakedness. We have used the words 'costume', 'clothes', 'clothing', 'dress' and 'garments' in these introductory paragraphs. There are yet more English words: the archaic 'raiment' and the specialist 'apparel', still used by garment manufacturers, the more neutral 'outfit', the colloquial 'glad rags', 'gear', 'kit' and the somewhat derogatory 'garb' are just some of the various general synonyms, which would be used when a more specific register is required. Garrett (1994) uses the term 'attire', which her readers will readily associate with the upper echelons of society. In Chinese there is a similar range of general terms: Tao Fangxuan's book about Zhang Ailing and her love of clothes reveals five on just one page: 衣裳, 着装, 服饰, 便服, 衣衫 (Tao 2009: 115).

At a more specialist level come the terms that relate directly to 'fashion'. English fashion terminology often has recourse to French (France being the fount of all fashion wisdom) and writers on Chinese fashion may choose this pathway. In his article on the key role of Suzhou in the fashion industry, Carroll (2003), uses the terms 'demimonde', 'passé' and 'à la mode' in his more general paragraphs. His approach throughout the article is to foreignise, for while using these general French terms, wherever possible he retains specific Chinese terms in pinyin. This is a strategy adopted by other specialists writing in English on the subject. Carroll is writing in English, rather than translating, but as a front-line researcher, is presenting material that may be new to readers: he exercises a technique that translators could emulate. His opening paragraphs on the development of fashion in Shanghai quote a Shanghai newspaper: 'fashion *(shimao)* clique' (2003: 443). Carroll's example, taken from the 'Free Talk' section of *Shenbao* (The Shanghai News) on 21 June 1912, relates *shimao* to Republicanism. With this first mention using an English equivalent followed by transliteration, he has established the term and its meaning, in its historical context, and proceeds to use '*shimao* (时髦)' throughout his article, situating the notion firmly in China. Later in the same article, he discusses the terms '*shimao*' and a later term 'contemporary clothing (*shizhuang*)' (时装), once more firmly contextualising and explaining, and at the same time making the specialist term a new coining available to the non-Chinese-speaking expert. Writers and translators who, by contrast with Carroll, use transliteration without some kind of explanation or contextualisation may not be helping the non-Chinese-speaking reader.

Garrett, well known for her highly accessible publications on traditional Chinese clothing, often takes the transliteration approach, as in the case of '*ao* and *ku*' (women's top and trousers). At first mention, Garrett describes a garment: ' … the *ao*, an upper garment which was cut like a man's but elaborately decorated, made from self-patterned silk damask with wide plain and/or embroidered bands at sleeves, neck, hem … ' (1994: 87). This is lengthy, and if it were translation would be decidedly 'thick' but it is essential information, and obviates the need for 'translation' of the term. In subsequent mentions, the author is free to use the term *ao*, without elaboration, progressing to '*ao* and trousers', and then to '*ao ku*'. All Garrett's terms are glossed at the back of the book. In many cases Garrett uses the magic word 'or' as in 'the *pao* or gown' (ibid.: 11). Where a term can be defined in a single word or brief phrase, this is probably the clearest method of combined transliteration and explicitation, leading eventually to coining of an appropriate foreignised term.

Semantic fields

The layer of more specific terms for the shapes of clothes and the way in which they cover the body (dress, trousers, cape, jacket etc.), may be culture-specific, and require explicitation techniques such as those used by Garrett (above). The next layer of terms might deal with the function of the garments: wedding dress, suit trousers, rain cape, blazer. In Chinese some of the more common traditional garments are 马褂 (*magua*), 长袍 (*changpao*),长衫 (*changshan*), 旗袍 (*qipao*), 旗衫 (*qishan*), 背心 (*beixin*), which label the garments in terms of style. All these words fit into what is known as a semantic field, which can pattern and structure the relationship of the words and their referents.

A semantic field is 'a distinct part of the lexicon defined by some general term or concept' (Matthews 1997: 360). A lexical field will cover a group of terms in one language: boots, shoes and sandals in English, for example, and 靴、鞋、拖鞋 in Chinese. A conceptual field will cover the broad notion of 'footwear' (鞋类) in more than one language (Matthews 1997: 360).

Within a semantic field there may be a hierarchy of terms and or concepts: 'footwear' is a hypernym (an overarching term), and boots, shoes and sandals are all hyponyms (subordinate terms) of the wider term. For the specialist, distinction between hyponyms is part of professional expertise, and translators need to be party to this expertise.

Members of semantic fields, whether hyponyms or hypernyms, are determined by the features that characterise them and distinguish them from other members of the field.

Thinking about the semantic field may help a translator to decide on what strategy to use – whether to retain the term in transliteration, or to generalise, describe, find an equivalent term in the target language, or explicitate in a footnote or parenthesis. When a certain kind of garment or accessory found in the source culture is not known in the target culture, the translator will think about the appearance and functions of an item and search for an appropriate way of expressing them in the target language.

Let us take the term 马褂 (*magua*) as an example. It would not be appropriate to translate it literally as 'horse jacket', even though its possible genesis among the horsemen of north China is clear in the name. To retain it as '*magua*' in the body of the text requires contextualisation or explicitation. Otherwise the reader would be left to guess from the context (as discussed in the Introduction), unless he or she is conversant with Chinese culture. The information of semantic field might aid the translator in the search for the mot juste. A '*magua*' belongs to the semantic field of clothing; it is usually of woven fabric; its hemline is a little below the waist; it has sleeves; it is fastened at the front, centrally, and has a 'mandarin' collar; it is worn by men, and worn over a long gown (*chang shan* 长衫). Finnane's term 'riding jacket' (see below) could give an impression of the tweeds and 'pinks' worn by English riders and huntsmen. Garrett explains at first mention that it was originally Manchu 'riding dress' (1994: 68). Given that the context of this term is likely to be that of China pre-1949, the general reader will already be exercising a 'pre-1949 China' schema, and will be ready to process 'jacket' as a Chinese jacket; it bears distinct similarities to the kind of upper, outer garments worn by men in Europe, but has Oriental characteristics. The specialist reader, however, who might be a costume designer, a museum curator or a props specialist, would want to have specific features, so as to create a precise image of the garment. The specialist reader might prefer 'thick translation' like Garrett's description of the *ao* (above) because he or she is in search of accuracy rather than easy reading.

Needless to say, this discussion begs the question of non-verbal, visual paratext in the form of helpful photos or other graphic illustrations. Why not simply use the Chinese term in pinyin and add a photo or drawing? The reasons are clarity on the one hand and economics on the other. Not every photo or drawing makes things clear. Not every historian or costume researcher has a good sense of the visual. If the terms are found in translated histories or fiction, there may not be any provision for illustrations. Finally, publishers work to a budget, and illustrations cost money. It is the translator's responsibility to 'draw' verbally for the reader.

Semantic fields and consistency

Clothing is without doubt an area of enormous economic and aesthetic interest that requires a highly specialised vocabulary. In other specialist areas some attempt would be made to standardise, for the sake of safety and legality. Apart from workwear such as surgeons' gowns and engineers' helmets, clothing is not normally an area associated with life or death decisions, and there is not always consensus among writers on the terms that they use. The terms listed below, used in English-language writing on Chinese clothes, show just how varied and confusing the situation is.

Magua (马褂): Garrett (1994) defines it, and uses her 'progressive' technique, from explanation, through transliteration plus 'or + equivalent', finally to stand-alone transliteration; Finnane uses 'horse [riding] jacket (*magua*)' (2007: xviii), and thereafter 'riding jacket'; Carroll uses the adaptive 'short mandarin jacket' (2003: 457).

Doudou (兜肚/兜兜): Finnane uses the Chinese term '*doudu*' and explains it as 'a sort of apron for the upper body' (2007: 162); Garrett's approach is similar, but more explicit and less coy: 'a small triangular apron to cover the breasts and stomach. Known as a *doudou* … ' (1994: 89); Harrison, investigating Taiwan women's adoption of Chinese dress, calls it 'square breast covering' (2003: 350); Hua succeeds in charting the development of the *doudou* graphically, without mentioning its name, by simply captioning it as 'women's underclothes in past dynasties' (2004: 92–93 tr. Yu and Zhang), but her translators, referring to its use in the Ming dynasty, call it a 'lady bellyband' (ibid.: 57).

Qipao (旗袍): Yu and Zhang, translating Hua, leave the non-Chinese reader somewhat bemused: 'The cheong-sam in Chinese is called "flag robe", which means the flag people's robe. And the flag people are how the middle land Han people referred to Manchu people' (2004: 93); Garrett deals with it more sympathetically as 'a one-piece garment called a *qipao*, literally "banner gown", as it resembled the style worn by Manchu women in the past' (1994: 104); Finnane is more succinct: ' … *qipao*, the high-collared one-piece garment … ' (2007: 5); Jones, translating Zhang Ailing, writes of 'a *qipao* or "banner gown" after the eight military banners under which the Manchus had invaded China … ' (2003: 435). An exhibition of the history of the *qipao* held in Hong Kong in 2010 establishes the use of the term in the title of the show: *The Evergreen Classic: Transformation of the Qipao* (歷久常新: 旗袍的變奏). The bilingual brochure uses the transliteration *qipao* throughout, but in the first sentence of the introduction, points out that it 'is generally known as the *cheongsam*' (Hong Kong Museum of History 2010), illustrating a change of use no doubt influenced by Hong Kong's return to China.

Huapendi xie (花盆底鞋) commonly known as 'flower pot shoes'; they are also called 'horse hoof shoes' (马蹄鞋). Garrett does not provide a term, but describes this footwear as 'an exaggeratedly elevated shoe with a concave heel in the centre of the instep' (1994: 61); Hong (2011), writing in the *Epoch Times*, explains that the 'pot-bottom shoe' or 'horse-hoofed shoe' was so-called because of the shape of the sole. Other English terms applied to this style include 'platform shoes' and 'pedestal shoes'.

This extraordinary range of interpretation and explication of a few very iconic items of traditional Chinese clothing illustrates the need for some standardisation and consistency in the translation of fashion scholarship.

Denotation and connotation

Technical terms and specialist vocabulary will not necessarily be affected by the grammar or the context of the sentence in which they occur, as they will often have a fixed and very specific meaning within a technical or specialist text. Let us take as an example the English word 'buttonhole': in other contexts it could be a flower, or it could describe the action of someone persuading, cajoling or forcing someone else to carry out a task; but in a text about fashion or tailoring, it can only mean one of two things: the hole in the fabric, or the loop attached to the fabric, through which a button is pushed in order to secure a garment around the body. 'Buttonhole', like all the other terms that refer to parts of garments, fabrics, styles, structural techniques, colours and textures, belongs in a semantic field.

In practical application, semantics covers two broad functions of use: denotation and connotation. Denotation is a straightforward labelling or pointing out: 'words are names, or labels for classes of entities (...) which exist in the world, external to language and independently of it' (Lyons 1981: 152). Connotation creates 'a set of associations between that word or phrase and whatever is distinctive about its typical contexts of occurrence' (ibid.: 150). The denotative meaning of 'suit' in the context of clothes, for example, is a set consisting of jacket and matching trousers, or matching skirt; the connotative meaning of 'suits' (often plural) may be the group loosely defined as urban professional male, in other words, those who wear a suit to work, and who aspire to a certain lifestyle.

Translating dress, behaviour and rank in Chinese history

The first example text in this chapter deals with the historical significance of dress, and is taken from the book entitled *A Detailed Discussion of Chinese Costume*, by Gao Ge (高格 (2005) 细说中国服饰，北京，光明日报). The reader of the Chinese text is given guidance in the form of a 'How to use this book' section (如何使用本书). The instructions in Chinese explain that the book is an ideal publication that brings together knowledge, science and practical use; it points to the illustrations that go deep into the dazzling culture, and help the reader to understand the main text and, at the same time, be entertained. The book covers Chinese costume (mostly that of nobility and wealthy sections of society) from the first bone needle used to sew skins, to 1930s Western-style fashions on the Bund in Shanghai.

The reader is also guided by very small amounts of paratext; the blurb is minimal, but there are brief statements on the fly leaves, which leave us in no doubt of the author's mission:

从服饰，可以看到历史和社会生活；从服饰，可以看到文化和艺术；从服饰，可以看到民族精神和风貌。

(Gao 2005)

> In costume, we can see history and social life, culture and art and the spirit and style of the people.
>
> (Authors' translation)

Costume has always pushed the boundaries, not only of fabric manufacture and the design and craftsmanship of jewellery, but also of the display of wealth and prestige. One of the topics addressed in the book is the cultural significance of hats and other accessories. Fashion historians have pointed out cultural differences in hat-wearing: 'European men doffed their hats to show respect, the Chinese kept theirs on' (Brouillon 1855, cited in Finnane 2007: 56). In many cultures, if not all, the head and its covering are of ritual and social significance. It is only in the detail that differences are apparent: 'doffing' the hat might well be compared to the 'putting on his hat three times' described in Example 4a, below.

One of the early chapters of Gao's book is entitled 美丽人生从冠开始 'Beauty starts with the hat'. This title could, of course, be translated in a number of more prolix ways: 'beautiful life starts with (or at) the hat'; 'a beautiful life starts with head gear'; 'a beautiful person starts with/at his hat' and so on. The message is the same, that what a self-respecting person, who has respect for others, wears on his or her head, is of great significance. The author illustrates the impact of hat-wearing with the story of Zi Lu, a disciple of Confucius who would rather have died than take off his hat (君子死，冠不免); he was indeed mashed to pulp because he did so (被人剁成了肉酱) (Gao 2005: 48).

In the following example, we will see how emphasis and redundancy in the source text are dealt with by means of explicitation or concision in the target text.

Example 4a

> 冠是古代男子成人的标志。几乎每一个民族都有自己的成年礼。古代汉族男子到了20岁就必须按照 "始加，再加，三加" 的程序行 "加冠礼"，再取一个名字之外的字，以此来宣告自己已经成人 。
>
> (Gao 2005: 48)

The following reference, or 'literal' translation gives the full flavour of the source text:

> A hat, in ancient times, was an adult man's mark. Almost every tribe has its own adult rituals. In ancient times, when a Han man reached the aged of 20, he would have to carry out the 'putting on a hat ritual' according to the 'first putting on, again putting on, thrice putting on' procedure, and take a 'zi' in addition to his 'ming', and thereby announce that he himself had already become a man.
>
> (Authors' translation)

A more fluent version might look like this:

> In ancient times a hat was a mark of maturity for a man. Almost every tribe has its own distinctive rites of passage. When a Han male reached the age of 20, he would have to carry out the ritual of putting on his hat three times. This, in addition to taking an adult name, would announce that he had become a man.

> (Authors' translation)

This account moves away from description towards a discussion of the significance of the accessory, and the translator has to think about strategies with regard to emphasis and redundancy. The writer is expanding and explaining, and the translator may need to create additional expansions and explanations for the benefit of the target reader, but at the same time reduce the text in order to eliminate 'un-English' elements that would detract from the message. If the translator really wanted to highlight the hat, and make it the most important element of the sentence, the hat could be end-weighted as follows: 'In ancient times the mark of maturity for a man was his hat'. This is not obligatory (nothing in translation is obligatory!), for a great deal depends on context. In some contexts, it would be very desirable to start the paragraph with the hat, rather than the person.

Having set the scene with two short, general sentences, the writer then goes on to describe a specific ritual that illustrates the importance of the hat. Now, the 'Han male' becomes the grammatical topic of a complex sentence that describes the ritual. If we repeat 'ancient' we contradict ourselves: we are talking about a young man, so we cannot say 'an ancient Han male'. Do we need to repeat 'ancient'? Probably not, as we have introduced the 'ancient' schema to the reader, who is now ready to be immersed in 'ancient' topics, and in any case, 'would' makes it clear that we are talking about the past. As we noted in the Introduction, the translator must take account of the reader's ability to infer. The ritual is both described and named, and in English, either the describing or the naming is redundant: 'the ritual of putting on his hat three times' succinctly deals with this. 再 gives the translator the opportunity either to continue the sentence or to break off and start a new one. We have used a relative pronoun to link the clauses, but it would be possible to render it as follows: ' … three times. In addition to taking an adult name, this would announce. … ' In this case, the pro-form 'this' maintains the coherence between the two shorter sentences. In the authors' translation, we have reduced 一个名字之外的字 to 'take an adult name' but some translators might prefer to provide a parenthetic explanation within the text or a footnote on the Chinese traditional naming system.

The following excerpt gives us a glimpse of the significance of headgear in the court of Wu Zetian, the Empress Wu (624–705). This passage is not characterised by any specialist costume terms, but it does present one or two syntactic and lexical challenges.

Example 4b

> 前面已经提到过古时候男子的帽子是有等级之分的。　一般来说贵族男子都戴冠，而平民只能戴巾。但是到武则天的时候，她反其道而行之，让内府特制了一种叫做"武家诸王样"的头巾，赏赐给那些归顺于她的宠臣。

> (Gao 2005: 90)

In previous pages we have described how men's headgear was a mark of rank. Generally speaking, nobles wore hats and ordinary people wore head cloths. During her reign, however, Empress Wu Zetian reversed this custom, granting her favourite, loyal courtiers the right to wear a head cloth called the 'military princes' style', which was specially made in the inner courts.

> (Authors' translation)

A notable characteristic of this short text is the typical absence of grammatical subject. In English, we have no choice but to insert some kind of subject, and the most natural subject for 已经提到过 is 'we'. It draws the reader in and helps the reader to identify with the writer and the subject matter, and is a common convention used in non-fiction. An impersonal passive would be possible, but awkward. The next sentence requires some re-structuring in order to achieve a coherence of subject and reference chain.

> 但是到武则天的时候，她反其道而行之，让内府特制了一种叫做"武家诸王样"的头巾，赏赐给那些归顺于她的宠臣。

> (Gao 2005: 90)

The Chinese syntax is ordered chronologically, but in English there would be some subordination designed to retain the importance of the granting of the favour of the special headgear. The expression 'By the time of X' leads the reader to expect a change of subject, and it could be disruptive to find that Wu Zetian is the subject of her own time. The time phrase could simply be omitted, as long as we give Wu Zetian her title 'Empress'. We could alternatively render the time phrase as 'during her reign', which provides better coherence with 'Wu Zetian' as the subject of the sentence. In the Chinese structure, Wu is the grammatical topic of the sentence, and this role is sustained right through. In English, however, this seems rather long winded; we have therefore reversed the clauses, and introduced a passive: 'which was awarded'. The expression 让内府 presents a degree of challenge: did the Empress 'allow', 'cause' 'instruct' or even 'force' the making of the head cloths? 'Having' takes a middle way: to have something made implies agency without involvement, and we have taken this a step further, rendering the phrase as 'specially made'. How fully does the translator need to tackle 内府? It was the department of the Imperial Household which looked after objects and the manufacture thereof. Some dictionaries give 'cabinet', but this is not what is required in the context. What is key here is the use of upper case: we know that upper case denotes a title, so this must be a particular part of the imperial, or emperor's, household. The full force of 那些归顺于她的宠臣 can be achieved through the use of 'favourite' and 'loyal'. Note that 那些 ('those') is not entirely necessary in English, as 'the' has the necessary anaphoric force. 'Head cloth' is sometimes rendered as 'head wrap' (Tophat n.d.).

Descriptions of historical costume show how culture-specificity is not simply a matter of geo-political difference, but also of time difference. The translator must convey the historical period and avoid anachronism; the connotative force of the text must be kept without subjecting the text to ridicule; the essence of the lexis in form and function must be retained, but not made awkward.

Fashion and celebrity in the twentieth century

Clothes and fabrics changed with the times in China, absorbing influences from foreign regimes like the Mongols and the Manchus, and responding to politics and evolution. Possibly the greatest change has been that of the transition from Empire to Republic at the beginning of the twentieth century, a period that saw educational, political and employment opportunities available to a broader cross-section of society, including women. The great thinkers of the time, such as Lu Xun, wrote about fashions (Lu 1927/1980: 353). The translator Yang Xianyi wrote about the quandary he faced in 'what to wear' to best identify himself as modern but Chinese (Finnane 2007: 178). The new freedoms were manifest in the great celebrities of the time, one of whom was the novelist Zhang Ailing (Eileen Chang), one of whose best-known works in the Chinese speaking world is *The Chronicle of Changing Clothes* (更衣記).

Zhang's scrupulously detailed descriptions of dress, particularly that of women, are central to her stories of the urban middle class in Shanghai in the early part of the twentieth century. The clothes featured in her fiction frequently mirror her own wardrobe, as demonstrated by Tao Fangxuan in *Clothes and Zhang Ailing* (霓裳. 张爱玲) (Tao 2009). Like Coco Chanel, Zhang was proudly eccentric and lived her ideals of fashion. Zhang's writing about clothes has been analysed, in terms of her own character and the way in which she used clothes to portray the characters in her novels and short stories. Tao Fangxuan reveals Zhang's use of fashion to reinforce sex and romance. Here is what Tao says about the *qipao*:

Example 4c

> 張愛玲時代上海灘的旗袍種類數不勝數，長衫式、高領式、高開式、直筒式、短袖式、荷花式、蓋膝式 – 到張愛玲筆下的男子，無論是有條件或無條件的愛，無不籍由對衣裝的觀感而生發。
>
> 正是看到流蘇一身月白色蟬翼紗旗袍，范柳原才說出：難得碰見像你這樣的一個真正的中國女人 – 繼而愛上了她。

(Tao 2009: 99)

In Zhang Ailing's time, one could see innumerable styles of *qipao* on the Bund in Shanghai: long gowns, high-collars, high splits, straight sheaths, short sleeves, lotus neckline, over the knee. ... Whether their love was conditional or unconditional, the men in Zhang's fiction never failed to be moved by a woman's clothes. It was only when Fan Liuyuan saw Bai Liusu in her organdie *qipao* that he said, 'It is rare to meet a real Chinese woman like you,' and promptly fell in love with her.

(Authors' translation)

This brief quotation is explicit in its assessment of the *qipao's* sex appeal, and of its identification with China. Two paragraphs later, Tao states:

Example 4d

只有中國人能理解這種美，一種獨特的文化符號，一個別致唯美的民族心理語言。

(Tao 2009: 100)

Only Chinese people can understand this kind of beauty: it is a unique cultural symbol, a distinctive, aesthetic language of the psychology of ethnicity.

(Authors' translation)

Whether or not this is true is not a matter for this chapter, but it illustrates perfectly the relationship between clothes, ethnic identity, psychology and sex appeal.

The language of these two quotations is noteworthy in two respects: the first one relies on a very simple list to create a vivid, varied image of women's dress, and the second relies on a series of abstractions to express a strongly ethnocentric notion of the importance of that same style of dress. In both, the lexical items belong to a specific semantic field: a field that is contiguous with a schema or frame built by the writer, into which the reader must venture.

Even readers who have never been on the Bund in Shanghai will have an image of that great commercial city, possibly as a hotbed of commerce, fashion and glamour. Shanghai has represented China in news and literature for well over a century, and the very mention of it in a text will conjure some kind of image for a reader.

Contemporary fashion

In the 2010s it is sometimes difficult to tell what is Chinese fashion and what is not, so global has the commodity become. Modern telecommunications have created a situation in which designs drawn on one side of the world may be simultaneously viewed on the other side, and fashions for both sexes change with alarming rapidity. The major Western trend-setting magazines are published in Chinese, and there are Chinese equivalents, which are equally glossy and glamorous and have a huge circulation. They provide visual and verbal affirmation, mainly for the young, of the current desirable 'look'. How do trendy Chinese talk about their clothes and accessories?

The Chinese edition of *Elle* interviewed Li Jing (李静), one of the most 'stylish' (最具风格) TV personalities in China in 2008, a year in which patriotic feelings reached a peak in China, not least in Beijing (Li 2008: 74). Li talks about the habit of following fashion (追逐时尚) as a part of her work, due to the requirements of the small screen: she cannot be seen twice in the same outfit. She therefore relies on her costumier (服装师) to help her select styles that not only suit her looks and personality, but are also this season's latest fashion, or 'look' (本季流行元素). She reflects on a garment that led to later problems, the 蛋型裙. This is literally, the 'egg-style' or 'egg-shaped' skirt. What was it called in English?

Fashions return to haunt humankind. The gathered skirt is timeless, and now goes by the name of 'umbrella skirt' (伞形裙) in China. A standard skirt extends from the waist (or thereabouts) to the knee or below, and is always 裙. The dress, which extends from the neck (or thereabouts) to the knee or below, has been consistently known as the 'linked' or 'all in one skirt' (连衣裙). The flares of the 1970s were known as 'trumpet trousers' (喇叭裤) in Hong Kong and have re-appeared in China as 'wide-leg trousers' 阔脚裤. The terms have changed in English too: we no longer wear 'flares', but 'boot cut' or 'wide-leg' trousers. In spite of, or perhaps because of, globalisation, styles merge and blend across national borders and across decades. The styles per se do not necessarily change significantly, but the language that defines them has changed with the times, and translators are obliged to keep up. Clothes are a specialist area, and often become a necessary object of translation, not only in the fashion world, but in history, anthropology, literature, trade and economics, and not infrequently in courts of law, when victims or assailants are identified by the clothes they were wearing at the scene of the crime.

Practical 4.1 Applying semantic fields

This excerpt from *A Detailed Discussion of Chinese Costume*, by Gao Ge, describes dress and occupation:

> 《清明上河图》是北宋张择端的名画，它从一个侧面极其生动地反映了当时汴京繁荣兴旺的景象。画面人物有数百人，白行百业、农工士商、各色人物无不具备。

> 画面中，凡是体力劳动者担夫、小贩、农民、船家等，都有一个共同的特点，那就是上衣都很短，大多是短襦或短衫，不超过膝盖，或者刚刚超过膝盖。他们头戴巾帕，头巾也是比较随便的，甚至还有的没有戴头巾，直接露出发髻。这类人的脚下一般穿麻鞋或者草鞋。

官吏、商贾、文人、有钱的市民则穿交领长袍或圆领襕衫，头戴巾子或幞头，下身穿长裤足蹬靴履。他们的衣袖虽宽窄不一却比较适中，没有太宽的，也没有太窄的，但衣身都比较宽松。

从画面看，宋代平民的服饰，不论是颜色、配饰、衣料还是式样，都是受到严格的限制的，   各行各业的服饰式样也有详细规定，不可以随便地改变和逾越。所以，在宋代，从穿戴上不但可看出等级差别，还可辨认出每个人的职业是什么：披肩子，戴帽子的是卖香人；穿长衫，束牛角带，不戴帽子的是当铺的管事；穿白色短衫，系青花手巾是卖干果的小孩.

(Gao 2005: 123)

i Group the lexical items that are included in each semantic field.
ii What are the equivalent semantic fields in English? How do they differ from the Chinese?
iii Does the time factor affect translation? Would it be appropriate to use anachronistic expressions in a translation of this text?

Practical 4.2 Construction and manipulation of a garment

The true complexity of headgear lies in how to secure it to the head. How would you translate the following text for a book on historical costume?

商周及后来的冠，一般只有一个冠圈，   在冠圈上装一条不太宽的冠梁，   带上冠以后冠圈与冠梁将头发束住。为了防止冠从头上掉落，在冠圈两边设有丝绳做的冠缨，用冠缨在下巴下面打个结系紧。

(Gao 2005: 48)

Practical 4.3 Garment care labelling

One of the commonest, least noticed text types is one of the most powerful: that is the instruction manual. Nowadays, every garment carries a miniature instruction manual, the label found sewn into the seam or below the collar. It has to be translated from the language of the manufacturing nation to that of the purchasing nation. It is now common to see labels that have been translated into six or more languages, depending on the export destinations. The garment label is one of a number of universal genres that is succinct and invisible, but crucial to the functioning of a multi-billion dollar industry. It is in effect, a contractual statement, for it re-assures the purchaser and wearer and protects the manufacturer, by stating the origin of the garment, the fabric of which it is made, and how it should be cared for. Even in such a small text, semantic fields are evident: in these cases, the fields of fabrics and cleaning methods.

Translate the following manufacturer's labels, bearing in mind that they have to be fitted on a very tiny label and sewn inside the garment in such a way as to be invisible and intangible.

i

　　成份含量: 麻100%;
　　洗涤说明: 可以水洗; 不可氯漂;低温熨烫; 悬挂晾干

ii

　　标准: 81007 - 2003
　　面料: 涤纶 66%; 锦纶 34%;
　　里料:涤纶 100%
　　洗涤说明: 中温整烫; 只可用手洗;不可漂白;普通干洗;洗后脱水凉干;
　　不可曝晒;不可扭干.

5 The role of the Chinese nursery rhyme in disseminating traditional values in a modern world

As might be expected, given the size of its population, China boasts a huge canon of nursery rhymes and children's songs. While translations of the great Chinese classical poems are many and eminent, translations of the rhymes are relatively few and little known outside China. Apart from the publications of Headland (1900) and Johnson (1971) we are not aware of any significant anthologies in English translation. New rhymes come and go, reflecting changes in society, and the old rhymes linger, passed on by parents, grand-parents, carers and teachers. The new rhymes come on a wave of political and social change, and are abandoned on the next wave of change. Reflecting politics, life and language over the centuries, the rhymes are the bedrock of children's literature. The hundreds, perhaps thousands, of rhymes in the Chinese canon are an Aladdin's cave of literary treasure, deserving of a wider audience and updated translation.

Nursery rhymes as a poetic genre

In *Thinking Chinese Translation,* we discussed issues surrounding the translation of poetry. Poetry is esteemed as a great literary genre. In pre-republican China, as in many other societies, it was the preserve of the literati, often considered difficult and abstruse. With the establishment of vernacular writing (*baihua* 白话) in the early years of the Republic, writers began to create prose and poetry specifically for children. Reformers like Hu Shi and Lu Xun and their contemporaries began to create new literature, drama and poetry in vernacular Chinese. Their aim was to break the monopoly on learning held by a conservative Confucian elite, and make China a modern, scientific nation.

Until that time, however, children would learn the tried and tested classical poems, and alongside them, they would learn the parallel canon of nursery rhymes. Nursery rhymes are universal. They are rhythmic, rhyming chants introduced by parents, grandparents, older siblings and other carers to infants, and are among a baby's first lessons about life and language. They are distinguished from, but occasionally overlap with, the rhymes which in English are known as playground rhymes. The difference is that nursery rhymes are consciously and deliberately passed down by adults to babies, while the more mischievous playground rhymes are transmitted by and among children. Chinese anthologies of children's rhymes (儿歌 *erge*) contain hundreds of examples, from all the regions of China; some of them are thousands of years old, while some have been written to respond to more recent history, such as the Japanese occupation in the 1930s and 1940s and the ideological demands of post-liberation China. Now, in the second decade of the twenty-first century, Confucian values have regained a foothold in Chinese society, and some of the traditional rhymes have regained a relevance that they lost between 1949 and 2000.

At the beginning of the twenty-first century, educators driven by a strong Confucian ideology are championing the use of traditional rhymes to instil traditional family values in children (Lei 2002). Even though the subject matter may be childlike, the intention of the anthologies is usually 'improving'. Some of the anthologies are published in Taiwan, some in the People's Republic of China, but all include traditional rhymes from the Chinese mainland. The rhymes, some nonsensical, some poignant, some harshly realistic, constitute an important body of literature: a traditional canon that underpins later learning of classical poetry and literature. They deserve a wider platform among non-Chinese speakers. Existing translations tend to be sentimental and romantic, as will be shown below, and new translations of a wider range of rhymes would leaven the existing fare.

There has been keen discussion in greater China about the terminology and definition of the various kinds of rhyming or rhythmic songs and recitations that make up the children's canon. Songs sung by and to small children were not necessarily designed for that purpose. In all cultures, very adult songs become popular, and are repeated by adults, heard by children, giggled over, and repeated again, thus creeping into the children's repertoire. Iona and Peter Opie note that 'children [...] are conservative and exact, and tend to be in touch with the non-working (oldest) members of the family, who themselves delight in recounting their earliest memories' (Opie and Opie 1951/ 1997: 14), which of course include the rhymes. On the other hand, there are songs that have been composed specially for children, to sing them to sleep, to comfort them when they are hurt, or to educate them.

Family hierarchy and numbers in Chinese rhymes

Although the subject matter of Chinese rhymes is broad and varied, one of the most common themes is the distinct family hierarchy of age, generation and gender. In anthologies, dating from the 1920s to the early 2000s, but containing rhymes of much earlier origin, themes of Confucian family values and relationships, dominance and precedence pervade the rhymes. Occasionally anthologists do comment on the pathos of the rhymes, but sometimes soften the blow for the modern audience, explaining away the apparent cruelty, or interpreting it, like Headland (see below), as cute and childlike. Anthologies of rhymes collected in the 1970s (Zhu 1977) and 1990s (Sheng and Wu 1999) show that even though society had changed, rhymes that depicted subservient women and younger siblings were still common, and still being taught to young children.

Owing to the broad subject matter and variety of sub-genre and form, we can select only a fraction of representative rhymes. We will focus on two aspects of the rhymes that differ to a greater or lesser degree from British rhymes, and their implications for the translator. First, pronominal reference and the effect that the Chinese zero pronoun has on the 'voice' of the rhymes, and, second, the role of numbers in the discourse of the rhymes. In spite of their apparent transparency and universality, numbers can be highly culture-specific and highly idiomatic.

The subject matter of the traditional rhyme is more or less limitless, and in order to restrict the scope for the purposes of this chapter, we will concentrate on rhymes that deal with family relationships and those which contain numbers relating to generation or precedence within the family. Many of these rhymes refer explicitly or implicitly to the way young women and children are treated, and the way they are expected to behave. Numbers constitute a nomenclature system for family hierarchy. While similar hierarchies exist in many other societies, the nomenclature is culture-specific, and may present challenges for the translator.

The rhymes quoted in this chapter are replicated in a number of anthologies, published both in the People's Republic of China and in Taiwan. Most anthologies of rhymes state explicitly in their introduction or preface that they are designed for moral and educational purposes. The transmission of these age-old ditties is intended to teach small children about the natural world, the world of work, social relationships and good behaviour (Lei 2002; Yin 2007; Zhu 1977). Most of the older rhymes describe a world that no longer exists, and newer rhymes have been created to reflect more modern attitudes, for example that married couples do not always have children. But the rhymes serve now to instil a sense of the traditional culture that is being lost to the instantaneous virtual culture that surrounds children everywhere. In the People's Republic of China, literature, including fiction, biography, poetry and drama, is one way of teaching the many only children about the former extended family and its functions as a system of care and support. The family in China now is 'top-heavy': young people may still have a number of uncles and aunts, but have very few cousins and even fewer, if any, siblings. Modern Chinese children may only know of the extended, hierarchical family through their reading, or through films.

The rhymes carry a mixed propaganda. They state what the situation is, for example that girls will be married to men they have never met, for the sake of family stability. At the same time, they warn young people of the hardships to come, and implicitly extol or condemn the hierarchical Confucian framework, depending on the ideological trends of the time. A very large proportion of the rhymes are about marriage and the social, economic and cultural activities surrounding marriage. Some of these are to do with the preoccupations of the unmarried man or woman: the dreams and hopes, or the known restrictions. Others state the case of the marriage: the role of the matchmaker, homesickness for the parental home once the wife has left to live in her husband's home, the behaviour of in-laws, characteristics of a husband and characteristics of a wife. These are listed exhaustively in Liu (1925).

The rhymes could therefore be as challenging to a translator as classical literature such as 'The Water Margin' (*Shui Hu Zhuan* 水浒传). In the translations of the rhymes suggested here, we have in mind an English-reading audience of children and adults, in the twenty-first century. We do not wish the rhymes to be seen as romantic, sentimental poems, but as frank, saucy reflections of the reality of Chinese life as it was many years ago.

Sub-genre, category and content

The sub-genres of Chinese children's rhymes and songs (兒童詩歌) are stated above: the cradle songs (搖籃曲), children's rhymes (兒歌), nursery rhymes (童謠) and folk songs (民歌). Within these broad and overlapping sub-genres are categories that are characterised by form or content; sometimes a particular type of content is associated with a particular form, for instance the Moonlight rhymes (月光光) and the Little Cabbage rhymes (小白菜). The Moonlight rhymes deal with the notion of admiring the moon, and worshipping or praying for good fortune (Zhu 1977: 80–81); the Little Cabbage rhymes deal with the sad situation of being orphaned and then being displaced by a step-parent and step-sibling (Zhu 1977: 94). Certain genres deal explicitly with the position of women and girls: there are 'small feet rhymes' (as illustrated in Example 5a below, taken from Headland's anthology); 'going home' rhymes, which describe a young wife going home to visit her parents; Third Sister rhymes (三姐) vary in form, but invariably start in the same way, with the characteristics and privileges of big sister, then those of second sister, and finally the destitution and misery of third sister. The sub-genres, categories and their content appear to be common throughout China, but exist in a variety of regional forms (Zhu 1997: passim).

The discourse of the rhymes

The discourse of these rhymes varies: in some cases there is an explicit didactic element, teaching girls how they should behave, what is expected of them, and what they can expect from their family situation. In other cases, the warning is implicit, the messages couched in understatement. Occasionally there is a subversive tone, as in the case of the young woman who beats the matchmaker for arranging a bad husband. Voices vary from rhyme to rhyme: the rhymer may be a young woman, hoping or despairing, or simply narrating; it may be a mother-in-law berating; it may be a motherless child sorrowing; it may be a generalised third party telling a tale, describing an event or instructing children in a game. Some rhymes, such as the Cowherd song quoted below, are dialogues. The genre may be childlike, with rhythmic and rhymed forms, but the content is often very serious, and there is almost always implicit or explicit warning of how things are for young women and children.

Translating numbers in the rhymes

In addition to the rhymes that are intended as counting rhymes and aimed at educating children in arithmetic, there are numbers that express and teach relationships. There are numbers that express weights, measures and distance, and these also serve to exemplify and teach, not only about the worth of material goods, and the times and seasons, but also about hierarchical relationships.

In dealing with the translation of the Chinese rhymes, we have to consider a multi-layered transfer. First, the transfer of culture-specific items and ideas from Chinese into English may include the regionally specific. Second, some culture-specific notions are to do with transfer across time, for there are artefacts, activities, customs and roles described in the rhymes that are no longer current in Chinese life, and may be unknown to many young people. Third, the transfer may be from a male-dominant, age-dominant hierarchical culture into a modern 'equal opportunities' culture. Another crucial consideration is the implication of the rhyme. Often the seemingly concrete description or narrative tale may hold implicit information that is easily apprehended by the native speaker audience, but may not be so clear to a target audience. An example of this is the case of 'small feet', discussed below. The linguistic structure of the rhymes is consonant with mainstream classical poetry and folk song. There is a tendency to economy of personal pronoun, time reference and gender reference with strong, simple rhymes and rhythms, all of which contribute to the implication of assumed knowledge.

The voice of the rhymes

It is likely that the authorship of Chinese rhymes involved both sexes: we do not necessarily know who composed the originals. It may be possible to posit an inferred author as narrator, in terms of the 'voice' of the rhyme, and vicarious, or proxy authorship, as rhymes are deliberately transmitted by adults or older children. The inferred author of the rhymes, as noted below, may be the young woman or girl as unfortunate victim, the mother as doting parent, the mother- or sister-in-law as irritated members of the host family, the young man as admiring suitor, and many more which we will not deal with here. Anthologists and commentators have been of both sexes, and early in the twentieth century, at least one female scholar, Liu (1925), was studying the sexual discrimination that is implicit and explicit throughout the canon. In translating the rhymes, we have to look sensitively at the question of 'fidelity'. Belsey and Moore (1991: 1) point out that 'for the feminist reader there is no innocent or neutral approach to literature: all interpretation is political', a point of view that is inevitably applied to translation. Simon states that 'feminist translation ... reframes the question of fidelity' (1996: 2). A controversial issue in feminist translation studies is whether to work only on 'sympathetic' texts, or to work also on 'antagonistic' texts (Simon 1996: 30). Chinese rhymes are often composed from a point of view that condones, if not supports, the Confucian family system that places the female and the young in inferior positions in the hierarchy, a point of view transmitted by the vicarious author. In terms of modern attitudes towards equal opportunities, we might therefore regard the rhymes as 'antagonistic' texts. Some existing translations, such as those of Headland, below, appear, by their softening approach, to be condoning Confucian attitudes. But this perhaps should be the very reason why we translate an antagonistic text.

Headland's *Chinese Mother Goose Rhymes* (1900) is probably the most well-known translation of Chinese children's rhymes. The parallel text anthology of 151 rhymes aimed to 'make a translation which is fairly true to the original, and which will please English-speaking children' (ibid.: Preface). Headland notes the 'keen and tender affection' of the Chinese rhymes, and he hopes that 'they will lead the children of the West to have some measure of sympathy and affection for the children of the East' (ibid.: Preface). The anthology is illustrated with charming photos of Headland's contemporary China: a paratext that contributes to Headland's romantic renderings. We cannot condemn Headland, for his contribution to the collection and dissemination abroad of a valuable literary resource is unmistakable. But he was of his time, writing in the last days of Imperial China, at a time when Chinese women were only just beginning to share the privileges of education, and at a time when European women still did not have the vote. Perhaps now it is time to re-present the rhymes afresh, in such a way that foreign readers see the important historical and sociological information contained in the canon.

Headland's anthology begins, perhaps unwittingly, with two rhymes that represent cultural traits typical of the China of the time. In 1900, the Qing dynasty was still in power, though weak, and Chinese society was still shaped by Confucian ideology and practice, though 'modern' ideas were infiltrating from the West. The first rhyme in the anthology is about how sweet a baby boy is; the second rhyme is about a girl with small (i.e. bound) feet, crying. The fifth rhyme in the collection is 'Of what use is a girl?', translated without any softening features.

If, as in Headland's translation, (Example 5a below), we simply say 'little feet' and give the impression of cute sentimentality, we are perhaps being faithful to the form of the rhyme, but we deprive the child and adult target reader of valuable information: a girl with small feet, who weeps, is a girl who has bound feet and is in pain.

Example 5a

小脚儿娘爱吃糖
没钱儿买
搬着小脚儿哭一场

> The small-footed girl with the sweet little smile
> She loves to eat sugar and sweets all the while.
> Her money's all gone and because she can't buy,
> She holds her small feet while she sits down to cry.

> (Headland 1900: 8)

This example reveals a great deal about judgements made in translation. Typically for a Chinese rhyme, there is an absence of function words (虚词). In the case of this rhyme, causal and temporal links are not explicitly stated in the source text. The reader or listener supplies the pragmatic links. By introducing overt causal and temporal links ('because' and 'while') Headland has attributed the girl's weeping to having no money to buy sweets. A more realistic, informed, viewpoint might attribute the weeping to the pain of bound feet. Headland infers that the girl had money, and no longer has it. This is not entirely justifiable, as, for all we know, she never had any money at all. The verb 搬着 *banzhe* in the source rhyme seems to suggest some kind of manipulation, or fidgeting: the girl could be massaging or flexing her feet. A more realistic translator might also use causal or temporal links between clauses, but would place them so as to achieve a different message. Perhaps the greatest liberty taken by Headland is the addition of a smile. In addition to considerations of content, we have also to consider form: Headland has rendered the Chinese rhyme as an English rhyme that works well, but has increased the length from 19 characters (19 syllables) to 38 words (43 syllables). In effect, the length of the rhyme is doubled, and Headland has created, perhaps unwittingly, a sentimentalised, neutralised version, where the unstated implications of the text are not only explicated, but over-translated. In this case, we would venture to suggest, a rendering more sympathetic to girls, as shown below, would reframe the translation in a much more 'faithful' manner:

Example 5b

> The girl with small feet
> loves sugar to eat
> has no money to buy:
> She rubs her feet and starts to cry.

> (Authors' translation)

This rendering may not be as poetic as Headland's, but it keeps close to the rhythm and rhyme scheme of the Chinese, and provides a rhythmic chant suitable for a child target reader. It avoids the issues of cause and effect, leaving the reader or listener to make his or her own inferences. A translator would be justified in translating 小脚 as 'bound feet'. For a very modern audience, reading cultural allusions that are distant not only in space, but also in time, a footnote about bound feet might be desirable (Pellatt and Liu 2010: 162, 173). For older readers, a paratextual illustration in the form of a photograph of bound feet might be a useful addition to the text.

Mother-in-law and daughter-in-law

Prior to the reforms of the twentieth century in China, women were expected to follow the Confucian principle of the three obediences and four virtues (三从四德). Until marriage, a woman had to obey her father, after marriage she had to obey her husband, and after widowhood, she had to obey her son. The four virtues were moral behaviour, proper speech, modest manner and diligence. On marriage, a woman became a member of her husband's family, and her place as daughter in her own family would be taken by the wife of her brother. Young wives might be unhappy on at least two counts: bad treatment by their in-laws and displacement in their maternal family.

Many rhymes are woven around these themes, sometimes from the viewpoint of the young, badly treated, lonely wife, sometimes from the point of view of the mother-in-law or sister-in-law. Zhu devotes a section in his anthology to 'being a daughter-in-law' (做媳妇) and includes the following Beijing rhyme (Zhu 1977: 121) in which we are party to the mother-in-law's view.

Example 5c

> 长得真拙！
> 长得真拙！
> 不会拿针去穿线，不会拿帚去刷锅，
> 一顿吃了八个大窝窝，比着汉子还吃得多得多。
> 会吃会穿不会做，比我女儿差得多，
> 全是妈妈不会养，偏偏留下这个没奈何。

(Zhu 1977: 121)

> How clumsy, how clumsy my daughter-in-law!
> Can't thread a needle to sew a seam,
> Can't scour a pan to make it gleam,
> But when she eats *wotou*, she'll eat two times four,
> That's as much as a man or maybe more.
> She can eat, she can dress, but she can't do a chore,
> Nothing at all like the daughter I bore.
> All due to her mother who couldn't teach her
> And brought up this clumsy, helpless creature.

(Authors' translation)

The number eight might be a random choice used for euphonic reasons, but may have deeper implications. Eight is an auspicious number in Chinese culture, so there may be some irony attached to a mere daughter-in-law eating this number of *wotou* (a dense, coarse dumpling of maize, sorghum or millet). A mother-in-law, watching her family budget, would be observant of how much family members eat, so here, the number expression is used to denote the magnitude and immorality of the daughter-in-law's apparent greed. Needless to say, every mother favours her own offspring over others, a phenomenon that is often reflected in the Chinese rhymes. It is also interesting to note that a woman, who might be carrying out quite hard manual labour, is not expected to eat as much as a man. I would suggest that the use of the number in this rhyme is not random, but purposeful, and deserves explicit translation. A further implication lies in the choice of 窝窝 *wowo* or *wotou* as it is more likely to be eaten by the poor than by the wealthy. A contemporary Chinese audience of any age would have inferred that the in-laws' family was not wealthy, and might be due some sympathy. This begs the question of footnotes and translators' notes, introduction or preface, which will be dealt with at the end of the chapter.

The following rhyme, by contrast, is composed from the daughter-in-law's point of view. It comes under the category of 'Cockerel with a curly tail', which is named after the title of an old song form often associated with this type of daughter-in-law's complaint.

Example 5d

> 鸡公仔，尾弯弯，
> 做人新妇试艰难，
> 一早起身都话晏，
> 眼汁唔周入下间。
> 下间有个榴罗仔，
> 问过亚娘炒或蒸？
> 蒸蒸炒炒 唔中意
> 大声吵闹细声弹。
> 大把揸盐都话淡，
> 指甲挑盐又话咸。
> 三朝打烂三条棒，
> 四朝跪烂四条裙。
> 只有一条花裙未跪烂，
> 留番去探外家亲。
> 去到外家三餐饱，
> 归来饿得面皮青。

(Ma 1996: 185)

Cockerel with a curly tail
It's hard to be a man's new mate,
When I get up early, she says I'm late.
Holding back the tears

I go downstairs
To see to all the kitchen needs.
There are pomegranate seeds–
Should I fry them or should I steam them?
No matter what, mother-in-law is steaming
She's yelling or nagging, and I know I'm not dreaming.
If you give her salty, she says it's got no taste,
If you give her plain, she's says there's salt to waste.
In three days, she's worn out three rods beating,
In four days, I've worn out four skirts kneeling.
I've one skirt left that's good to wear,
To go to back to my parents, and when I'm there
I get three good meals. But when I come back
I'm so starved my skin is blue and black.

(Authors' translation)

The first thing to note about this rhyme is the inevitability of inference. The audience must infer the identity of the narrator and the identity of the person who is so dissatisfied as to do the beating and expect the kowtowing. Typically, the rhyme uses the zero subject sentence structure common in Chinese, and any rendering in English, except perhaps a symbolist or minimalist approach, would require a grammatical subject for each sentence. We have assumed that the voice is that of a daughter-in-law who is ill-treated by her mother-in-law. Using the third person voice is a possibility, but this would require some kind of distinction between 'she' the wife and 'she' the mother-in-law. The rhyme could even be rendered as an explicit warning using 'you' and a future tense. Note the pun in line 7: 'to steam and fry' (蒸蒸炒炒 *zheng zheng chao chao*) could be a homophone of 'to fight and quarrel' (争争吵吵 *zheng zheng chao chao*).

The numbers in this rhyme are significant. They measure the extent of good or bad treatment. The new wife is subject to beating and is made to kowtow, in deference or apology. The 'three meals' are an idiomatic statement of normal, good treatment in her own family home (in British English they might be termed 'three square meals'), compared with the starvation she suffers in the in-laws' home. Like many rhymes, this one explicitly describes a situation that was common, and condoned. Conditions in China have changed beyond all recognition; women do not lead lives like this now, but nevertheless, the translator of the rhyme has a duty to show society as it was, and can use the numbers as the metaphors they are intended to be: rather than saying 'my mother-in-law beats me very hard', the implied author, the young woman, uses the subtle, vivid metaphors of wearing out numerous rods and skirts.

Third sister

Within the maternal, or natal, family, as daughters descended in age, so their status in the family decreased. The oldest daughter might get a good dowry, and a reliable provider for a husband, but the more the daughters, the less wealth the family had, and the less able they were to procure a good match. Zhu has a section on 'Poor Third Sister' (1977: 89) in which he explains that the Third Sister rhymes are found throughout China, and catalogue the scorn, discrimination and misery experienced by 'Third Sister'. Third sister is representative: she is not necessarily the last in the line of sisters, and there are also rhymes about Sixth Sister. Zhu quotes a Chinese proverb 'burglars don't bother with a home that has five daughters' (盗不过五女之门) (ibid.: 89), a succinct comment on the economic realities of a family with many daughters, itself a typical example of a Chinese proverb that uses a number to express a family's economic situation. In Example 5e below, features of several subgenres of rhymes are included: the rhyme starts with a reference to 'moonlight', which is often used for the sake of rhythm and '兴', (what we might call 'interest' or 'catchiness': see Chapter 6 on transcreation of Chinese poetry). The form is made up of parallel repetitions of descriptions of the three sisters in descending order of age, wealth and status. There are many rhymes of this type that drive home for the reader the difference between siblings in status, income and marriage outcomes.

Example 5e

> 月亮走，我也走，我同月亮提花篓，
> 一提提到大门口，打开大门摘石榴，
> 石榴上头三张图：三个大姐同梳头。
> 大姐梳的盘龙髻，二姐梳的插花头，
> 三姐不会梳，梳个狮子滚绣球。
> 大姐戴金簪，二姐戴银簪，
> 三姐没得戴，戴根豆芽菜。
> 大姐回来杀只猪，二姐回来杀只羊，
> 三姐没得杀，杀只孵鸡 婆煮汤吃；
> 吃又不吃，尝又不尝，躲在湾里哭一场。
> 大姐坐轿回，二姐骑马回，
> 三姐走路回，走一里，哭一里，扯根禾包拭眼泪。

(Zhu 1977: 91)

> The moon travels on and I travel too,
> Flowers in my basket, all for you.
> Carry them along to the big front door,
> And pick a pomegranate, just one, no more.
> In the shiny fruit, three pictures there:
> Three pretty sisters, combing their hair.
> Big Sister wears hers in a dragon coil
> Sister Number Two has flowers in her hair,
> Sister Number Three has no hairdo at all,
> Just rolls an embroidered lion ball.

Sister Number One has a pin of gold
Sister Number Two has a silver hairpin,
Sister Number Three has nothing to wear,
So she puts bean sprouts in her hair.
When Big Sister comes home a pig is slaughtered
A sheep is killed for the second daughter
All third daughter gets is a sitting hen.
Her appetite gone, she sits by the river
Sobbing her heart out, all of a quiver.
A sedan chair carries Big Sister home
And Sister Number Two rides a fancy roan,
Sister Number Three walks, trudging all alone,
Wiping her tears as she weeps and walks
With a little handful of rough rice stalks.

(Authors' translation)

In some areas of China, a girl would have her hair pinned into the dragon style as a sign that she was about to be married. In some 'Third sister' rhymes, the number of loads of dowry, for example, is listed. In the following rhyme, framed as a dialogue, we hear a younger sister's own voice:

Example 5f

看牛郎，看牛郎，
可见我家姐姐娘，
喔也，见了她。
桃李树下洗衣裳。
油菜花，黄又黄，
大姐俊，细姐麻。
大姐嫁妆十八担，
细姐嫁妆空油罐。
行一步，哭一声，
旁人问我哭什么，
哭我爹娘心儿不公平。

(Ma 1996: 89)

Cowherd, cowherd answer me,
Have you seen my sister, older than me?
Oh, yes, I saw her under a tree,
Washing clothes in the shade of the peach and the plum.
The rape seed's yellow, yellow as can be,
Big sister's pretty, pretty as they come
Younger sister's pockmarked, ugly as can be.
Big sister's dowry is eighteen big loads
Younger sister's dowry is an empty oil drum.

Go step by step, shed tear on tear
Passers-by ask me what I fear.
Parents are not fair, I fear.

(Authors' translation)

The number expression in this rhyme makes explicit the huge difference in treatment between one sibling and another. The identity of the first person narrator (我) is explicit, and this helps the translator to find a voice. While it is not absolutely certain that this is third sister bemoaning her own fate, the implication is very strong. In this translation we have resisted an explicit rendering: 'I' could be another sibling, but as in the source text, the implication is that this is third sister's voice.

Little Cabbage orphans

'Little Cabbage' (小白菜) rhymes are a category that deserve some attention. They are almost always concerned with the death of a parent (usually the mother) and the advent of a step-parent. The age of the orphan is usually specified as two or three years old, or sometimes older, as six or seven. Zhu points out that at the age of seven, the child's feelings will be very different from that of a very young child (1977: 96). The child will have a greater sense of apprehension about the step-mother, and a greater sense of the obligation to suffer in silence. The central message of the rhymes is that sooner or later, a step-mother arrives on the scene and bears a child who will supplant the orphan in her own parent's affection. The gender of the orphaned child is not usually explicit in the rhyme, but, it is generally accepted that the orphan is always a girl. Sometimes the age of the new step-mother is specified, and it is not necessarily much older than that of the orphan. These rhymes are usually expressed from the point of view of the orphan.

Example 5g

小白菜哟，遍地黄哟。
两三岁哟，死了娘哟，
只好跟着爸爸过哟，
又怕爸爸讨后娘哟。
讨个后娘三年整啊，
生个弟弟，比我强哟。
弟弟吃的白米饭啦，
我是吃的大粗糠啦，
弟弟穿的绫罗缎啦，
我是穿的破破烂哟，
弟弟跟着爸爸睡哟，
把我丢在床沿外哟。

噫哟，唉哟！
想起我娘哭一场哟。

(Zhu 1977: 95)

Little cabbage, yellowing and sad,
When I was two, my mother died.
My father and I we led our life
I was always afraid that he'd find another wife.
After three years there was sure to be
A baby boy who was better than me.
Baby brother eats fine, white grain,
And I just get the coarsest bran;
He wears the finest satin cloth
I get the rags that folk cast off;
He sleeps with father in the bed so wide
And I'm thrown out to sleep at the side.
Alas alack, alas alack,
I cry for my mother who won't come back.

(Authors' translation)

Headland's rendition of a similar Little Cabbage rhyme about, a seven-year-old, is as follows:

Like a little withered flower,
That is dying in the earth
I am left alone at seven
By her who gave me birth.
With my papa I was happy,
But I feared he'd take another,
And now my papa's married,
And I have a little brother.
And he eats good food,
While I eat poor,
And cry for my mother
Whom I'll see no more.

(Headland 1900: 45)

Headland's translation is faithful, rhythmic and evocative, but omits the brief three years it takes for the child to be displaced in the family, and also omits the expression 比我强 'better than me', which is a strong indication that the orphan is a girl. While there is no explicit statement of the gender of the orphaned 'little cabbage', for the Chinese audience, it is undoubtedly a girl, since, within the Confucian family, an older son's place in his father's esteem would be unlikely to be usurped.

Brothers at work

Chinese rhymes are, naturally, peopled by boys as well as girls. The following example shows us a family of ten sons, each following a different occupation.

Example 5h

> 大兒大，說實話，不扯謊，不亂罵。
> 二兒二，會扯鋸，鋸得光，作隻箱。
> 三兒三，不好玩，沒得事，好扯談。
> 四兒四，曉得事，不靠人，自照顧。
> 五兒五，常習武，是好漢，打戰鼓。
> 六兒六，裁淡竹，淡竹多，筍子足。
> 七兒七，學作筆，賣了錢，買飯吃。
> 八兒八，餵雞鴨，糞肥田，肉好吃。
> 九兒九，喜走路，走一步，還能夠。
> 十兒十，把布織，織一天，幾十尺。

(Zhu 1977: 213)

Number one, oldest son, always says a true word, never says a bad one.
Son number two can wield a saw, saw to a shine and make a box so fine.
Number three son is not much fun, nothing else to do, chats the whole day
    through.
Son number four, knows so much more, counts on no one, independent
    to the core.
Number five son is the military one, a fine upstanding chap who plays a
    drum.
Son number six cuts bamboo sticks, if the bamboo's thick there are
    shoots to pick.
Son number seven's writing is so nice, he sells it for cash to buy the rice.
Son number eight feeds all the fowls, for manure on the fields and meat
    for our meals.
Son number nine wanders where he will, step after step, it's his only skill.
Son number ten weaves away, making metres of cloth all in one day.

(Authors' translation)

Zhu's notes on this rhyme point out its narrow range of characters, which makes it suitable for the very young. It will 'bend the mind' (勵志) towards language (1977: 213). It is very simple in structure and in rhyme. There are virtually no function words (虛词), and all the cohesive links are carried in the lexis, or indicated by the editor in the punctuation. Translated into coherent, rhyming English, as above, it risks being very wordy. In order to preserve the simplicity and the rhythm, it might be possible to adopt a minimalist approach, using, where possible, only English content words. Would a note on 'glaucous bamboo' (淡竹) be useful for interested parents?

Thick translation: Aims, readership and the provision of footnotes or an introduction

The great difficulty of translating nursery rhymes is the very ambivalence of the source texts, which, as we pointed out earlier, can be rude, crude and horrific, as well as instructive or subversive. At this point I will return to Headland's aims, stated in the brief Preface to his anthology, to 'make a translation which is fairly true to the original, and which will please English-speaking children' (1900). Headland himself toned down the rhymes, and there is a great temptation for any translator to make the target text cute, on the one hand, and neutralised on the other. Should we offer children a saccharine, bowdlerised version of the source text, or should we give them an honest, informative version? In translating nursery rhymes, a form of propaganda used by adults to inform and instruct children, should we not also consider the adult reader and selector of the rhymes? A translation can be as rhythmic and as entertaining as the original without letting go any of the educational and instructional implications. What Headland chooses to render as 'keen and tender affection' (above) is, in the source text, often rampant misery. Nursery rhymes the world over are notorious for their candour, vulgarity and cruelty, and this is why they are so well loved and well used. Children are sometimes delighted by wicked words and ideas, and it is the responsibility of adults to allow them truthful access. For this reason, translators may wish to consider Simon's notion of re-framing fidelity (1996: 2; see above). In conveying accurately in translation the wording of many of the Chinese rhymes, we may provide a more truthful picture of the way women's lives were lived in earlier phases of Chinese society, and will indeed 'lead the children of the West to have some measure of sympathy and affection for the children of the East'.

Traditionally, nursery rhymes have been regarded as fun activities that aid a child's development of language and motor skills. They have been used to lull babies to sleep, and are common in circle games and for counting out. For adults they are nostalgic, and for academics they are a rich source of historical and sociological information. Some quite cruel ideas and behaviours are sometimes described in rhymes that children sing in innocence. In the Chinese rhymes, the status and treatment of women and children is laid bare, and the translator can choose, or not choose, to reflect realistically the narratives of the rhymes. Existing translations are not always as honest as they might be. While it is not always easy to be faithful to the rhyme scheme or the rhythm of a rhyme in such a way as to make it attractive and singable for the target audience, it is possible to transmit the sometimes unpalatable content.

The numbers contained in the Chinese rhymes are used for reasons of rhythm and rhyme, but are also crucial conveyors of meaning. Number expressions in Chinese nursery rhymes convey relationships: between members of the family; between wealth and poverty; between good treatment and bad treatment; the passing of time; youth and age, especially 'rites of passage'.

These rhymes cry out for a faithful translation: not a translation that clings to the rhyme and rhythm, though that would be a bonus, and not a sentimentalised gloss-over, but a translation that reflects the reality of women's lives in traditional Chinese society, as they are told in the rhymes. Their status as the property of children also demands fluent, rhythmic and entertaining translation, as they are designed to be read, recited or sung. The Chinese and European custom is to present nursery rhymes in bold easy-to-read print, to enable reading, and with bright, colourful illustrations to draw a child's attention, aid understanding and motivate. Small, source-language nursery rhyme anthologies do not usually have an introduction, as the adult readers who relay the rhymes have sufficient cultural and historical understanding to provide a paratext for the child. In the case of scholarly collections of rhymes, a significant amount of paratext accompanies the core texts, as in the case of the Opies' various works on rhymes and games, and in the case of Zhu Jiefan's anthology. If rhymes are to be translated, as we have pointed out above, there may be many cultural, historical and linguistic issues that need to be explained. Footnotes or endnotes disrupt reading, and in the case of rhymes or children's stories, would be undesirable for the listening child: children are fierce critics, and disapprove of any mis-reading or interruption. What is called for in an anthology, and seems to be the preferred option for poetic genres, is a 'thick' introduction, prepared with adults in mind, which goes to the heart of the text, leaving the reading of the text itself untrammelled. Hermans writes of 'thick translation' as

> bringing about a double dislocation: of the foreign terms and concepts, which are probed and unhinged by means of an alien methodology and vocabulary, *and* of the describer's own vocabulary, which needs to be wrenched out of its familiar shape to accommodate not only similarity but alterity.
>
> (Hermans 2003: 387)

McRae makes a strong case for translators' introductions as a way of presenting background information about cultural and linguistic differences (2012: 80). We can deliver the rhymes as rhymes for the child reader or listener, but we also need to take into consideration the underlying cultural messages. This need justifies translators' introductions or prefaces and accompanying notes and explications for the interested adolescent and adult reader. The target audience of a nursery or children's rhyme is varied, and has complex requirements that demand sensitivity and skill on the part of the translator.

Practical 5.1 Rites of passage for girls

In Confucian China girls married early, often betrothed as infants or very young children. The following example shows a young woman, already married, returning to her parents' home. Translate the rhyme, considering the following points:

i   How significant are the ages stated in the rhyme?
ii What do you feel is the underlying message of the rhyme? How explicitly
    should the tone of the rhyme be conveyed?

> 蝴蝶儿穿花裙
> 十三岁做新人，
> 十四岁拖儿胞女上爹门，
> 长竹竿晒红裙，
> 短竹竿打媒人，
> 不是媒人故，
> 是爹娘做错了人。

(Ma 1996: 93)

Practical 5.2 *A new kind of family*

Rhymes of the twentieth century were influenced by political change. The following rhyme of the 1960s depicts a rather different kind of 'family' from that of
the traditional rhymes. Translate the rhyme, bearing in mind the following points:

i   What are the relationships between the characters depicted in the rhyme?
    What do these relationships tell us about the society and politics of China
    during this period? How would these 'family members' be best referred to
    in English?
ii There are historical and cultural references in the rhyme. To what extent
    should these be explained to a modern non-Chinese audience of parents
    reading the rhyme to or with their children?
iii Prepare two translations for publication: a bouncy, rhythmic version aimed
    at children and a 'thick' translation for parents.

> 送奶奶
> 好八连，八连好，
> 开荒种地上西郊。
> 上西郊，脚步齐，
> 来回要走几十里。
> 几十里，走得快，
> 回来遇见老奶奶。
> 老奶奶，走亲家，
> 肩上挑的大南瓜。
> 大南瓜，重又重，
> 奶奶累得走不动。
> 走不动，汗水淌。
> 八连叔叔来帮忙。
> 来帮忙，送到家，
> 好像儿子送媽媽。

(*A Selection of New Children's Songs and Nursery Rhymes* 1964)

6 Transcreation as a means of delivering poetry to an Other audience

Rap adaptation and sinophonic poetry

Of all areas of Chinese translation, one of the most debated is that of Chinese poetry. In this chapter we will look at the creative potential of very 'close' rendering at one end of the spectrum, and adaptation, or transcreation, at the other end. In both cases reviewed here, the translator-writers take a course that deliberately and openly creates a target text that is different from the source text. We take as examples the work of Jonathan Stalling, whose novel approach uses literal translation of found poetry, and an adaptation or transcreation of the poem *Journey to the Peach Blossom Spring* by Wang Wei as a rap-style narrative poem, a clear departure from the source text.

The canon of classical Chinese poetry is well known outside China to intellectuals, and mostly to sinophiles and poetry aficionados. This is particularly true of the poems of the Tang dynasty (618–907), which have been frequently published in China in a collection of 300 items. Ezra Pound is mostly famous and occasionally infamous for having 'translated' a small number of them into very appealing, minimalist symbolist-type poetry. Pound's versions stand out as examples of real English and real poetry, compared with many awkward, arrhythmic, inaccessible versions.

While it is perhaps superfluous to translate a Tang poem yet again, the sheer volume of extant, unsatisfactory versions permits illustration of the obstacles to transmission in acceptable foreign-language versions. The poems, which in Chinese are highly readable, are often terse and earthy. Many existing translations, especially by Chinese native speaker translators, are at best pseudo-Byronic, and at worst awkward, ungrammatical and overly sentimental.

Transcreation is a long-established tradition in many cultures that transmits cultural knowledge and values in accessible, exciting, attractive modes to new audiences: words to pictures, pictures to music, music to movement and each mode in new forms within itself. Transcreation from one language to another is one of the many modes, and we suggest that it may serve some literary forms and audiences better than translation which attempts to be 'faithful', 'accurate' or source culture-oriented. In this chapter, we suggest that transcreation of classical texts in modern guise may be beneficial to transmission of a culture and genre which might otherwise remain unknown outside intellectual circles. Chinese classical poetry, which has been interpreted in very varied forms over hundreds of years, may be a good candidate for an overtly adaptive or transcreational approach.

About transcreation

Transcreation may be said to be at the extreme domestication end of the domestication–foreignisation spectrum. On this spectrum, foreignisation is regarded as bringing the reader to the foreign text by means of so-called 'literal' or word-for-word techniques. The notion of foreignisation implies respect for the author and the culture, and non-interference in the text. A foreignised translation does not make concessions to readers. Domestication is the more liberal use of techniques such as paraphrase, synonyms and reconstruction to bring the foreign text to the reader on the reader's own cultural terms (Venuti 1995: passim). Nida and Taber's notion of dynamic equivalence is perhaps the best-known practical domestication approach. Their aim was to reproduce in the target language 'the closest natural equivalent of the source language message' (1969: 12), in meaning and style, rather than form. Dynamic equivalence is close in spirit to transcreation.

Transcreation comes in various guises: as adaptation, re-writing or re-telling, and Lefevere in 1975 talked about such an approach as 'version' (Lefevere 1975: 76). Applied to literature, where we would expect a degree of creativity in any transfer from one language to another, 'transcreation' seems the most appropriate nomenclature.

The term has been used to label the re-telling of stories and myths in the Indian tradition. Gopinathan uses the simile of a shadow, which exists attached to, and totally like its object, but constantly changing in form and intensity depending on the light source (Gopinathan 2006: 236). He describes transcreation as a 'rebirth or incarnation (Avatar)' and 'an aesthetic re-interpretation of the original work suited to the readers/audience of the target language in the particular time and space' (ibid: 236). The usefulness of transcreation lies in its scope for universality, and the scope it offers for explaining and expanding the content of the source text. For Gopinathan, it 'breaks the myth of untranslatability' (ibid.: 237).

Gopinathan's examples are the Hindu myths, but the great European fairy tales are also splendid examples of transcreation as transmission: we hand them down from generation to generation in countless different verbal versions, and non-verbally in pictures, cartoons, opera, ballet and pantomime. Transcreation is a universal way of transmitting knowledge of the ways of the world to succeeding generations. A perfect example of transcreation for a modern audience is Roald Dahl's *Little Red Riding Hood and the Wolf*, which becomes a funny, racy poem in iambic tetrameter rhyming couplets, in his provocative book *Revolting Rhymes* (Dahl 1982).

Chan (1998) provides a perfect Chinese illustration of what he calls adaptation, but which is so extreme that we might include it in transcreation. He describes in some detail a range of Chinese versions of Aesop's fables, showing how they were domesticated for the Chinese nineteenth-century market. In some, 'virtually all traces of the original story [were] eliminated' (ibid.: 66–67). Although the 'plot line' remained unchanged, the target version became significantly longer than the source (ibid.: 66–67). The impact of at least one version of the fables, by Thom, revealed the complexities of accul-turation: while Thom claimed that the Chinese target text was aimed at non-Chinese learners, ultimately, the receptor audience was Chinese (ibid: 60). In being foreignised for foreign learners, the version became domesticated for Chinese native readers (ibid.: 60).

Recently, the term 'transcreation' has been adopted by the advertising industry. Stibbe provides a definition of the practice as an instrumental technique:

> Transcreation is about taking a concept in one language and completely recreating it in another language – it is normally applied to the marketing of an idea, product or service to international audiences. The language, therefore, must resonate with the intended audience.
>
> (Stibbe 2009)

It is noteworthy that Stibbe uses the word 'service'; this is a word unusual in discussion of translation techniques, where discussion of fidelity, equivalence, skopos, etc. are more common. Service is a principle that rightly should inform translation. If we aim to transmit ideas, attitudes, information and passion to younger audiences, we must offer them a service in ways that are recognisable, acceptable and perhaps even inspiring to them.

Tymoczko (2007) has argued against the use of the word 'translation', recognising the wide range of re-telling and re-crafting of language in cultures other than that of Western Europe. Critics and translatologists demonstrate time and time again that translations believed by their creators to be 'faithful' or 'accurate' are nothing of the sort. Loffredo and Perteghella, for example, highlight the view, held by scholars like Benjamin and Derrida, that literary writing and translation are interdependent, and that translation does not involve slavish copies, but transformation, modification and mutation (2006: 7). We believe that honest and intentional adaptation or transcreation may serve literature far better than 'faithful' but awkward translation.

Some critical analyses of poetry translation

Lefevere makes a detailed analysis of a number of nineteenth- and twentieth-century translations of Catullus 64, which penetrates even deeper than Wein-berger's comparison of translations of Wang Wei (below). Lefevere takes conventional translation strategies, manifest in the work of a few selected translators, and one by one demolishes them. He shows how 'literal' transla-tion cannot necessarily offer the 'nearest possible equivalent' and that in order to achieve accuracy, the translator must 'smuggle[s] "explanations" ... into his translation' (Lefevere 1975: 35–36), or is forced into painstakingly explaining in footnotes (ibid.: 27). For instance, a 'metrical' approach, which follows the metre of the source poem, turns out to be a 'rigorous straitjacket' (ibid.: 37). Using prose to translate a poem may appear to be liberating, but is also unsatisfactory, for 'prose is unable to direct the reader's attention towards certain words in the way that poetry can' (ibid.: 43), or produces a 'shady no-man's land between poetry and prose' (ibid.: 45).

Lefevere is perhaps most damning on the subject of translating in rhyme:

> The Catullus who emerges from the rhyming translations can only be described as a clumsy poetaster, definitely not in command of his medium, who makes words mean what they do not, bores the reader with a heavy deadbeat rhyme, is verbose, prudish, and more than a bit pedantic … the rhymer has merely succeeded in transmitting a caricature.
>
> (Lefevere 1975: 61)

Lefevere is on less firm ground when he criticises blank verse, for he makes certain sweeping statements that can only be justified in the examples he cites (ibid.: 62, 66). The 'version', which Lefevere defines as having the substance of the source text, but in a changed form, has a 'greater communicative value' but relies on 'shock value' (ibid.: 76). Though for Lefevere, this is criticism, it may be exactly what suits transcreation as a tool for transmitting Chinese poetry. It can allow for expansion and paraphrase of the source text. It can use digressions to tell the listener the essential background stories that would otherwise be in bottom-heavy footnotes. He notes that the translator is free to replace the unfamiliar not merely with the less familiar, but with the completely familiar (ibid.: 89). This, surely, is a method of transmission that reaches out to the target audience.

Much of what Lefevere says of the nineteenth- and twentieth-century translations of Catullus, including the 'very delicate equilibrium indeed between the sublime and the ridiculous' (ibid.: 92), can be said of nineteenth- and twentieth-century translations of Chinese classical poetry. The comparison is apt, in terms of time and culture gaps. Lefevere's later work (1992) shows how translation as re-writing takes the influence of the original work to wider audiences (Lefevere 1992: 9).

Holmes, in his discussion of poetry translation, proposes the 'metapoem', that is, 'the poem intended as a translation of a poem into another language', which is a 'fundamentally different kind of object from the poem from which it derives' (Holmes 1994: 10). Holmes highlights the role of the metapoet as critical, poetic and analytical:

> It is these three factors – acumen as a critic, craftsmanship as a poet, and skill in analysing and resolving of a confrontation of norms and conventions across linguistic and cultural barriers: in the making of appropriate decisions – that determine the degree to which the metapoet is capable of creating a new verbal object which, for all its differences from

the original poem at every specific point, is basically similar to it as an overall structure.

(Holmes 1994: 11–12)

Holmes, like Lefevere, categorises types of poetry translation quite rigidly: mimetical form, analogical form, (both form-derivative forms), content-derivative form and extraneous form (ibid.: 26–27). Holmes classifies 'extraneous form' as 'deviant form', casting 'the metapoem into a form that is in no way implicit in either the form or the content of the original' (ibid.: 27). It allows the metapoet 'the freedom to transfer the "meaning" of the poem with greater flexibility' (ibid.: 28).

Both Holmes and Lefevere approached the issue of poetry translation from a European perspective. The problems of rhythm, rhyme and structure that they enumerate have great relevance for the task of translating Chinese poetry into English, and it may be that their categories of 'version' and 'extraneous form' may be the most intuitive and appropriate approach for this language pair. In discussion of the hierarchy of correspondence, Holmes mentions briefly, and without elaboration, 'correspondence of appeal' (ibid.: 86) a criterion that ought to apply to poetry. It would, however, defy measurement, or any kind of normalization.

Boase-Beier and Holman, discussing the constraints of translation, note that the 'burden' of constraint opens up the possibility of creativity for the translator (1999: 13). Jones emphasises the 'problematic' nature of poetry translation for 'novice translators' noting that the special characteristics of poetry make 'difficult-text operations the norm during translation' (2007: 67). Are constraints and difficulties due to a perhaps unconscious obligation on the part of translators to ape the original? Given freer rein, might translators, even novices, produce more creative and reflective versions of source texts? Jones partially answers this by remarking that 'one could define creative acts in poetry translating as those strategies that try not to reproduce source text features, but to generate new features to suit the target text as a poem in its own right' (2007: 69). He notes that in his experiments, poetry translation typically involves multiple drafts (2007: 70). This may suggest a degree of labouring at the text rather than inspiration and creativity, but the idea of generating new features echoes Holmes's notion of freedom to transfer with flexibility.

The analyses of poetry translation reviewed above all support the principle of translating creatively, freely and in ways that will appeal to the target audience. Spontaneity, creativity and the sheer motivators of fun and joy, or despair and tragedy, are the factors that drive not only the poet but also the poet-translator.

Translation from Chinese to English: Inevitable adaptation or transcreation

There is a strong tradition in China of translation by Chinese native speakers into English. This is in part to do with the relative isolation of China during the middle part of the twentieth century, and partly to do with the relatively small number of non-Chinese speakers who learn Chinese (Pellatt and Liu 2010: 3). It is at odds with the European tradition, in which it is normal to translate into one's first language. This practice of second language translation has led to some very strange versions, and has led to very conservative attitudes towards poetry translation among Chinese and foreign translators. Levy, for example, appears politely scathing about Pound: 'Poets such as Ezra Pound have exploited their impressions of Chinese poetry and poetics for their own artistic ends, to lend an exotic legitimacy to individual attempts at innovation within their own tradition' (Levy 1988: 6). Levy is not alone in perceiving Pound's versions not as translation, but as something else inspired by Chinese poetry. But Pound's *Cathay*, a very slim volume of 19 poems, informed and inspired in a way that has probably not been seen before or since (Yang 2005: 10). Pound's work is a kind of transcreation that succeeded in transmitting where 'faithful' translations have not.

Transcreation is more likely to work when the perpetrator is working into the mother tongue. The first-language translator is able to transmit the ideas and information in language that the target audience will 'get', unlike a second-language translator, who, however excellent his or her target language, may not have such an extensive stock of nuance and idiom.

It is appropriate to note here that classical Chinese cannot be translated literally or faithfully, even into modern Chinese. Different scholars' 'literal' versions, provided for reference in academic texts, differ as widely as their 'finished' versions do. Any translation of a Chinese classical poem into English will necessarily involve a high degree of interpretation on the part of the translator, since the source text offers little of the cohesive grammatical framework found in European languages: no tenses, no articles, no case endings, few pronouns, no number, and originally, no punctuation. A prescriptive approach is thus inappropriate: it is up to the reader-translator of a Chinese poem to express the poem in the way he or she reads it, and that expression is likely to be more readable for the target audience if the translator is working in the mother tongue. Any translation of Chinese into English is to some extent a transcreation. This is excellently illustrated in Weinberger's *Nineteen Ways of Looking at Wang Wei* (1987). Weinberger shows how markedly different translations of the same simple quatrain may be, and how unlike the source text, in spite of the probable profound and sincere belief of each translator that his or her work is the most accurate.

Transliteration and found poetry

The concision, simplicity and implicitness of classical Chinese poetry are well known, and have provided much material for discussion and dispute over the centuries. Traditional Chinese poetry has strict rhyme schemes and regular metres, many of which are based on song. In the Preface to the *Book of Odes* (诗大序), this definition of poetry can be found:

Poetry is the fulfilment of intent; what dwells in the mind is intent, what comes forth in words is poetry. Emotions move in the core of one's being and take form in words. When speaking them does not suffice, then one sighs them or chants them; if sighing and chanting do not suffice, then unconsciously one taps them out with the hands, dances them, treads them and stamps them.

(quoted in translation by Levy 1988: 23)

Chinese poetry is not a sedate, fossilised textual genre, but a medium for movement and sound as much as for words, images and meanings.

Stalling's approach is not strictly translation, but rather a form of found poetry. He has discovered a medium in the popular, but perhaps mis-conceived, language teaching method which uses transliteration. English is rendered in Chinese characters that give a rough approximation to the sound of the English to be learned. To some, this is verging on the iconoclastic and irre-verent. Combining the found 'English' in Chinese characters with a coherent Chinese message, rendered as coherent English, and sung to an audience, he has created a new artistic form of great beauty, to 'chant and weave the English and Chinese together' (Stalling 2011: 8). The following example, provided in the introduction to Stalling's book *Yingelishi*, shows how it works:

Example 6a

请原谅我
　　please forgive me
　　pu li si fo gei fu mi
　　普利私
　　　　佛给浮谜
　　　　Vast private profits, Buddha offers impermanent mysteries

(Stalling 2011: 5)

Stalling acknowledges the richness of Chinese homophones, which enables this creative approach, and it is easy to see how the method can be developed to create longer narratives and discourses. Exploiting the sound of the Chi-nese syllables musically led to the development of substantial musical perfor-mance, carried out at Yunnan University in 2010 (Stalling 2011: 7). Through this creation, Stalling has achieved the chanting and musicality first noted in the introduction to the *Shijing*, as quoted by Levy above. The title of the work is instructive: 'Yin ge li shi' (吟歌丽诗) sounds like the word 'English', and means 'chanted/sung songs, beautiful poetry'. Stalling points out that 吟 means more than just singing, it is the recitation of Chinese poetry as if it were song (ibid.: 3).

In this mining of sound and meaning, Stalling has in some way taken the audience back to Chinese poetry as it was (and should be) and at the same time has crossed cultures. His feeling is that 'one must intervene in the normal cultural ways of hearing … to house heterocultural ways of hearing that will move us toward greater transpacific consciousness' (ibid.: 7).

The following excerpt from the sinophonic poem 'Tragedy Strikes' (当悲剧降临) illustrates the way in which Stalling has 'heighten[ed] the tragic humour of Sinophonic English's failure as a medium for clear expression' (ibid.: 9).

Example 6b

    哦， 我的天啊！

      oh, my god!

      o mai gao de

      噢！卖糕的

          Oh! a cake peddler!

  抢劫！

      robbery

      rao bo rui

        娆波

          睿

          Beautiful waves

             wisdom

                (Stalling 2011: 77–78)

A monolingual English native reader will be able to follow the 'story' of the final English rendition which is the newly created poem; the bilingual English reader will appreciate both the Chinese transliteration of the English and the rendition of the Chinese transliteration. Stalling's layout is worth discussion. The lines of the found poetry which constitute the source text are aligned left, and each successive modification is further indented: translation of the found expression, transliteration of the English translation in pinyin, transliteration of the found expression in characters and finally translation of the transliterated characters. This layout is a non-verbal indication of the process and progress of the making of the poem.

The communicative role of transcreation

Among some readers there is a received notion of Chinese poetry as a refined, untouchable, sacred genre, against which one cannot blaspheme, an attitude that has not helped to disseminate Chinese poetry widely. Although Chinese poetry is popular in sinophile circles, it is not commonly read by the broad British masses. If it were translated for them, or even better, by them, it might gain acceptance in the same way that Chinese food has. The embracing of Chinese cuisine has been largely due to its transcreation as a down-spiced high street commodity. Similarly, the adaptation of the Chinese story of Mulan as an animated film, and the film version of Jin Yong's *Crouching Tiger Hidden Dragon* (卧虎藏龙) have been enjoyed without bewilderment by a large section of the non-Chinese-speaking public all over the world.

Cross-cultural food, film and many other popular versions of high-brow and low-brow literature and culture, are all down-spiced, sexed-up transcreations.

One of the intentions of transcreation is to reach a different audience from that served by the source text. The target audience may be younger, older, or weaker (as subjects and customers), stronger or more powerful (as rulers and purveyors), or in some way novices, either in terms of language or culture. The service that transcreation provides is to present the source narrative in such a way that the target reader or audience identifies with, understands and responds to the message. This may mean recreating the narrative in terms of time, space, register and appeal.

Anachronism and displacement

All translation, however 'close' or 'free', at least risks, and more often than not entails displacement and anachronism. We always translate at a time after the event, and for readers situated far from the event (Lefevere 1975: 84). These two facets of translation intensify the degree of change already required by difference in language and culture. Adam Thorpe, describing his translation of Flaubert's *Madame Bovary,* makes very clear the diachronic issues of literary translation. He decided to base his translation on the nineteenth-century English styles of Henry James and James Joyce although they were writing later than Flaubert (Thorpe, 2011: 20). Thorpe believes in 'the modernity of the past' (ibid.). All writing is cutting edge modern at the moment of its inception. He acknowledges the difficulty of rendering Flaubert in an idiom that is not his own. It is just as problematic for translators of Chinese to provide an eighth-century 'English' equivalent for *Journey to the Peach Blossom Spring*: to use any time setting is both anachronistic and adaptive. While we may endeavour to adhere to the times and seasons expressed in an ancient poem, any language that we use will be 'out of sync'. The Byronic approach so popular in China in the twentieth century is no less anachronistic and culturally distant than a twenty-first-century setting.

Register and readership

Transplanting a text into a different language and culture inevitably involves a choice of register. One of the great advantages of a minimalist or symbolist approach such as that of Pound is that register more or less disappears. A surrealist approach, as in the case of Yang and Holton (Pellatt and Liu 2010: 177), and a 'found art' approach as in the case of Stalling, might have the same effect. A less economical approach would require decisions on the use of register, for, like temporal and spatial setting, register pins the text down to a certain time, place, implied narrator and target reader. The implied target audience of translations of Chinese poetry has, with a few exceptions, been the well-educated elite, in other words, a narrowly targeted readership. There have occasionally been successful translations that appealed to a different or wider audience, such as Brian Holton's Scots translations of Du Fu (Holton 2010). There is no reason why other sections of society should not be targeted in this way, and encouraged ultimately to make their own translations. Chinese is now taught in local authority schools all over the UK, and almost every university in the land teaches Chinese at some level: young British adults are au fait with current Chinese pop, rock and hip hop, and have a right to access to ancient pop, rock and hip hop. Chinese poetry and poets are wonderfully well documented. We know enough about poets' ages, circumstances, employment and talents to have at least some insight into their lives. Their work was in and of its time and we often have enough information to be able to re-tell their poems in forms contemporary with our own culture.

The appeal of rhythm and rhyme

Rhyming, rhythmic stories in the first language have an honourable pedigree and great popularity almost everywhere in the world. Chinese has the performance or recitation forms of *dagu* (大鼓), *xiangsheng* (相声) and *kuaiban/r* (快板). Russian has Pushkin's *Eugene Onegin*, English has Spenser's *Faerie Queene* and Chaucer's *Canterbury Tales*, Browning's *Fra Lippo Lippi* and *Pied Piper*, Longfellow's *Hiawatha*, Nabokov's *Pale Fire* and Seth's *Golden Gate* among others. Many of these well-known rhyming narratives are transcreations of older stories, or have given birth to a new series of transcreations. The Scots literary tradition includes the practice of 'flyting', which means quarrelling, or contention, and was a competitive oral poetry making among Scots poets in the fifteenth and seventeenth centuries (Siddons 2011). Siddons reveals that American rap (discussed in greater detail below) can be traced back to Scottish slave owners who taught their slaves the art of flyting (ibid.). The language of flyting was sometimes frank, ribald and rude, like rap, but as one of the many rhyming traditions of the world, it can serve to support the notion that narrative and rhyming poetry from other language cultures may be a good subject for cross-cultural adaptation.

We noted above Stibbe's inclusion of 'service to international audiences' in his definition of transcreation (2009). China currently exploits stereotypical tradition in order to 'sell' or serve its culture to western nations. Confucius, food and buildings are high on the list of selling points, but where poetry appears (in language textbooks, on culture websites etc.), it is not well served by its translations, because of the tradition of twee romanticism and glaring linguistic errors. Fluent, idiomatic transcreation, rather than 'close' translation, might enhance its appeal, retaining comprehensibility, and attracting and inspiring through creative and artistic techniques.

Creative features of transcreation

Transcreation of a source text encompasses a wide range of possible re-telling strategies: language, style, mode, time setting and location. At one end of the spectrum it may be a monolingual verbal re-telling: Wang Wei's poem *Journey to the Peach Blossom Spring* was itself based on a preface and poem by Tao Qian 372 (?) – 427. At the other end of the spectrum, it may be a representation in dance or pictures, such as a ballet version of Romeo and Juliet, or a cartoon version of the early Chinese novel *Shuihu Zhuan* (水浒传 thought to be by Shi Nai-an 施耐庵) translated in various versions, including *Outlaws of the Marsh* by Sydney Shapiro and *All Men are Brothers* by Pearl Buck.

The motivation for transcreation to a different mode may be the interest of the artist or writer, or the target audience. There may be political or pedagogical motives, or the work may be part of a project for which funding is sought. Classical Chinese poems may not have been written as educational tools, but they have certainly been used as such in later centuries (Yu 1980: 4). Short poems often appear in Chinese language textbooks aimed at British school children, but they are mainly of the twee variety, and poorly translated. A transcreation that abandons any pretence of 'faithful' translation may be a much better way of getting the message across.

Narrative in Chinese poetry

While there is not always a clear distinction between the lyric and the narrative in Chinese poetry, some poems are very definitely narrative. The main distinguishing features of narrative poems are point of view, characterisation and sequence of events (Levy 1988: 17). Narrative poetry tends towards propositional language rather than imagistic language (Levy 1988: 26). Needless to say, many Chinese poems combine lyricism and narrative, and Wang Wei's *Journey to the Peach Blossom Spring* is one of these. Levy's view (ibid.: 26) is that the specificity of the narrative actually makes the narrative poem more subjective, while the implicitness and impersonal character of lyric poetry provides greater objectivity for the reader. This is true, to the extent that the reader of the narrative can envisage specific persons, times, places and actions. So while the lyric poem may invite a symbolist, minimalist or at least economical treatment, avoiding pronouns and tenses, narrative poems tie the reader, and certainly the translator, down to decisions on specifics. As noted above, any translation of a Chinese poem will have anachronisms, displacement and problems of register. For the sake of communication to a new audience, and for the sake of creativity, the translator is surely justified in choosing modern, rhythmic, rhyming genres that specify persons, places, actions and times.

In addition to having the usual formal characteristics, all Chinese poetry is expected to have recognised desirable or required qualities. Among these are *fu* 賦, *bi* 比 and *xing* 興, which together encapsulate the essence of Chinese poetry: there is some discussion as to the best translation of these terms, but *fu* means unfolding (of events or plot, and eventually came to be the name of a poetic form), *bi* indicates comparison – that is metaphors, similes and figures of speech, while *xing* is the resonance of the meaning.

The adaptation or transcreation discussed below is based on Wang Wei's *Journey to the Peach Blossom Spring*. This poem is an eighth-century monolingual transcreation of Tao Qian's fourth-century preface plus poem. This in turn is a transcreation of the story of Liu Tzu-Chi, who heard of a community of people who had survived the wars at the end of the Qin dynasty around 200 years BC. Liu intended to go and look for them, but never did. Tao Qian's preface tells the story, while his poem is a reflection on matters inspired by the story. Wang Wei created his own poetic version, depicting the community as utopian, and hinting that the journey was a spiritual one.

Wang was a devout Buddhist, and much of his poetry deals indirectly with spiritual matters. Yu believes that 'Wang Wei's work is a fulfilment of several key Symbolist aims' (Yu 1980: 22), but we do not have space to discuss this somewhat anachronistic notion here. *Journey to the Peach Blossom Spring* is, however, narrative and descriptive. It is only towards the end of the poem that we understand that the journey undertaken by the protagonist might have significance of an allegorical and spiritual nature. A person in a fishing boat sails along a river, goes into a cave, and comes out in a beautiful land inhabited by strange people who wear the clothes of the Qin dynasty. They speak a strange language, but welcome the guest, who stays. He becomes homesick and leaves the utopia, planning to return, but however hard he tries, he never finds his way back.

The poem has been translated many times into English and other languages. The reason is that it is potentially accessible. It tells a story we can all understand and empathise with. It has a simple but profound message, which is probably universal. Unfortunately, existing translations are often couched in quasi-archaic language that does not appeal to youngsters, and very often not even to hardened old-China hands, as can be seen in the following examples:

Example 6c

驚聞俗客爭來集，競引還家問都邑

i

In sweet surprise, the dwellers hastened all
To hail and meet an earthly guest,
And each and all invited him to home,
Of news from old homelands in quest.

(Loh in Xu, Loh and Wu 1987/1992: 65)

This translation has a number of features that reduce its appeal to the purist and to the lay reader. The addition of 'sweet' to 'surprise' gives a cloying feel where there is none in the source text, which is spare and direct. Some of the lexis is inappropriately used: in English, 'dwellers' is most often prefixed, as for example in 'cave dwellers'; 'earthly' implies a contrast with aliens from other worlds, whereas the utopians in the poem are obviously of Chinese origin: it is a utopia on earth, rather than on some other planet. The most reader-unfriendly aspect of the translation is the uncomfortable syntactic inversion.

ii
Amazed to hear of the world's intruder
　　　　　　All vied to see him
And take him home and ask him
　　　　　　About his country and place
　　　　　　　　　(Robinson 1973: 35)

Robinson's version should be admired for its determined use of mono-syllables, which helps to preserve the concision of the source text, but the contrast in register between the first two lines and the second and third is bathetic in tone. It is not easy to see why Robinson has staggered the lines, as this layout does not reflect rhyme, rhythm or content in any meaningful way.

iii
Amazed to hear of a stranger from the world, they throng to see him,
Compete in hospitality and ask about his home town.
　　　　　　　　　(Innes Herdan 1972: 240)

Herdan keeps close to the meaning of the source text, and makes no attempt at rhyme or rhythm. Hers is a prose version, set out in lines as if it were blank verse. Of the three versions, it is probably the most readable and accessible: there are no uncomfortable grammatical inversions, the layout and punctuation are conventional, and the lexis is varied and evocative without seeming odd. While these translations all give the reader a rough idea of the content of the poem, Herdan's is the most readable, and none of them encourage sighing, chanting, treading and stamping!

Characteristics common to rap and traditional Chinese poetry

Journey to the Peach Blossom Spring is rhythmic, rhyming, narrative. It has a point of view, a sequence of events, and characterisation. It has 'unfolding', figures of speech, and it certainly resonates. In form, it comprises two sets of 16 lines, each line consisting of seven syllables (characters), equivalent to four beats. This regularity in form invites a rendition that also has strong rhythm and rhyme.

As in many Chinese poems, there are relatively few pronouns or personal references in Wang Wei's poetry. In *Journey to the Peach Blossom Spring,* the reflexive pronoun 自 appears, and Levy chooses to indicate that the whole poem is narrated in the first person (Levy 1988: 14). Other translators narrate in the third person, but as Yu points out, the absence of personal reference in Chinese 'offers the poet means unavailable to the Westerner to avoid reference to a particular speaker' (Yu 1980: 28). This works in the translator's favour, as it provides a freedom to change voice throughout the poem, and, as can be seen in the rap-style version below, this is what our rapper does.

Rap is now an established poetic form. It grew out of the tradition of 'signifying' or 'playing the dozens' in the USA, when men of Afro-American descent would gather and tell their stories. It is a form that not only tells stories, but also expresses feelings. Like Chinese narrative poetry, it has a sequence of events, characterisation and very definite points of view, depending on the individual MC (rap performer). 'Rap is associated with story-telling, complexity of meaning and intention' (Bradley and DuBois 2010: xxv). It is an oral poetry: MCs would base their performance on a 'rhyme book', but songs would be transcribed from performances, rather than the conventional reading from a previously written version (Bradley and DuBois 2010: xxiii). This is reminiscent of the story-tellers' prompt books that preceded the early novels of China. Rap may include verbal duels (Bradley and DuBois 2010: xxiii), again reminiscent of the poetry couplet challenges and contests traditional in China and Japan, and elsewhere in the world. Rap is usually performed in songs of 16 lines, or bars, each of four beats, not unlike Wang Wei's poem. The regularity is sometimes broken, but always retains a rhythm. Rap often expresses the individual and the other, like the boatman and the utopians in Wang Wei's poem.

Rap is a very popular form, and has undergone some quite significant changes: it is now performed by whites and Asians, including women, in many languages, including Chinese. 'Rap's tradition is as broad and deep as any other form of poetry, but like any other literary tradition it contains its shallows, its whirlpools, and its muddy waters' (Bradley and DuBois 2010: xxix). Bradley and DuBois hold that no reasonable person can regard it as a fad or a gimmick, now that it has a history of thirty years of studio-recording (2010: 11) and an even longer history of performance in the community.

The similarities between rap and Chinese poetry, and between rap and many other traditional rhyming, rhythmic story-telling forms, offer scope for transcreation from Chinese to English. On the title page of his book *Chinese Poems,* Arthur Waley wrote: 'A taste for Chinese poetry is not hard to acquire. It is as easy to enjoy as chop suey, and has in fact something of the same quality, being many flavoured and subtle, yet full of honest nourishment' (1961). Waley provided that 'honest nourishment' for English-speaking fans of Chinese poetry in the first half of the twentieth century. Perhaps rap can provide it in the twenty-first century, for it is a rich, energetic form that speaks of and to ordinary people, and is a mature poetic genre:

> When a rap lyric appears on the page, aspects like rhyme schemes and enjambment suddenly become apparent; our attention is heightened to the point of awareness of similes and metaphors and other species of figurative language. It can be a remarkable aesthetic experience on its own, and one that carries over again when the song is heard in full.
>
> (Bradley and DuBois 2010: xxxv)

Meanings, forms and fashions change with time; the translations of the nine-teenth and twentieth century were not timeless, and many now seem ugly and awkward in their use of idiom that translators then thought conveyed the 'feel' of the Chinese poem. A poem has a different 'feel' for every individual reader, and as time goes by.

Rap might be used as a form for poetry transcreation where existing styles of translation are off-putting or inadequate. It might be more attractive to younger people put off by the stuffiness and pomposity of 'traditional' Chi-nese poetry translation and show them that the messages of poetry are not fossils. If attracted by a rap transcreation, they might be drawn to do their own translation, thus looking closely at the source text. Because of its length, and its tradition of asides, rap is ideally suited to the adding of paratextual information: what might otherwise be expressible only in footnotes in a con-ventional translation. In the rap version provided here, such a paratextual explanation is given (transcribed within brackets) of the alien utopians left over from Qin times.

Rap is a story-telling medium, a long, shapely costume ideal for tran-screating a long shapely poem. Its four-beat bar equates to the 7-syllable line of the old style *shi* (古体诗 *guti shi*). The rap tradition is strongly reminiscent of Chinese traditions of story-telling and chanting performance noted above (*dagu, kuai bar, xiangsheng*), and of worldwide narrative story poems. Its chanting delivery is suitable for Chinese poems that were designed for or stemmed from singing and chanting. Rap is common and accepted by young people in China now.

In the West, as in China, poetry may be a spiritual, meditational experi-ence: William Sieghart, speaking on *The Verb* (BBC Radio 3, 4 March 2011) told how his misery at boarding school was relieved by his discovery of poetry. He noted that people are often frightened of poetry because they find it 'fusty and dusty'. He himself found in rap 'the most exquisite poetry'. There may be two messages here: first, that some Chinese poetry presented escape, relief, and spirituality for those who wrote and read it, and can do so now; second, that many established translators of Chinese poetry have made it far more fusty and dusty than it really is, but it can and should be accessible, as shown in Weinberger's *Nineteen Ways of Looking at Wang Wei*. Translations of Chinese poetry do not need to be agonisingly stilted and romanticised; they can, if so desired, be agonisingly modernised.

Practical 6.1 *A critical review of* Yingelishi

Read Stalling's *Yingelishi* and, if possible, access the musical performance.

i   Discuss the poet's aims, as set out in the introduction to the book.
ii What are your responses to the bilingual poetry?
iii Reflect on who Stalling's audience might be and how they would react to sinophonic poetry.

Practical 6.2 *A critical review of a transcreation of* Peach Blossom Spring

i   Write a critical review of the rap version of *Peach Blossom Spring* given below. Consider features such as the length, the rhythm and the rhyme scheme.

ii Make your own translation or transcreation of the poem, using English or international forms such as sonnet, ballad, villanelle etc.

Journey to the Peach Blossom Spring by Wang Wei

桃源行
王维

渔舟逐水爱山春，两岸桃花夹去津。
坐看红树不知远，行尽青溪忽视人。
山口潜行始隈隩，山开旷望旋平陆。
遥看一处攒云树，近入千家散花竹。
樵客初传汉姓名，居人未改秦衣服。
居人共住武陵源，还从物外起田园。
月明松下房栊静，日出云中鸡犬喧。
惊闻俗客争来集，竞引还家问都邑。
平明闾巷扫花开，薄暮渔樵乘水入。
初因避地去人间，及至成仙遂不还。
峡里谁知有人事，世中遥望空云山。
不疑灵境难闻见，尘心未尽思乡县。
出洞无论隔山水，辞家终拟长游衍。
自谓经过旧不迷，安知峰壑今来变。
当时只记入山深，青溪几曲到云林。
春来遍是桃花水，不辨仙源何处寻。

Peach Blossom Spring Rap by Pul'ka (transcribed 2010)

The hills are alive
It's spring, doncha know,
As the boat runs fast
On the downstream flow.
Cuttin' the water clean as a blade,
The fisherman's boat goes
Slicing through the glade.
Huggin' the bank in the oncoming spring
He looks at the mountains, just lovin'
The peach flowers danglin'
Dense as the stars, but soft
Crowdin' in on the river and waftin'
All over the pebbly ford.
His eyes all dazzled
By the blooms ablaze
His oars went slack and he sat amazed,

Not knowing how far he'd drifted from home
Only that he was all alone.
He sailed right down to the end o' the stream
Alone as a dreamer dreamin' a dream.
A mountain cavern came an' swallered him whole
And the boat tumbled on in a glorious roll
Through windin' caves and curious boulders
Till he felt a draught of air on his shoulders.
The hulking stones of the mountainside
Stood back and the cavern opened wide
On a warm golden plain that met the horizon.
Far in the distance he suddenly sees
A whole lotta towering, canopied trees,
Lean and splendid and growing proud,
So tall they definitely pierced a cloud.
Then closer by, an' he nearly didn't see,
All nestled in the flowers and among the groves,
Was a bustling village of a thousand homes.
The fisherman left his boat and began
To greet all the villagers, woman and man,
By mentioning the name of the dynasty of Han.
But they all stared, not knowing a word
Everything he said sounded so absurd.
For they themselves were a blast from the past,
Like a history pageant or even the cast
Of a play or an opera telling a tale
Of incidents on a magnificent scale.
Now they were all dressed in the clothes of the Qin
(and here I'll insert a bracket or two
And an explanation especially for you:
The Qin were a tribe of two thousand years ago,
They conquered all the kingdoms in the vicinity
To create the great Chinese polity).
Back to the story, bear with me.
These alien folk who dressed so strange,
Lived within a very small range.
Wu Ling Springs was the name of their place,
And they had opted out of the rodent race
To till their fields and gardens fine
Beneath the moon and the soughing pine.
Their doors are closed and quiet now,
But the day has broken and mired in mist
The dogs and the chickens cannot desist
From crying aloud as the day breaks through.
Around the village the folk all smile,

For they didn' know a stranger would arrive
And the news has brought their faces alive.
They're rushin' all around and they all crowd out
Come in, come to us, they all shout.
They're questioning him so fast and crazy,
Where is he from, their knowledge is hazy
Of any other world that's beyond their ken.
In the morning bright the boatman saw
Thousands of petals strewn on the floor
Up and down the streets to every door.
The villagers got busy with brushes and broom
To sweep the lovely litter and make some room
For the stranger boatman to walk the alleys.
Finally at dusk the streets are clear,
and out to ceilidh our boatman sallies.
They were runaway folk who had it up to here
With the hassle and struggle. They said 'no fear'.
And they left the world by a fairy-tale track,
Saying no no no we will never go back.
Deep in the valley we don't know f ... -all
We're free as the spuggies, and we're not in thrall
To the horrible binds of human livin'
All that workin' and talkin' all takin' no givin',
All those guys down there stare up at our space
With their dead stupid eyes
Stickin'out o' their face
'cos all they can see is cloud covered hills,
That are way outside their cheap kinda thrills.

Now back to our boatman, we mustn't forget,
We can't let him out of the story just yet.
He's a bright young man with attitude
A realist with no time for pseuds
And he thinks, this place ain't hard to find,
I'll keep the address at the back o' my mind.
My heart's full o' dust of the real hard world,
And I'm thinking all the time of my life unfurled
In my own home town, my stamping ground
With friends and family all around.
He left the cavern and the mystery state
And got back home just a little bit late.
But however high the mountains between
Himself and the paradise he had seen
He was always beckoned mysteriously,
Like the sailor who's called by the sound of the sea.

Without regret he said his goodbyes,
He was hopefully plannin' a reprise.
There was a journey ahead and he knew darn well
It would take some time to enter the spell
Of the magic land he once had known.

He was no fool, he remembered the route
His sense of direction was extremely acute.
But how was our savvy traveller to know
That the peaks and the valleys he saw not long ago
Had changed their faces, alarmingly so.
Hey, gimme a break, where have they gone?
The landmarks I need so I can travel on?
In his mind he recalled deep clefts, high crags,
Where he'd find those cute guys in their ole-fashioned rags.
Surely it would be round the next meander,
Once more left, then a right-hander.
He wouldn't care how long it took
(he was a fish on the end of a hook).
The spring came again and he was still searching
This way and that, in his boat, lurching,
From doubt to faith and back again.
Those natural landmarks were never the same.
The peach blossoms covered all o' the stream,
Laughing at the traveller's hopeless dream,
His faith and hope and tenacity.
His only thought was where could it be,
That land of pleasure and plenty and peace?

His quest for paradise will never cease.

7 Absurdity and irony in modern Chinese literature

Laughter, and the humorous speech or behaviour that provoke it, are universal, yet perhaps not universally welcomed by all, owing to the range of motivation, target and effect, among cultures and among individuals. Humour ranges from the farcical to the implicit, and it may provoke a range of reactions. Much has been written about the translatability of play on words and cultural differences, but here we will focus on the translation of satirical, critical writing, which may not appear to present great linguistic or cultural challenges, but which needs careful handling with regard to tone. Absurdity and irony are points on the wide spectrum of humour and play a pivotal role in public and literary discourse.

Absurdity and irony are funny: we don't necessarily laugh out loud, but we smile wryly and nod wisely as we recognise the truths of stupidity, negligence and sheer wickedness expressed in a funny story. Humour is subject to broad and fickle definitions. Ostensibly, humour induces laughter, but as Billig shows, laughter is not always 'good' and may be designed to ridicule its target (2005: 2). Billig explores three main approaches to a theory of laughter, each of which may be said to reflect common sense reality. He argues that one of the theories at the basis of humour, first formulated by Hobbes, is superiority, including self-mockery (ibid.: 52), an attitude that is not always welcomed in a world of equality and political correctness, but is the basis of much satire. Billig suggests that mockery that disparages or degrades others, may have the effect of discipline (ibid.: 39). A second theory is that of incongruity: we laugh at things that are unexpected, either verbally or visually, where similarities are unlikely in the context, and where dissimilarities coincide. Incongruity, like mockery, is a useful weapon in satire directed against those in authority. On hearing or reading the joke or the jibe, we recognise the disjuncture between the situation as it should be and the absurdity of reality. Billig's third theory of laughter is release: human beings feel relaxed, unstressed and happy when they laugh (2005: 5). The very physiology of laughing and the relaxation of the muscles and nervous system experienced in the process were believed in Victorian Britain to have good effects on health (ibid.: 90–91). Yet humour can be cruel, and if individuals or groups want to criticise authority, that cruelty is a crucial part of political and social practice. It is almost certain that these theories or categories exist in parallel, integrated in a complex web of human ways of dealing with the sometimes unpleasant realities of life.

Billig begins his account of laughter with an evaluation of positive and negative humour. There are those who believe that humour is and must be positive. This might include the approach found in authoritarian regimes that do not allow ribbing of their great and good, showing only a positive, cheerful face to the general public. Yet in these regimes, there is usually a butt of jokes, an 'Aunt Sally'. This target is often the Other, that which is outside, opposite and opposed to Self, implicitly different, implicitly either dominant or dominated. The Chinese have never been averse to laughter, and the universal tools of satire, absurdity and irony have always been an integral part of Chinese literary history and culture. Chan notes the 'spate of so-called condemnation novels' (谴责小说) of late nineteenth-century satirists in China (1998: 66). Jest is one of the tools of change and progress, and not least of rebellion.

Billig notes that Francis Bacon believed that 'religion, matters of state, great persons should be exempt from jest' (2005: 14), and we have only to look at the era of Mao in China to see that, while the leadership figures were supposed to be beyond criticism or satire, stereotypical figures of Japanese and Americans, and the domestic 'class enemies' (landlords and capitalists) were reckoned to be justifiable targets. During periods of heavy censorship and top-down guidance of literary endeavour, the objects of lampoon and critical innuendo have been 'Other', but the art of satire has remained. At the time of writing, in a period of relative liberalism, writers are aiming their darts at the time-honoured domestic targets of hypocrisy, bureaucracy, corruption and inefficiency.

The butt of humour may be the helpless, the disabled, the unintelligent and the rural, to whom the humorist feels superior, or, on the other hand, someone who is ostensibly superior. As we shall see from the examples below, the anomalies of the inferior/superior distinction have been expertly used by Chinese writers: so often, the apparently superior official or intellectual is mocked by the apparently inferior narrator or protagonist, to both comic and critical effect. The very suggestion that the protagonist of a story is 'helpless' or 'stupid' alerts the reader to the probability that what follows may be implicit, but hard-hitting criticism of authority.

There have been suggestions that humour helps to maintain social order – mockery is criticism and censure, and while authoritarian leaders may not like their subjects to laugh, the laughter helps to maintain equilibrium. We do not like to be laughed at, and mockery will act as a disincentive to undesirable behaviour. Nowhere is this more manifest than in the great political and social satires of the world: *Vanity Fair, The Scholars, Don Quixote, Candide.* The reason for the use of amusing irony to criticise, particularly in political terms, is avoidance of the risk involved in outright condemnation. Yet this notion has also been linked to the relief theory. Satire is a time-honoured tool of dissent, and it is alive and kicking in China today. Link has pointed out that it may be more diplomatic for a regime to treat satire as humour, rather than as serious criticism, on account of its 'safety valve' effect (Link 2012). It is to their even greater detriment that hyper-sensitive leaders and regimes censor humour.

The physical and verbal in comedy

A combination of buffoonery and wit, or farce and wordplay, constitute the bulwark of great satirical writing. Billig notes the historical distinction (in Great Britain) between 'wit', which was to do with wordplay and elegant conceits, and 'humour', which was to do with jokes against the person (2005: 62). In Chapter 1 we saw how visual artists combine language and visual puns to express ideas. One of the best-known combinations of verbal and visual joke is that of Ai Weiwei dropping his ancient ceramic vase: it combines the unexpected or incongruous (we would not expect such a revered figure to drop such a precious object); the ridiculous (a crazy artist doing something no conventional person would do); and the pun: Ai is an iconoclast – he breaks icons. One could also read into the situation the juxtaposition of inferior and superior: Ai, as one human being in the great scheme of things, could be said to be 'inferior' to 5,000 years of history symbolised by the vase; he demonstrates, however, that he is superior to the small, manmade, vulnerable artefact. In the same way, writers of fiction and non-fiction combine situation and language to lampoon the not-so-great and not-so-good.

The relevance of the joke

The fundamental underpinning of humour and irony, in various situations and forms, is implicitness. The reader infers from the writer's or comedian's 'tongue in cheek' (stating the opposite of what is true) and understatement (stating the outrageous unemphatically). This may often involve the use of incongruous register (usually artificially high or formal) and a degree of intertextuality or allusion that is designed to 'involve the reader in a re-creation by hinting at half-hidden meanings that the reader is expected to recover and then use for a deeper understanding of the work' (Leppihalme 1997: 8). Billig suggests that in order to deal with the unexpected and incongruous aspects of humour, we are forced to change our cognitive framework swiftly and radically (2005: 63), and having a sense of humour requires the ability to shift (ibid.: 65). Gottlieb notes that the ambiguity of irony differs from that of wordplay in its pragmatic nature, having to do with the intentions of the speaker, 'beyond the denotative meaning of the words' (1997: 209). Gutt writes of 'the higher investment in processing cost' the reader must put into expanding the context for its implications (1991: 105).

Pelsmaekers and Besien (2002: 241) make the somewhat startling assertion that 'Irony and humour are not often discussed in one breath.' They are referring to academic discussion of humour and irony, but it is likely that in the real world, recipients (as opposed to targets) of irony, will at least smile at subtlety. Whether cruel humour is really funny is an argument that continues;

of course it is funny for the perpetrators, and less funny for the victims, but it can have a very significant effect. The perlocutionary force of irony starts with the reader's or listener's recognition of the incongruity or understatement, and triggers the realisation of underlying criticism. Sperber and Wilson note that irony entails 'the implicit expression of an attitude' and that the hearer needs sufficient information for the irony to be relevant (1986: 239). These notions of changing cognitive frameworks, perlocutionary force and relevance and attitude are core concerns for the translator. We have all experienced the failure of political or social jokes that depend on 'in-group' knowledge, and one of the translator's hurdles is to re-create in the target text relevance for the out-group target reader.

Home-grown Chinese satire covers a spectrum from the gentle stories by Wu Jingzi (吴敬梓), who revealed the shortcomings of the civil service in his work *The Scholars* (儒林外史) to the bleakly comic, poignant and sometimes heart-rending stories by Lu Xun. Since 1979, writers in China have enthusiastically re-adopted the traditions of satire. In this chapter we look at three modern text types: the short story, the blog and the full length absurdist novel.

Black humour as described by Wang Meng

Wang Meng, born in 1934, is a prolific author of short stories. He had his fair share of criticism, having undergone labour reform as a result of a critical short story. He was re-instated in 1980 and was Minister of Culture from 1986 to 1989. Wang's particular brand of humour is well known for uncovering the lies and excesses of the Cultural Revolution period. His writing is strongly political and reveals the wisdom of humanity in the face of political stupidity. He is a past master of the tongue in cheek.

The following excerpt is from a short story entitled 'An Anecdote about Section Chief Maimaiti: the Black Humour of the Uighur People' (买买提处长轶事：维吾尔人的黑色幽默). The narrator of the story is puzzled as to why Uighur twins Maimaiti and Saimaiti have aged so differently, in spite of a similar background. The scene is set for the black humour by their one-upmanship, each capping the other's claim of harsh treatment as a result of the 'Movement against the Three Evils' (三反运动, a movement against corruption, waste and bureaucracy 1951–52). The narrator concludes that Maimaiti looks younger because he has laughed at his misfortunes, whereas Saimaiti has not, and goes on to illustrate Maimaiti's attitude in a short series of anecdotes.

Example 7a

A member of Maimaiti's family is told that a prospective bride and groom must have a 'new-style wedding' (新式婚礼):

就是大家要念语录，学习 '老三篇'。就是要请专区、县和公社三级领
导干部讲话。就是新郎和新娘要向毛主席像三鞠躬，向各级领导一鞠

躬，互相一鞠躬。就是不能陪嫁和彩礼，要双方赠红宝书、宝像、砍土
镘、镰刀和粪叉。就是不能休息玩乐，新郎要在新婚之夜去浇水、开口
子、封口子，新娘要在新婚之夜用红黄二色油漆和木板，做出四个语录
牌 ...

(Wang 1981: 172)

[The new style wedding] shall comprise the assembled company reciting
Chairman Mao's sayings and studying Chairman Mao's 'Three Great
Essays'. District, county and commune leading cadres shall be invited to
speak. The bride and groom shall bow three times to the statue of
Chairman Mao, bow to each leading cadre once, and bow to each other
once. Betrothal gifts and dowry are not permitted. Each party may
bestow upon the other party a gift of the treasured little red book and a
statuette of the Chairman, a mattock, a sickle and a manure fork. No rest
or revelry is permitted. On the wedding night the groom will use his hose,
open the sluice and close the sluice. The bride will make four quotation
tablets using red and yellow paint on wooden boards ...

(Authors' translation)

For the family in the story and for the reader, this bureaucratic list is the
antithesis of what a wedding should be, and needless to say, later, the families
hold their own 'underground wedding' and the innocent Maimaiti is held to
blame for the whole episode and punished. How problematic is this description of a revolutionary wedding? It is densely packed with culture-specific
items, each a subtle vehicle of irony. 老三篇 is a political allusion: the three
well-known essays by Mao: 'Serve the People', 'Yugong Moves the Mountain'
and 'In Memory of Norman Bethune'. The allusive use of the number 'three'
reminds us, perhaps unconsciously, of the numbering of the great Chinese
classical writings, and exalts the three essays to the status of classics. But 'old'
(老) has a comforting, familiar ring to it. The 'new style wedding' still
demands that the bride and groom make their bows, and Wang reflects the
rhythm of the traditional kowtow in the rhythm of the repetitions of 鞠躬. In
the story, however, the bows must be made to a likeness of Chairman Mao, to
the officials, and reciprocally by the bride and groom. Gifts are to be given,
and they are still the traditional red, but now it is revolutionary red, embodied
in the book of Chairman Mao's quotations. Lastly, the bride must make
'quotation tablets' (that is, quotations from Mao), reminiscent, in a traditional context, of ancestral tablets or, in a Uighur context, quotations from
the Qur'an.

The definition of the new-style wedding is couched in a quasi-list, quasi-
regulation style, with each item in the list beginning '就是'. This subjectless
topic structure provides a wonderful opportunity for the English language
translator: the possibilities range from a simple definition, through various
prescriptive forms, using passive or active voice, and even using a mock legal
tone, for example 'The bride and groom shall ... '

Wang Meng did not need to exercise his imagination to produce this image: at the time, in the 1960s, countless couples and families were deprived of the romance and festivities normally associated with a wedding, and they would have keenly felt the incongruity of old practices adapted to the political circumstances of the time. Xinran's *China Witness* (2008: 104–6) shows how heartless and humourless those weddings could be. Wang's artistry lies in his retrospective view, in the deadpan bureaucratic listing, the subtle allusion and the rhythm of repetition.

The new ritual, as stated by the official, includes incongruity at the level of romance. Rather than spending the night in blissful union, the newly-weds must work. The bridegroom's duties of 'irrigation' (浇水) and 'opening and closing the sluice' (开口子、封口子) might well be regarded as rather saucy euphemisms.

It is not by accident that Wang Meng has chosen to set his story among an ethnic minority group. It means that he can make interlingual puns at the expense of bullying petty officials and military personnel, who were likely to have been of Han origin, and unacquainted with the local languages. Maimaiti is asked if he 'knows' (认识) a certain well-known author, that is, is acquainted with him, and replies that he 'knows' (知道), that is, he knows about him, because, in Uighur, the two expressions are used interchangeably. The consequence is that Maimaiti is thought to be a friend of the famous author and is labelled a 'black author' himself. He delights in the negative label, for it elevates him from unknown to high literary status.

Wang is a story-teller par excellence, weaving human frailty around the material culture of everyday life. His retrospective view of diurnal detail reveals the effect that central and local government policy and political attitudes had on ordinary people; at the time, 'the man in the street' could only observe, but a few years later, Wang was able to present the incongruity of the situation for a knowing readership, who would, likely as not, simultaneously laugh and cry.

Blogging for common sense

One of the greatest advantages of the blog is that it reaches the internet-reading public more or less instantaneously. A serious blogger can react swiftly to current events and publish swingeing comments. Our examples are from blogs by Chen Xuan, who specialises in gentle, but persuasive mockery of the illogical behaviour of human beings: our tendency to be easily persuaded, and to go with the crowd. In the blog entitled 'Lost Values' (失落的价值), Chen pokes fun at the consumerism occasioned by 'festivals', using colourful images and astute observation.

Example 7b

> 朋友戏称，每到一个洋节日，就是"女人要月亮，男人摘月亮的时
> 候"。可不是么，如今的节日都成了商家牟利的好机会，也是考验男士

们钱包的一关。利用节日来消费和娱乐都是我们的正常需求，本无可非议。

(Chen 2010)

Friends joke that every time a festival comes round, women want the earth and men go to the ends of the earth to get it for them. It is indeed the case that festivals are a moment of opportunity for retailers and present a tough test for a man's wallet. But we cannot escape the fact that it is quite normal to exploit festivals for the sake of consumerism and entertainment.

(Authors' translation)

Chen's target of criticism is the excessive consumerism encouraged by retailers, who find an excuse in every 'festival'. When the foreign festivals (洋节日) come round 'Women want the moon, and men go out to gather the moon' (就是 "女人要月亮，男人摘月亮的时候"). The moon is significant, for, as Chen goes on to point out, later in the blog, it is associated with the Chinese 七夕, or seventh day of the seventh month, the night when the Weaving Girl and Herd Boy constellations come together, and is now often seen as a Chinese equivalent of Valentine's day. In Chinese folklore, the Weaving Girl and the Herd Boy fell in love, but could not continue to be together because she was supernatural and he was human. Forced to separate, they found themselves in heaven, divided by the Milky Way, and only able to meet once a year. This allusion might not fit well in an English version. In English it would be more common to say that a person wants the earth: should we foreignise slightly and translate 'moon' as moon, or go with a more idiomatic 'earth'? How should we render 商家牟利的好机会? We could stick with 'a good opportunity for business' or we could try something a little more piquant, for example 'retailers have an eye on the cash register'.

The blog gathers momentum, depicting the Chinese family spending Chinese New Year in front of the television busily engaged in slagging off the ever more tedious programmes (除夕晚上一边看越来越没新意的春晚一边吐槽成了全国人民的娱乐形式), pastimes not unknown in the rest of the world! Chen describes the embarrassment of sitting through the 'romantic meal' offered by a restaurant, and finally, in a moment of bathos, shows Chinese customers queuing for the New Year sales.

Chen's style is sardonic: we grin as we read, for these are scenes we have all witnessed or been part of: they are to do with human nature. The tone of such writing cannot be serious, there must be an edge of humour if the satire is to succeed. This may require a slight shift in register, making the target text a little more formal. Formal accuracy is not crucial to translation of such a text; the translator may find it preferable to aim at a vivid and witty rendering that departs from the wording of the blog, but retains the wryness.

Absurdism in the twenty-first century

Often, the key to humour and particularly to irony, is the intertextuality that gives power to the point being made: allusions to the comic and the absurd already extant in a culture highlight the comic in the text being produced. Yan Lianke (阎连科) in his full-length novel *Ode to Elegance* (风雅颂) continues the Chinese tradition of *The Scholars* (儒林外史), Lu Xun's *The True Story of A Q* (阿Q), and *Kong Yiji* (孔乙己); also to some extent the great 'journey' novels: *Don Quixote, The Travels of Lao Can* (老残游记) and James Joyce's *Ulysses*. At the time of writing, we are not aware of an existing translation of *Ode to Elegance* and have coined this title for the sake of convenience.

Like Wang Meng, above, Yan has written humorously about the Cultural Revolution period, in, for example *Serve the People* (为人民服务 2005). The title of his full-length novel *Ode to Elegance* (风雅颂) published in 2008, is a direct allusion to the Chinese classical *Book of Odes* or *Book of Songs* (诗经). Yan uses the motif of weighty classical literature (literally, in the case of the principal character's own scholarly writing, 一部伟大的专著) to parody and satirise modern China. Understatement is core to Yan's irony, as is the notion of obsession: the protagonist and first person narrator, Yang Ke, is serially obsessed with a number of issues, including his great scholarly tome and later with the saving of fallen women.

In this novel, Yan's barbs are directed primarily at the academic world, and also at officialdom and business. Incongruity and the superior/inferior dichotomy are at the heart of the story, as we see Yang Ke scorned and sidelined in continuous confrontations with his wife, with senior academics, with officialdom in the city and with the peasants and small businesses in his hometown. We understand deep down that Yang is an intelligent man, but he is gullible, diffident and lacking in the cynicism needed to survive in the modern world. Yang Ke is a quixotic hero, acutely aware of his superiority as a university professor, yet vulnerable to embarrassment and ridicule. His naivety and fantasies invite comparison with James Thurber's Walter Mitty. Yan's writing is only mildly absurdist, a technique that works well, for the reader is lulled into a sense of reality, then suddenly alerted to startling, acid incongruity.

Whereas Wang Meng's style is one of fairly unadorned narration and dialogue, Yan uses a range of marked stylistic devices. *The Ode to Elegance* is crafted in a poetic, scholarly way, almost parodically reflecting the poetry of the *Book of Songs*, yet lapsing into very colloquial language in the dialogues and monologues. Yan's very distinctive style consists mainly of the following literary devices: *chengyu* and metaphor, which in many cases overlap, together with similes; synaesthesia; reduplication and repetition; obsession, very often created through the use of numerical values and idioms; and cross-purposes dialogue. Interspersed throughout the writing are scholarly footnotes provided by the narrator on poems mentioned in the body of the text, a subtle mockery of academic practices.

Translating chengyu *(成语)*

Yan's descriptive passages of places, people and events are over-larded with *chengyu*, with very perceptive descriptions of the natural environment, sometimes apparently serious, yet sometimes seeming to ape scholarly or poetic style. Rohsenow makes clear the difference between *chengyu* and *yanyu*: while *yanyu* (谚语) are the 'heritage of thousands of years of China's … peasant-based culture', *chengyu* are 'fused literary idioms or set phrases' (Rohsenow 2002: xi). *Yanyu* are usually metaphorical or allegorical in nature, illustrating types of behaviour or situation, and the results that ensue from it. While deeply embedded in Chinese culture, as a rule, because of their metaphorical qualities, and their close relationship to daily life, they are not difficult to translate.

Chengyu, however, are notorious among translators: they are dense in meaning and implication, and frequently require many target language words for an adequate rendering. Xing, who labels *chengyu* 'fixed expressions', advises teachers that their use is 'not fundamental in communication', but rather 'the icing on the cake' (2006: 50). Her words are a model for the translator of *chengyu*: we can render these succinct, colourful expressions in terms of their surface meaning, retaining their metaphorical and cultural colour, or we can achieve 'fundamental communication' by rendering them according to their actual illocutionary meaning. In his exhaustive *Grammar of Spoken Chinese*, the English term Chao uses for *chengyu* is 'literary clichés' and he notes that the internal structure of *chengyu* is literary, as opposed to spoken, and that 'it should be considered a part of the language' (1968: 489). Chao's observation may sound obvious, but it serves as a reminder to the translator, who must integrate any rendering smoothly into the target language.

A *chengyu* is potentially a stand-alone expression, yet, integrated into the stream of speech or of writing, still fits in perfectly with the syntax of the Chinese sentence of which it is a part. This perfect jigsaw effect is largely due to the concision of literary Chinese, in which explicit grammatical links are minimal. Chao's examples include 非驴非马 (ibid.: 490), 'neither a donkey nor a horse'. The Chinese has no pronouns, no verb, no articles. Integrated into a sentence, it would act adjectivally: '这非驴非马的办法一定会失败的. This method, which is neither one thing nor the other, will certainly fail' (ibid.: 490). Translators' difficulties with *chengyu* have much more to do with constructing a sound target language sentence than with meanings or with any cultural considerations. The translator of *The Ode to Elegance* not only risks doubling or trebling the word count of the target text, but also risks losing the spontaneity and colour of the images created by *chengyu*. Very often, it is syntactical manipulation that compels us to use more words than we would wish.

Yan's motive in using *chengyu* is probably to underline the first person narrator's self-importance as an academic, and the reader cannot help thinking of Lu Xun's character Kong Yiji, who 'used so many archaisms in his speech that half of it was barely intelligible' (Lu, tr. Yang and Yang 1980: 53)

(他对人说话，总是满口之乎者也，叫人半懂不懂的) (Lu 2002: 422). Yang Ke's utterances in conversation are intelligible, but the impression the reader has of his inner speech and of his lectures is similar to that of Kong Yiji's speech. Throughout the novel, Yang Ke overtly relates his own life and work to the *Book of Songs*. His lack of success contrasts with his own self-esteem, and the author's studied use of *chengyu*, together with rhythmic reduplication, helps to highlight this incongruity. It is with this in mind that we approach translation of Yan's narrative.

Example 7c

Crossing the university campus, Yang Ke finds himself caught in a sandstorm. As he battles against the wind and gritty sand, his gestures become a quixotic battle against a personified storm. He braces himself:

> 可我那时候，头脑清醒，打兴正浓，用双脚的趾头紧紧地抓住地面，
> 站稳脚跟，拳脚相交，挥臂抡腿，不停地朝它们掴着和踢着。
>
> (Yan 2008: 58)

> But I was clear headed and spoiling for a fight. I stood my ground, ducking
> and diving with fists and feet; I circled and wheeled, my toes gripping the
> ground, firm as a rock, tireless. I faced up to them, punching and kicking.
>
> (Authors' translation)

The reader has a vivid image of the protagonist as a practitioner of the martial arts, ducking, diving, using circular defensive movements and attacking '它们', the grains of sand swept in the storm, with blows of the feet and hands. The allusion to martial arts contains within it a small allusion to the propaganda of Mao's era, 正浓. The reader knows that this unassuming academic would not stand up to a human opponent in this way, and is conscious of irony. The translator needs to retain this deadpan irony, using idioms that reflect a false or imagined bravery. Crucially, the syntax of the target sentence needs to be fluently crafted to create a motion picture of the imagined fight.

In our version, so as to avoid repetition, particularly of 'standing firm', we have taken certain liberties with the rendering. In one case (不停地), we have moved the phrase and translated it as an adjective, 'tireless' rather than an adverbial 'ceaselessly'. The grammar of each four-character *chengyu* has been varied to fit into the English target sentence. We have used alliteration to reflect the wonderful rhythmicality of the Chinese source text.

'At that moment' (那时候), at the beginning of the Chinese sentence, marks a contrast with the narrator's feeling of helplessness in the face of the storm, and is redundant in the English text, as long as there is a contrastive 'but'. Given the literary nature of the source text, it would be possible to indulge in a much more adaptive version, perhaps alluding more directly to Chinese martial arts or even boxing, as follows:

But I stood my ground, a left hook here, a right hook there, dancing like a butterfly, stinging like a bee, I faced up to them.

(Authors' translation)

This version conjures up Western-style boxing, with a well-known allusion to Mohammed Ali's technique, and domesticates the text, by comparison with our first version, which stays with the source text, leaving the reader with a sense of Chinese-style martial arts, but in a fluent, readable target text. The adventurous translator will find many lively verbs to reflect Yang Ke's battle with the storm: a defensive fighter will parry, ward off, dodge and duck; an attacking fighter will lunge, punch, swipe, cuff and take swings at an opponent. They might also lash, bash or thrash in the cut and thrust of the fight.

Translating metaphor and allusion

The quixotic nature of the fight is heightened by the author's use of anthropomorphism and zoomorphism, as he likens the sandstorm to a crowd of mad women, and to a tiger. The sandstorm has a head, waist and legs, at which Yang Ke lunges and hacks. These similes need no alteration in the target language: women, mad or sane, remain a constant motif in the protagonist's life, and a tiger, in terms of colour, weight and ferocity, is a perfect metaphor for a sandstorm. The mention of the tiger grounds Yang Ke's struggle with the sandstorm in Chinese literature, for the reader inevitably associates it with the story of Wu Song killing the tiger in *Water Margin* (水浒传). Yan uses very different, and rather more varied epithets than we find in *Water Margin*, but the allusion is there, and reinforces the physical comedy of the situation.

Translating simile

Throughout the novel, Yan uses simile constructions such as 和 … 一摸样 and 如同, 'the same as' and 'like'. This helps to heighten the unreality of the narrative: not only the first person narrator, but the other characters in the novel are constantly likening the situation to some other non-existent or unlikely situation.

Example 7d

The narrator undertakes to coach Xiao Min (小敏) the orphaned daughter of a late friend, for university examinations, but she says:

读书写作业时， 我和受罪一摸样，可我洗衣服，把手泡在水里时，滑溜溜的洗衣粉沾在手心上，心理的快活和我小时候跳绳踢键[sic]一摸样。

(Yan 2008: 241)

When I study or write essays, it's like a punishment, but when I wash clothes, when I plunge my hands into the water and feel the slippery suds in the palms of my hands, I feel the same happiness I felt when I skipped and kicked shuttlecocks as a small child.

(Authors' translation)

This is dialogue, and does not require elegance, but sincerity and realism: the translator must voice an 18-year-old's feelings. In the translation above, we have used 'as a small child' but a rural English-speaking 18-year-old would probably say 'when I was little', or 'when I was a kid'. It should be noted that the character used for shuttlecock in the 2008 edition of the novel is 键, which is now commonly used in Chinese writing, but it is likely in the context that this should be 毽.

These contrasting similes intensify the girl's implied wish to give up school and become a wife. The reader knows from the musings of the narrator that he would like to marry her, and we can infer the anomaly in his behaviour: he is encouraging her academic efforts, yet sees her as the object of his desire. The girl implies her wishes, the narrator implies his, and the reader understands the mismatch between the two. In cases like this, there is no need for major shifts in the translation.

Translating synaesthesia

Synaesthesia is a neurological condition in which sensations experienced by stimuli to one of the sense organs are felt by another organ, a kind of cross-over of the senses. For example, an aroma may be associated with a colour, and it is well known that some people associate days of the week and numbers with colours. The phenomenon has been used to good effect by European writers, notably Baudelaire, who created a theory of *correspondences* exemplified in his eponymous poem of 1857. Yan skilfully integrates synaesthesia into his descriptions of the physical world, at the point where it impinges on the psychological or spiritual, as in the following example:

Example 7e

那响器班也开始吹奏起来了，吹奏的是丧白事中最为愁伤的《大出殡》，铜乐声像玲珍的寿衣在风中飘着样黑亮而寒凉。

(Yan 2008: 207)

The wind band began to play. They played the most mournful of the dirges, 'the Grand Obsequies', and the sound of the brass instruments floated on the air, as black and as cold as Ling Zhen's burial clothes.

(Authors' translation)

Very little in this passage needs to be changed to suit the target reader: sadness, dirges and funereal music are common to many cultures. The apparent oddity of sound having a colour and a temperature jolts the reader out of the comfort zone, and nothing needs to be explained.

Example 7f

Similarly, in the following description, the sunset makes a noise:

黄昏悄然而至，有生有响地在寂静中铺展和呢喃。

(Yan 2008: 165)

Softly, the sunset arrives, and, in the silence, spreads, twittering audibly.
(Authors' translation)

The reader understands the implication of twittering swallows, and should be allowed to infer from the evocative synaesthetic description.

Translating reduplication

Reduplicative and parallel phrases are a common feature of this novel, emphasising the link with classical poetry, and moving the narrative along in lively rhythms.

Example 7g

From a distance, Yang Ke watches the wedding festivities of the girl he himself wanted to marry:

有帮着婚配的村人，正抬着一口蒸馍的大锅，从小敏家院里趔趔趄趄走出来，朝着村里趔趔趄趄去。

(Yan 2008: 248)

A villager who was helping with the wedding staggered out of Xiao Min's yard, carrying a huge pot, of the kind used for steaming buns, and staggered towards the village.

(Authors' translation)

This is a perfectly acceptable, close translation, but some translators might prefer to do without the repetition, which emphasises the weight of the pot and the gait of the bearer, and achieve the effect in some other way, for example:

A villager who was helping with the wedding party emerged from Xiao Min's yard carrying a huge pot, of the kind used to steam buns. Staggering under its weight, he made for the village.

(Authors' translation)

This description of the villager is closely followed by a description of the sound of crickets:

Example 7h

> 有知了在我的头顶呜啦啦地叫。
>
> (Yan 2008: 248)

Crickets make their sounds by rubbing their wings, and the notion of a cricket 'calling' (叫) would be a slightly tricky concept in English. The conventional colloquial term for stridulation, as it is known in the scientific world, is 'chirping'. We could talk about the buzzing of crickets, or humming, as insects and even machines hum without necessarily using their mouths. 'A cricket chirped/hummed above my head' is perhaps a little too succinct in the context, and we could say: 'Above my head a cricket chirped away', which reflects the reduplication in the source text and provides the reader with a sense of the ongoing noise. We could use onomatopoeic expressions such as 'shrilled' or 'sawed' to create a more irritating effect, if that is what is required.

Translating number expressions

Among the literary techniques used in the novel is the use of number idioms. Number expressions are common in Chinese language (Pellatt 2007), and in Yan's novel, they are used in what could be an obsessive fashion. Yang Ke is constantly using number metaphors and idioms and constantly counting and measuring. This is a trait that emphasises his academic position, and hints at a degree of autism or obsession, contributing to the depiction of him as the target of ridicule. Among the many examples are the following:

Example 7i

> 小敏他四爷等你等得心急火燎，一天到门口看你八百遍。
>
> (Yan 2008: 206)

> Xiao Min's Uncle Number Four has been waiting ages for you. He's so anxious he's been to the gate to look for you hundreds of times!
>
> (Authors' translation)

The '800 times' used in the source text is expressive, but is perhaps not quite the right expression for English. In Chinese, an auspicious number is preferred. English speakers would exaggerate the number in just the same way, but it would probably be '99' or '100' or '1000': a round number or a euphonic number would be preferred. In many cases, an English speaker would opt for the colloquial hyperbole 'hundreds of' or 'thousands of', rather than indicating a specific number. The impact of the hyperbole would be similar in both languages. An English version might omit Uncle Number Four's anxiety, as it is fully implied by the hyperbole.

Example 7j

The villagers regard Yang Ke as a scholarly freak, initially with respect, and later with suspicion and contempt. In the following example, his interlocutor uses a *chengyu* that is also a number idiom, to indicate Yang Ke's great learning.

感谢杨克教授学府五车.

(Yan 2008: 222)

The author quite frequently makes minor modifications in clichés, as in this example, which is usually quoted in dictionaries as 学富五车. 学府 is a seat of learning and 五车 means five cartloads of books. This *chengyu* comes from a story told in *Zhuangzi* (庄子) about Hui Shi, (惠施), who was such a great scholar that his books had to be carried in five carts. The reader is well aware by this point in the narrative that Yang Ke is seriously adrift from his career as an academic, and is also aware that the villagers, who may not have much schooling, but have wisdom and common sense, have sussed him out. In translating this utterance, it is important to keep the 'Professor Yang', so as to emphasise the academic calling. A suitable solution would be 'Professor Yang, you have read many books' or 'Professor Yang, you are a very learned man'. The translator must remember that this is a villager speaking, who might not use words like 'scholarly' or 'academic'.

Translating cross-purposes dialogue

Yang Ke's conversations are frequently marked by cross-purposes dialogue. The phenomenon of cross-purposes dialogue is common in daily life, for human beings approach the same topic from different egoistic perspectives, and on the basis of different personal schemata. In the case of Yang Ke, who is leading a double or, at least, deceptive life, the cross-purposes dialogue keeps the reader informed of both sets of assumptions: what is said and what is actually the case (see above).

Example 7k

The following dialogue takes place between the narrator, Yang Ke, and Xiao Min:

我说你虚岁十八了？
她说明天考语文。
我说没事的，你肯定比别人考得好。
她说人一到十八岁，就成大人啦。

(Yan 2008: 233)

I said, you're eighteen, counting Chinese style?
She said, I have a language exam tomorrow.

I said, no problem, you'll do better than everyone else.
She said, when someone reaches eighteen, they're an adult, aren't they?

(Authors' translation)

It is obvious to the reader that each interlocutor is pursuing a line of thought, without apparently attending to the speech or thoughts of the other, though they seem to be heading in the same direction. The dialogue is clearly set up for the reader to infer apparent conflict masking underlying ulterior motives on the part of both speakers. In this particular dialogue there are two significant considerations for the translator. The first is 虚岁. In traditional Chinese culture, a child is counted as one-year-old at birth, and a year is added each Chinese New Year. To convey the full meaning of the two character phrase would demand at least a sentence of explanation. Translating for an international audience, the translator could reduce the message to 'nearly eighteen' or 'going on eighteen'. An explication could be added 'counting from birth' or 'counting Chinese style, you're eighteen'. The dialogue here wastes no words, and a long explication might destroy the 'feel' of this encounter, all the more so as Xiao Min herself sees her age as eighteen. Young people often like to be considered older and approach each birthday with eager anticipation. Elsewhere in the context of the chapter, Xiao Min is described in the third person, and this is where an explanation of the 'counting Chinese-style' or 'Chinese birthday' can be given.

The second point of potential challenge for the translator is the particle 啦, in 她说人一到十八岁，就成大人啦. Xiao Min is dropping massive hints: she wants to leave school and get married, but dare not say so outright. In English a question tag, such as 'don't they?' would imply that she is trying to get Yang Ke to understand the situation. But the hint of the source text must remain a hint in the target text.

Example 71

The following example is part of an episode in which the protagonist Yang Ke finds himself in a hotel with a dozen prostitutes whom he entertains by giving a lecture on the poems of the *Book of Songs*. They are bemused and astonished that here is a man who is apparently not interested in sex:

> 她们有些吃惊地望着我，说杨教授，你不喜欢床上那事情？我说我真的半年没有给清燕大学上课了。她们说天呀，天下还有不愿做那事情的男人哩。我说别说话，你们现在都是大学生，都是研究生和博士生，我们集中起来讲一节古典文学课，讲一节《诗经》欣赏课。

(Yan 2008: 193)

They were somewhat mystified, and stared at me: Professor Yang, aren't you interested in 'bedroom activities'? I said, honestly, I haven't given a lecture at Qing Yan University for six months. They said good heavens, is there a man in the world who is not inclined to that sort of thing? I said stop talking. You are my undergraduate, graduate and doctoral students, and we are going to concentrate on classical literature. We will have a *Book of Songs* appreciation class.

(Authors' translation)

In contrast to the dialogue between Yang Ke and Xiao Min quoted above, the author has set out the conversation in uninterrupted paragraph form, perhaps to give the impression of a lively, continuous banter. Yang Ke is undeterred: he appears to ignore the prostitutes. No explanation is needed from the translator, who can have fun exploring the kind of language a group of teenage prostitutes might use, and the pomposity of the naïve professor. 吃惊 is often, mistakenly, translated as 'to be shocked', but in this excerpt, while the girls are likely to be amused or bemused, intrigued, puzzled, astonished, or simply surprised, the word 'shock' could be used, as it would illustrate the incongruity of the situation: most people would be shocked by prostitutes' behaviour, but here the tables are turned, and the girls are 'shocked' by the abstemiousness of Yang Ke. The euphemism 'bedroom activities' (床上那事情) offers the translator a wide variety of possibilities: for example, in her English language fiction focusing on Chinese marriage and family, See (2006) uses the alliterative, but unambiguous term 'bed business'.

Yan's brilliantly crafted book is in many ways a gift for the translator: everything in it is implicit, yet nothing is opaque. The challenges lie in producing a target text that tells the reader all, yet explains nothing, a text that reflects the rhythms and sensations of Yang Ke's faltering progression through a life of vicissitudes. Characters like Yang Ke are found everywhere in the world, and the criticism aimed at them through irony and absurdity is universal. In many cases, no great 'foreignisation' or 'domestication' techniques are required; only fluency and understanding of the character and the context.

Practical 7.1 Mocking bureaucracy

Re-translate the excerpt from Wang Meng's short story in your own way. Do you need to add anything to make it funny and ironic in the target language? Do the culture-specific items require footnotes or explanations?

就是大家要念语录，学习 '老三篇'。就是要请专区、县和公社三级领导干部讲话。就是新郎和新娘要向毛主席像三鞠躬，向各级领导一鞠躬，互相一鞠躬。就是不能陪嫁和彩礼，要双方赠红宝书、宝像、砍土镘、镰刀和粪叉。就是不能休息玩乐，新郎要在新婚之夜去浇水、开口子、封口子，新娘要在新婚之夜用红黄二色油漆和木板，做出四个语录牌 …

Practical 7.2 Translating for blog readers

i Access Chen Xuan's blog to get a feel for the style and content: http://blog.
sina.com.cn/s/blog_49b2fed20100w3s7.html

ii Translate the following excerpt from the blog, retaining the situational
humour.

记得我曾一度为约会总得花钱而感到无奈，尤其是有一回在绿茵阁咖啡
厅点了个所谓的"浪漫情侣套餐"更是搞笑到雷人，每上一道菜服务员
都要大声报一遍"浪漫情侣套餐"，当真是有些尴尬，加上当时我和他
都没什么钱，彼此暗中算计着要不要点果汁，哪还有半点浪漫。

8   Drama translation

A case study of collaborative translation

Drama is a field of activity so deeply associated with and embedded in translation that its metamorphosis, from its source language and culture to other manifestations which may, occasionally, be almost unrecognisable, is something that theatres and audiences take for granted. Drama translation is, however, a complex business: the adaptor more often than not is given credit for work that the translator has done, and the wording and mise en scene of the original may be radically altered. Translators of drama are scandalously under- or unrecognised (Hale and Upton 2000; Espasa 2000; Bassnett 1991; Brodie 2012), yet they underpin international creative industry. Johnston has written of the 'infinite Shakespeares' (2007: 84), and most of the world's core, established drama has been subject to varied and innovative treatment, starting, of course, with translation of the script into a target language.

Academic discussion of drama translation often hinges on the 'literary' versus 'performance' dichotomy, and Bassnett notes that 'a notion of theatre that does not see written text and performance as *indissolubly linked,* will inevitably lead to a discrimination against anyone who appears to offend against the purity of the written text' (Bassnett 1980/2002: 120). That kind of discrimination ignores the fact that plays in their original language are written to be spoken, and ignores the fact that speech varieties are part of the literary canon. Bartlett, interviewed by Johnston, said 'I don't translate plays to get them onto the page. I translate plays to get them into the mouth' (Bartlett 1996: 68).

There is a wide spectrum of adaptation, re-writing and borrowing in the theatre, and variety is not necessarily undesirable: Johnston suggests that perhaps, 'as English-speaking audiences' own ability to understand Shakespeare's language continues to erode, the future of vivid and meaningful Shakespeare productions lies within the cultural and post-colonial re-animations of translators abroad' (ibid.: 84). The business of theatre is to make 'the strange familiar and the familiar strange' (Hale and Upton 2000: 8). Drama is by its very nature creative, and to deny breadth of vision in its transfer from one culture to another would be to imprison that creativity; to encourage innovation and difference may be to preserve and enhance the original.

Cameron (2000: 17) takes up Lepage's coining of the term 'tradaptation' applied to old texts in new contexts. Cameron, discussing English productions of Indian and Pakistani dramas, calls into question the assumption that cultural borders are to do with national borders and geography, and that some received notions of indigeneity exclude the contexts of migration (ibid.: 19). In an increasingly globalised world, drama in translation can belong to everyone. Bowman, seeing no distinction between translation and adaptation, claims that 'the practice of theatre rules' such that translation or adaptation, for example into a vernacular language, is perfectly possible (2000: 28). Bowman illustrates through examples of culture-specific items how some (such as *Lucozade* and *Scottish Football Today*) may be kept, and some (such as *Coca-Cola* and *baloney*) have to be jettisoned (ibid.: 30).

The issues that beset any translation work are compounded in drama translation by the destination of the target text: production on stage. Bassnett (1980: 121) shows how the translator of drama is faced with a multiplicity of considerations not found in the task of translating texts that are designed purely for reading. While actors must first read a script, it is only once they have internalised it and begun to act it out that the meaning of the script takes shape. Hale and Upton note the 'several dimensions': the visual, gestural, aural and linguistic signifiers that have to be integrated into the translation and ultimately the production (2000: 2). Beyond these relatively graspable aspects of an actual stage situation, which is a tangible representation of an implied reality, is the suspension of disbelief that the actors aim to provoke in the audience. The dialogue exists in a world of sound and vision, rather than text; the inaudible, invisible stage directions contribute to a new three-dimensional and visual reality into which the audience is transported by means of the dialogue and the action.

In terms of working practice, these considerations force the translator into certain decisions about rendition. The work of the great dramatists of the world (Aristophanes, Shakespeare, Racine, Molière, Goethe, Chekhov, Ibsen, Lao She, Havel, Pinter) is usually regarded as literature, and studied by school and university students in its written form. It is very often held in worshipful respect by theatre audiences, who would be horrified by the thought of a translation that was anything less than 'faithful'. This is the great dichotomy in drama: it is thought of as literature, yet it is intended to be a transient, malleable and provocative entertainment in the hands of the actors. A translation presents a new 'framework for mise en scene, guiding director, actors, designers and finally audience towards a particular spectrum of interpretation' (Hale and Upton 2000: 9).

Culture-specific items, cultural markers and realia in drama

As Hale and Upton point out, theatre 'embodies and enacts cultural markers' in a 'cultural milieu' (ibid.: 7). Yet, how is the translator to bring a drama 'faithfully' to an audience whose language and idiom, clothes, artefacts, religion and humour may not coincide with that of the play? Should we foreignise or domesticate, to what extent, and in what way? Bowman also suggests that languages have their own 'emotional laws that cannot be transgressed in the act of translation' (Bowman 2000: 31). To what extent this is true (are human beings so emotionally diverse?) and to what extent this idea problematises translation are moot points. It turns out that Bowman's argument hinges on grammar, in the gender of derisory terms, and Latinate forms, which are colloquial in vernacular French, but formal in Scots (ibid.: 32). Yet Bowman uses the 'c' word, which is undoubtedly 'feminine', in his translation of expressions of derision (ibid.: 26). If one were seeking for a 'literal' translation this could be construed as a problem, but at the level of speakablity or performability (see later sections) it would probably be ironed out in discussion with actors. The very roundedness of drama supports the translator or adaptor. Even when Chinese characters are speaking on stage in English (or vice versa) the culture-specific items – the non-verbal signifiers – will provide the required 'otherness' (Hale and Upton 2000: 8). Rozhin discusses the possibility of providing a glossary of 'realia' in theatre programmes, as frequently practised in Polish theatres (Rozhin 2000: 140). She suggests that substituting items in the target culture for very specific items in the source culture (for example 'English *scones*') 'simplifies the play', depriving the audience of the 'true depth' (ibid.: 141). She further proposes literal translation, loans or calques, but her examples seem invalid, in that they have religious connotations that are not restricted to the Polish context (ibid.: 142). As we discussed in the Introduction, it may be dangerous to assume ignorance on the part of the audience. A great deal depends on what 'true depth' is conveyed through the play. Rozhin claims that she has 'neutralized' her translation of *Greenpoint Miracle* (ibid.: 149), but it is probably not possible truly to neutralise language at all, particularly in translation.

Drama often treats universal themes, but is usually set in a particular time frame and a particular cultural, historical or political situation. Given that playwrights addressing a historical theme are dealing with the past, translators dealing with a historical playwright have at least two time perspectives to consider: that of the period in which the dramatist created the play, and his or her intentions relating to that period, and the period in which the play is set.

Performabilty and speakability

Our discussion so far has dwelt upon the rather special and complex nature of drama translation. It is a vehicle that enables the dramatic conventions and messages of the stage to be performed, usually through the medium of speech, in another culture and language. While for centuries, the scripts of great plays have been regarded as literature, it is now recognised by drama translation practitioners that a key quality of drama in translation is performability. The notion has been famously rejected by Bassnett (1991) and is championed by Johnston (2000) and Espasa (2000), among others. Once we have a definition, we have a tool for practical use, and Espasa provides a reasoned discussion of how performability may be defined. Espasa's method is to 'look at what theatre directors and performers do to the text so that it becomes performed, and then look at the criteria that make it performable' (2000: 49). Johnston states that translation of a play is 'reconcretization' or 'transubstantiation' rather than a mere translation of words (2000: 86) and cites his experience of working in radio drama as a way of producing 'verbal visibility' (ibid.: 92).

Translation, adaptation and collaboration

We noted above that theatre practice is often to commission a translation, then hand it over to a monolingual adaptor, often a well-known poet or playwright, who will make it 'performable' (Bassnett 1991: 101). The big name is associated with box office takings, but the monolingual adaptor may have at best a limited understanding of the source culture of the play. This is what Perteghella calls 'collaborative translation' (2004: 11). An excellent example of the way in which collaboration works in theatrical adaptation is the 2012 Royal Shakespeare Company production of *The Orphan of Zhao*. James Fenton acknowledges three individuals who contributed the basic translations of Chinese sources for his English language adaptation of the play, and two individuals who gave theatrical advice (Fenton 2012: Acknowledgements). In dealing with Bassnett's remarks on the growing collaboration required to realise performability, Espasa notes that a 'complex chain of participants ... need not be an obstacle to translation. ... but is a specific feature of theatre' (2000: 58). A dramatic text needs the participation of the agents involved: playwright, director, actors, back-stage crew and, ultimately, audience. Anderman suggests that 'the combined effort of director and actors working together on a play in their own language tends to result in an authenticity of expression to which the audience responds' (1996: 181).

The development of modern Chinese drama as revolutionary tool and political critique

The stereotypical Chinese drama is the Shanghai opera *kunqu* (昆曲) or Beijing opera *jingju* (京剧), the highly costumed, symbolic drama sung to musical accompaniment, either in theatres or in the open. These forms and their regional variants use archaic language and traditional stories, often to express political or ideological notions, but in themselves are not necessarily ancient or unchanged. Chinese drama over the last few centuries has developed and expanded the range of forms and themes employed. Chan (1973) notes that the Yuan *tsa-chu* (杂剧) play, which developed in a period when China was ruled by an oppressive foreign regime, 'opened up a whole realm of experience not previously explored in Chinese literature – the secrets of the heart without the sanction of custom or the rationalization of orthodox doctrine. It was, moreover, deeply rooted in common life ... ' (Chan 1973: 14). Society, politics and styles change, and, as Chang notes, in the eighteenth century, literary drama gave way to popular mixed repertory: 'acrobatics and spectacle ousted the text' (Chan 1973: 17).

In the early years of the twentieth century, the *baihua* movement for language reform and the New Culture Movement provided a background against which writers and dramatists rejected the traditionalism of the stylised opera and injected literary form and content with earthy realism. They rejected the stylised, unchanging language, conventions and costumes of the traditional 'opera' (戏剧 *xiju*), along with its lofty themes and historical characters. Revolutionary writers aimed to write as ordinary Chinese people spoke, in order to pave the way for universal literacy, and to reveal the social and political injustices of the period. While heavily costumed musical drama in archaic language may equally well carry social and political messages, the contemporary dialogue, modern settings and costume of modern spoken drama (话剧 *huaju*) leave no doubt as to what its messages are.

The pioneers of the *huaju* (spoken drama) form were the revolutionary student groups inspired by Japan's embrace of modern Western drama. The Spring Willow Society first performed *huaju* in Japan. Modern Chinese drama was initially grounded in translation. At the time of the May Fourth Movement, the plays of Ibsen were seen as models for the new revolutionary form that would enable Chinese playwrights to develop an authentic dramatic style through the medium of colloquial language (Song 1999: 19). Hu Shi translated plays by Ibsen, and wrote his own vernacular Chinese versions based on the Ibsen model. He was followed by playwrights such as Hong Shen and Tian Han (Song 1999: 20).

The first three decades of the People's Republic altered the course of this new drama, as stage productions of all kinds were pressed into the service of the state, channelling the Party message through 'socialist realist' dramas (Gunn 1983; Cheung and Lai 1997). Predictably, plays of the 1980s depicted the new social situations and problems associated with reform and opening up. 'Slice of life drama' (生活切片戏剧) typified by Lao She's *Teahouse* (茶馆 1957), once more became a popular, well-developed vehicle of social criticism in the years following the Cultural Revolution. Drama, the most public of literary genres, was more susceptible to scrutiny, yet still benefited from the increasing relaxation of controls on creativity.

With this expansion of creative effort, came adventurous dramas, known as 'exploration plays' (探索剧) equivalent to 'experimental' in English: the term 'exploratory' being less ideologically loaded (Cheung and Lai 1997: xvi). Cheung and Lai point out that these plays may not seem very avant-garde to Western audiences (ibid.: xvii), but were part of the development of realistic, modern, apolitical drama in the twenty-first century. By 2000, Chinese television had adopted and developed soaps and historical drama, a trend that almost certainly contributed to stage drama.

Choice of drama

The selection (or de-selection) of any text, whether it is fiction, non-fiction, drama, or poetry, entails not only overt, conventional artistic decisions, but also assumptions of a social and psychological nature about the intended audience, and political concerns about the audience and the authorities under whose aegis it is to be written, read, performed or translated. Meech points out that a play, in contrast to a novel, is a public activity: 'a thousand people in one place applauding a comment spoken by an actor is a powerful force' (Meech 2000: 129). Drama is a sharp socio-political weapon, and in translation must retain that sharpness. The great plays of global renown have almost always carried a political message, either support of a regime, or barbed attack that has sometimes sent the regime tottering to destruction.

Lefevere illustrates how the very act of selection of dramas for an anthology is an act driven by ideology and power structures. The same applies to selection of drama for staging and translation. Lefevere notes that the 'hidden makers' of anthologies have 'hidden agendas' that create a living canon (Lefevere 1996: 140). He poses the question: on what authority does the anthologist base his burden of selection (ibid.: 141)? This is a profoundly important question, not only for the creation of anthologies, but for any publication, and in the case of drama, is especially relevant: the translation and staging of a play is an overt sign that those responsible for its selection, translation and staging condone, support and promote the message of the play. They do so in the expectation that the target audience already condone and support the message, will do so in the future, or will react to the provocation of the drama. Lefevere notes an 'inbuilt weighting toward the conservative' (ibid.: 142): selectors, either of individual plays or anthologies, prefer what is accepted by the general public and the authorities; all the better if it is tried and tested, and is recognised as 'establishment'. This approach is probably universal among publishers, governments and education authorities, but more strict and extreme in regimes that may be regarded as authoritarian or paternalistic. Choosing a play to translate is a political act: the decision reflects the translator's or agency's knowledge of the market and the audience, and also reflects their desire to influence the views of the audience.

Selections may not always be conservative: new plays are sometimes added to the repertoire, but in these cases, the editor or preface writer may edit out politically undesirable content, or provide 'judicious introduction' and 'judicious interventions' (ibid.: 147), which have the effect of adapting or toning down the intent of the drama. Lefevere notes how in the United States, at the time of his study, anything that was French or could be made to sound French was considered 'high culture' and thus made its way into anthologies alongside the broadly English-language repertoire (ibid.: 148). This general tendency to conservatism, albeit exoticist, does not stop progressive, activist and simply creative, innovative drama companies selecting for their repertoire plays that are new and provocative.

In the case of choice of Chinese play for anthology, staging or translation, attitudes and approaches inside and outside China have swung between extremes over the last century. Cao Yu and his near contemporaries Hu Shi (1891–1962) and Lao She (1899–1966) were writing in a form that was at the same time familiar and foreign for Chinese audiences. They brought to the theatre-going public familiar everyday scenes and issues, expressed in normal, colloquial Chinese (白话 *baihua*), spoken for centuries, yet eschewed by the reading intelligentsia. High drama at the beginning of the twentieth century was still the traditional *jingju*, a stylised form in archaic language, transmitting old tales of morality and virtuous romance. Hu Shi introduced the harsh realism of Ibsen and Chekhov through translation and adaptation, as part of the *baihua* movement to provide ordinary Chinese people with accessible literature and drama. The content of Cao Yu's *Sunrise* and *Savage Land* and Lao She's *Tea House* does not shock a modern audience, who have benefited from a century of literary and political revolutions and change, but at the time of their publication they were literary dynamite. There are now, in spite of China's modernisation, themes that shock and provoke, and there is a role for translation of provocative drama.

One hundred years after Cao Yu's birth, we have the luxury of being able to choose his dramas for historical, literary and celebratory purposes. Once rejected by the Chinese authorities for being too 'bourgeois', they are now a part of the literary canon and are studied in school. They can re-kindle in young Chinese audiences the decadence and hopelessness, the political will and optimism of pre-revolutionary China. To a Western audience, they are a window on the transition of Chinese culture from the traditional to the modern, and reveal the normality of Chinese people's emotions, reactions and behaviour. They are also exciting, funny and poignant, qualities essential to any play, regardless of its political intent.

Once the decision to stage a play has been taken, the deeply controversial issue of translation approach takes over. We are by now well accustomed to the complementary notions of domestication and foreignisation, and the spectrum of balancing strategies between them. The debate over which approach to take becomes all the more fierce in the case of drama, when the actor literally speaks through the translation. Some actors and dramatists would opt for no translation at all. Curran cites cases from her Japanese experience, of plays being performed for Japanese audiences by foreigners in the source language, or performed in the source language by Japanese actors. In the first case the audience might not understand the words, but might understand the acting, and in the second case, the actors themselves might not know what they were saying (Curran 2008: 3). Certainly in the staging of drama there is a physicality that transcends the text of the play, and some translators have tried to achieve this 'embodiment': the 'rhythm and tempo that will be expressed on stage through the actor's body and vocal chords' (ibid.: 1).

The very centrality of speech in drama exacerbates the foreignisation versus domestication debate. Curran notes Futabatei's obsessive attention to punctuation (ibid.: 3) in the translation of drama: a notable approach, considering that punctuation cannot be seen or heard on stage, and in addition, differs between languages. These decisions are not so much those of the translator, but the dramatist or director, who will have strong ideas about how the play is acted and produced. A crucial factor is the intention of the playwright, and the ideology to be conveyed. Translators, directors and actors have to face the fact that the original language will be lost in any case, and translation decisions hang upon the messages the playwright appears to convey via the dialogue and stage directions.

The paratext of drama: Translating stage directions

Dialogue spoken on a stage can only provide a fraction of the information available in, for instance, a novel. A film can provide flashbacks and imagined or remembered sequences in ways less feasible in drama, though multi-media productions may overcome displacement of time. The dramatist depends on his or her own skill of implication in writing the dialogue, and on the power of the audience to infer from what they see and hear. The paratext of stage directions aids the producers and actors in their visual, aural and dramatic production of the play.

Genette defines paratext as 'a zone between text and off-text, a zone not only of transition but also of transaction' (1997: 2). In the case of drama, it is a medium of control the playwright has on interpretation of the work, once it has passed into the hands of readers and actors. From the dramatist's point of view, the paratext can provide a bridge between script and actors, and between actors and audience. With the help of paratext, the actors are given enough information to enable them to create a new enacted world, such that the audience suspends its disbelief. The paratext of a play may consist of an introduction, a list of characters, scene setting, a prologue, stage directions and possibly even an epilogue. Most, if not all, playwrights provide paratext in the form of scene-setting and stage directions. In cases in which the playwright wants the actors and audience to use their imagination and creativity to re-create the action, plot and theme, this may be minimal, reduced to the indispensable instructions required to get actors on and off the stage, move them around and ensure that they are using the correct props. Chan describes a very overt form of paratext, the prologue *kai chang* (开场) of the Southern play, or *chuan qi* (传奇), in which the characters can explain themselves and give their version of the story (1973: 16). Dramatists frequently use devices such as prologue, epilogue or asides to the audience to provide information which might not come across in the dialogue.

Many forms of drama rely heavily on symbolism of make-up, costume, props, back-drop and language to convey a wide range of concepts, from character and action to notions such as the passage of time. The playwright uses stage directions to prescribe the physical elements of the production. Since the advent of widespread literacy, the immediate paratext of the play, and metatext in commentaries and manuals, often deal with symbolism. In a sense, everything in a drama is symbolic or iconic, and the playwright's stage directions are crucial to every staging, and every translation.

Dramatic paratext such as introduction, prologue and the list of dramatis personae, is used to prescribe a number of abstract notions and concrete properties, as follows:

- narrative or historical background to the play and its characters;
- costumes, props and sets that indicate a time frame, social setting or economic background;
- the personality, attitudes and age of a character.

Stage directions deal with all the physical context of the acting, apart from the dialogue, such as:

- facial expressions and make-up required to convey character traits;
- facial expressions and non-verbal noises required to convey emotions of the moment;
- actions and gestures required to convey character, plot and themes;
- movements across the stage;
- clothes and props that a character uses to convey these abstract traits.

Some playwrights are more prescriptive than others, and some directors may ignore the stage directions, preferring to stage an adapted version that lifts the play out of time or place constraints, or aims it at a new audience. Whether a director chooses to use the stage directions or not, a translation must provide them, in order that the director may make appropriate choices as to how to direct the play.

One of the impressions one has on first sight of a Cao Yu script (*juben* 剧本) is the overwhelming presence of paratext. This is part of Cao Yu's weapon: he was attacking the traditional values and habits prevalent at the time, revealing the awkward transition from old to new, and suggesting a way forward. The highly detailed prescription serves these purposes. *Beijing Ren* (北京人) was written as a contemporary play: it depicted society as Cao Yu perceived it at the time of writing. At the time the play was written, there would have been no problems dealing with the props, costumes and behaviour of the characters, for the audience would have been familiar with them. Now, however, Cao's directions depict a China that is unknown to many, except through television, films and old photos. The unfamiliarity of the China of seventy years ago is even greater for an international audience, and the translator needs to avoid any risk of using or provoking orientalist notions.

Speakability

While selection, publication, paratext and culture-specific items are of great concern to the translator, the core of the task is, of course the series of spoken exchanges that constitute a play. Speakability and playability are constituent

parts of performability. However elegant, poetic or accurate a drama translation is, it is only fit for purpose if it can be spoken by the actors. From a
pedagogical point of view, drama translation could be regarded as a link between
interpreting and translation: while the rendition is not contemporaneous,
simultaneous or spontaneous, it must seem so. An interpreter speaking the
words of a speechmaker from a soundproof booth is under an obligation to
reflect the live energy of the speech, an obligation that also applies to the
translator of drama.

Not only must the dialogues be rendered accurately, but all the implications
and subtleties of the source text must be relayed to the audience. Like the
soundproof booth of the simultaneous interpreter, the stage allows no space
for anything other than the spoken exchanges. The audience usually sit in a
darkened auditorium, and cannot consult their programmes during the performance; they require optimal, but not necessarily overt, information delivered
through the words and actions of the characters on the stage.

Register in drama

Of central interest to drama translators, register is culture-bound and sometimes very hard to convey in another language. Register indicates relationships, within a family, among a social or working group, and between ethnic
or national groups. It also indicates states of mind and character, and is a
strong cultural marker of time setting. The way in which a translator renders
register in a play can have great impact upon the messages conveyed. An
insult such as 你无赖 could be playfully or flirtatiously translated as 'you
rascal'. Translated as 'you useless bastard' it changes not only the attitude of
the speaker, but also the relationship between the interlocutors.

Register includes terms of address, one of the thorniest of the translator's
problems in any language. The absence of terms of address (Madam, Sir, Mr
So-and-so, etc.) and polite second person pronouns in normal British English
conversation is often mistakenly seen as 'informal' or lacking in courtesy. But
the formality and courtesy of English lie in its verb forms. In the case of
Chinese to English, the translator may have to displace the degree of formality or cordiality from the term of address in the source language to the verb
or some other part of speech in the target language. Addressing one's in-laws
in Chinese is simple and there are conventions: there is a whole set of terms of
address for one's own family and one's in-laws. In English, to call one's
mother-in-law 'mother-in-law' might be so polite as to be sarcastic: first
names, nicknames or alternatives to 'mother' (ma, mum or mam) would be
more courteous by virtue of their very informality. Every family differs in the
terms it uses.

In both the pilot study and the core study reported below, not only the
translator-actors, but also their audiences, found that register was at the heart
of speakability and performability. When the register was not right, it was
uncomfortable for the actors and noticed by the audience.

Case studies of collaborative drama translation

This review of issues in drama translation reflects the practical challenges and problems faced in two translation projects we carried out with students. In 2011, a group of student translators re-translated and carried out a rehearsed reading of Cao Yu's *Beijing Ren,* and in 2012–13, another group translated a new play culminating in a rehearsed dramatic reading. The first, informal project was used as a pilot study on which to base the second, more adventurous project. Both involved collaborative translation.

The pilot study: Translating Beijing Ren *by Cao Yu*

The playwright Cao Yu was one of the greatest proponents of *huaju* in the middle years of the twentieth century. As a young man he was a member of the Nankai New Drama Troupe, and played the part of Nora in an early Chinese production of the play, continuing the Chinese tradition of female impersonation, but in a new context. He is credited with bringing the *huaju* form to maturity, and is known variously as the Shakespeare, the Chekhov, or the O'Neill of China. The impact of his *huaju* play *Peking Man* (北京人 *Beijing Ren*) is attested to by its popularity and celebration in the 1940s and 50s, its banning in the 1960s and 70s, and its re-emergence since the 1980s. By the time it was written in 1941, modern drama was no longer quite so shocking, but it was still a powerful means of conveying pointed criticism. *Beijing Ren* is a typical, perhaps model *huaju,* performed in everyday vernacular Chinese, with no music, and based on contemporary themes of the 1930s. The scene is set in the home of a noble Chinese family, whose power and wealth have declined. The family is deeply in debt, and there is a great deal of domestic friction. The domestic story is set against the background of the discovery of 'Peking Man', (*Homo erectus pekinensis*) near Beijing in 1929.

The collaborative project of translation and dramatic reading of *Beijing Ren*, became the pilot study for the more structured collaborative translation of *Poison* by Wan Fang (the core case study, see below). The decision to translate *Beijing Ren* arose serendipitously. Through the good offices of Li Ruru, we were able to bring to Newcastle a series of centenary events celebrating the life and work of Cao Yu. In order to involve students, a play reading was organised. A major decision was whether we should read it in the original Chinese, for the benefit of Chinese students and students of Chinese, or whether we should read it in English, for the benefit of the broader community of students and general public. Good translations exist, created by highly respected translators. Using an existing translation, would, however, have deprived our students of translation of a golden opportunity. We therefore embarked upon a translation of our own.

It is a long play, taking about three hours in total. Owing to time constraints, both in the preparation of the translation and in the staging of the final reading, only the first act was translated. Not all the actor-translators were familiar with the piece, but some had studied it at school. Each 'actor' translated his or her own part, with some assistance being given to the student who translated and read the part of Zeng Siyi, the matriarch, and the core and dominant character in the first act. Translation of their own parts created an uneven work load among the group, but it meant that each translator-actor translated his or her part 'in character', and had intimate knowledge of that character's language and expression. Two students translated and summarised the relevant stage directions (a mammoth task when dealing with Cao Yu's writing) in order to provide background for the audience. Their summaries were read out just prior to curtain-up. Although each student translated his or her own part, it was necessary to collaborate and co-ordinate in order to achieve a coherent dialogue. Two members of staff helped with final editing. Our main problem was time, as we had only three weeks to translate the text and rehearse the reading. Students gave up their free time to translate and perform the dramatised reading, and we administered pre- and post-activity questionnaires to find out how they had approached and ultimately how they reacted to the translation activity, and the sensation of reading their translation aloud in public.

All the 18 students who were involved in the translation, production and reading were Chinese native speakers enrolled on a master's degree course in Chinese translation, and had at least some experience of translating from Chinese to English. They were all aged between 20 and 30. Nine students returned the pre-activity questionnaire. Out of these, seven had been involved in some kind of drama activity either at school or at university, but only four had read or acted in a Chinese play. Six had read a play or plays by Shakespeare, but none had read a modern English-language play. Five of them had engaged in some kind of collaborative translation work. Most of their experience of translating was in business, technical, scientific and academic texts, and only one of them had ever translated a play. All of them admitted to being nervous about speaking in public, including those who had some experience.

Fourteen post-translation questionnaires were returned, and showed that all of the students enjoyed doing the translation of the play, and one of them regarded it as good preparation for subtitling work. All of them enjoyed reading the play, though one pointed out that it would have been even better to perform it as a drama. Only two of the students said that they would not want to translate the whole play, and all of them said that they would be interested in translating and performing another play, especially a more modern one that would resonate with their lives and interests.

The questionnaire responses showed that generally speaking it was a positive experience, but the key questions for us were those to do with collaborative translation, actors translating their own parts, improvement of skills, and the open-ended invitation for comments and suggestions. Collaboration was a controversial issue: all the respondents felt that the interactive process was helpful and made it easier to 'understand the hidden information', but there was a feeling that ideally more time and effort would be required to create a really productive collaborative environment. The students all enjoyed the teamwork. They were overwhelmingly in favour of actors translating their own parts because it helped them to understand the role and create an individual. One or two of them, however, pointed out that it might lead to incoherence of dialogue (which we overcame through co-ordination and editing), and the major problem in translating their own parts was the uneven workload. All the students felt that they had improved their language skills, translating skills and public speaking skills through their involvement with the project, one specifying that they had learned 'diction improvement; sense-for-sense translation required in a play with a different culture; voice projection and interaction with the audience'. One of the more experienced students felt that they had gained additional experience rather than improved.

The most difficult aspects of the translation were culture-specific items and concepts; register and daily language; and terms of address for family members, illustrating that drama may be one of the most challenging types of translation. All the students involved would have liked more time, more discussion, more rehearsal and more preparation. Some would have preferred to perform the play rather than read it, and there were two innovative suggestions of multi-media presentation with dubbing and/or subtitling. One student suggested that the Chinese students should translate the play, and British students perform it.

We decided to stop translating towards the end of the first act, and when the translators performed the dramatised reading, they reverted to a bilingual style, in which very obvious utterances (such as swearing and quarrelling) were left in the original Chinese. This was a slightly controversial choice. Reactions to the bilingual nature of the later parts of the reading were unexpected. On the whole, fewer translator-readers were in favour than the audience, who enjoyed the novelty and challenge of the bilingual dialogue. We have to bear in mind that literary works, including drama, are often bi- or trilingual. Well-known examples are Tolstoy's novel *War and Peace* and the drama productions of Robert Lepage: any multi-lingual society will produce multi-lingual works of literature. Feedback from our audience suggested very strongly that when confronted by bilingual dialogue, members of the audience used their powers of inference, and enjoyed doing so. While one or two found the bilingual switching strange, the remaining audience (many of whom were English-speaking students of Chinese) found the bilingual approach stimulating. They found that the English side by side with the Chinese provided sufficient context for the Chinese to be understood, and were able to practise their listening skills. One native Chinese speaker member of the audience said that it was a 'rather fantastic way for the audience to appreciate the rhythms and beauty of both languages'.

Seventeen members of the audience (approximately one-third of the total) returned a questionnaire. All the respondents were very positive about the quality of the translation, the reading and their own enjoyment. All the audience respondents asked for more of the same play or more plays to be translated and read or performed, suggesting that there is probably a market for more accessible Chinese drama in the UK. The choice of *Beijing Ren* proved successful: this drama, dating back more than 70 years, still strikes chords, perhaps the more so since China has reformed and reverted to Confucianism as orthodox state ideology. Through the misery, anguish, frustration and anger of the characters, and the high comedy of their interaction, Cao Yu sends forceful messages about hypocrisy, snobbery and stagnation which are eternally relevant. His plays were revolutionary and became establishment, but are still fresh.

This small pilot project highlighted some of the challenges associated with the translation of drama, felt keenly by the student translators, and noticed by the audience. How could we convey a dysfunctional family in 1920s China to a 2011 British audience? The discussion that surrounded the project led to a second project to which we were able to devote more time and a more structured approach. We moved on from Cao Yu's great family drama to a family drama of the twenty-first century written by Wan Fang, which reveals the same degree of familial tension and friction, in a more modern context.

The core project: Translating Poison by Wan Fang (万 方)

In October 2012, we worked with a group of 31 Chinese-speaking students to produce a translation of Wan Fang's 有一种毒药 (A Kind of Poison), which we entitled *Poison*. The play is in a sense a 'slice of life' drama, but is also 'exploratory' in that it uses lighting and sound effects to create surreal dream sequences. The playwright, Wan Fang, is also a screen writer. The play was first performed in Beijing in 2005, and focuses on another dysfunctional Chinese family. It updates the social and economic concerns of the family to the twenty-first century, yet retains a continuity with *Beijing Ren* in its focus on a strong, yet embittered matriarch, a weak, ineffectual husband and a younger generation who deal with their lives as best they can. It is a play that, like *Beijing Ren* before it, smashes the stereotypes.

Bearing in mind that the translators were students, and neither professional actors nor professional drama translators, we began with a drama workshop. The workshop, led by Sarah Kemp of Theatres sans Frontières, centred around notions of conflict, fortuitously, as our chosen drama centres around the underlying frictions in families and couples. The aim of the workshop was to draw the student translators away from words to actions, and the word 'translation' was not mentioned. The student feedback showed how fruitful it can be to move away from words into images and action, and how this can ultimately aid the translation process.

The gradual move towards the notion of performability was continued in a workshop given by Professor David Johnston of Queen's University, Belfast, an acknowledged expert on drama translation. He demonstrated the variability in approach that is possible for a translator of drama, always bearing in mind the demand for a work that can not only be read as literary text, but performed on stage before an audience. As Chinese speakers, the students were inevitably forced away from the Chinese word to a wider consideration of drama. One student remarked that this talk said everything anyone needed to know about any kind of translation!

The third link in the chain between the physicality of acting and translation of the script was a workshop on modern Chinese drama, led by Dr Li Ruru, of Leeds University, a specialist in Chinese drama. Feedback indicated that even those who had studied play scripts as part of a literature syllabus had not, until now, appreciated the implications and impact of performance.

With the lessons of the pilot project to support our decisions, and the drama context provided by the workshops, we embarked on this project with a new set of strategies. This time round, the translation was done collaboratively: rather than each member of a pre-selected cast translating their own part, the whole team worked in groups of three on chunks of the play, giving everyone a more or less equal workload. Casting took place when the translation was finished, and everyone had a solid understanding of the characters in the play. Certain characteristics of the text, such as names of characters, currency, and colloquialisms were discussed by the whole team, and where necessary, translation decisions were made by vote. The whole text was edited and checked for consistency by a native English-speaking teacher, and throughout the project, the single English native-speaking student in the group provided advice on points of language and performance. The aim of the translation team was a rehearsed reading with possible publication. The project did not end with the completion of the translation: the team were involved in setting up the theatre event, the publicity and the production of a programme and audience questionnaire. In this way, in both the pilot project and the core project, the translators had an opportunity to see how their translation worked with reader/actors and with an audience.

Performability in action

At the point where the translation was finished, but had not been edited, the team watched a stage performance of the play in Chinese. This was a revelation: the same words that our translators had used as their source text were spoken on stage, but produced a very different effect from that they had experienced reading the source text. Our Chinese student team, unanimously, had read the relationship between the middle-aged couple as fraught, bitter and antagonistic, but they saw it played on the Chinese stage as affectionate and even flirtatious. By contrast, the relationship between the young married couple, which they had read as warm and romantic, they saw played as less warm, perhaps even aggressive. The student who took the role of the young wife in our students' rehearsed reading said that in the stage production 'Xiao Ya was always indifferent, thoroughly, and I hated her.' In reaction to this, she decided to play the role as warm and sincere. This contrast was a perfect example, first, of how schema affects a reader, and second, of how perform-ability and speakability work on the stage. Members of the student translation team suggested that the nature of the Beijing audience played a key role in the Chinese director's and actors' decisions to play the couples in the way that they did. Just as in the UK, Chinese theatre-going audiences tend to be middle-aged or older; they are the discerning intellectuals who appreciate live performance because it has always been a part of their culture, whereas their children enjoy a digital culture. It was, perhaps, a concession to a somewhat senior Beijing audience that the older couple's relationship was cast in a rosy glow, while the younger couple's relationship was tense and frictional. The decision of the students to take a different approach from that of the Chinese staging was evidence of performability in action.

Ultimately, the student translator-actors semi-performed and semi-read the play, aggressively, physically and to great acclaim from their audience, which was aged from three years old to late sixties. The majority of the respondents to the audience questionnaire were in their twenties, and made such inspiring comments as 'it rocks!'

The challenge of register

The biggest challenge relating to translation of the dialogue was register. It was necessary to find up-to-date idioms that were appropriate to a middle-aged businesswoman/mother, a middle-aged alcoholic man, and six younger adults. The team, of similar ages to the younger characters in the play, had to think about how members of a somewhat less-than-loving family would address one another: solutions emerged through the rehearsals, as the whole team watched, listened, commented and corrected. There was a realisation that beautifully constructed sentences don't happen in real dialogue, especially of the emotional kind.

Stage direction: A hidden tool of control

Whereas Cao Yu's stage directions are long, complex and detailed, Wan Fang's are brief and to the point, and relate overwhelmingly to sound and action on the stage. In the seemingly constant bickering that characterises the Gao family, tone of voice is crucial to the performance. 'In a low voice' (低声、低低自语) does not always convey the tone that the characters would use, and the team held lengthy discussions on the relative functions of muttering, mumbling, and whispering. A good idiomatic rendering of the 'contemptuous sniff' or 'snort' (不由嗤之以鼻) perpetrated by one character throughout the play, also stimulated intense discussion. Reactions of the characters to one another's remarks were often related to facial expressions of surprise, shock or bewilderment. Stage directions such as 'panic stricken' (怔住) and 'with a dull expression' (神情呆滞) could not simply be translated as the dictionaries pre-scribed; they needed to be contextualised according to situation, character and dialogue. Making use of the initial workshop on 'action', the team supported arguments with demonstrations.

The fierceness and naturalness of insults can be lost irrevocably if the wrong synonym or register is chosen. The general tone of the translation was youthful, and candid. While we did not feel obliged to warn the audience of 'strong language', many of the insults chosen by the translator-actors were rude, and sounded natural and appropriate in the context of a warring family.

Cultural considerations

At first glance it seemed that *Poison*, given its modern setting, with mobile phones and camcorders as props, would not present too many cultural challenges. There were, however, features that provoked discussion. The importance accorded to a bag of instant noodles, for example, was felt to be culture-specific. The significance of the noodles was conveyed by the actor through intonation and facial expression, rather than any marking of the translation. Frequently mentioned large sums of money posed another challenge, which was overcome by not mentioning a unit of currency: it was obvious from the context that it was money, and the audience was left to infer pounds, dollars or yuan, as they saw fit. There were at least two cultural allusions, the first of which was the implication that 'hairdresser' is seen in China as a euphemism for the sex trade: the equivalent in the UK would be massage parlour or sauna. The team felt that it was not necessary to highlight this implication, since the context was, in any case, about extra-marital sex. A second allusion was to birth: when asked where he came from, one of the characters responds 'I didn't jump out of a stone' (我不是从石头里蹦出来的), a literary allusion to the story of Sun Wukong in the Chinese novel *Journey to the West* (西游记). It was felt that it was not necessary for an English-speaking audience to know the allusion, since the context was clear, and translators opted for the equivalent 'I wasn't found under a gooseberry bush'.

Reactions to the core project

Feedback from the student actor-translators and the audience provided clear evidence that our collaborative approach to drama translation, backed up by the principles of performability and speakability, resulted in a workable translation and a successful, stimulating dramatic reading. In addition to a standard feedback questionnaire, the students were able to react to the module through the reflective portfolio by which the module was assessed. The students all found it a formative, stimulating, if sometimes unsettling experience. Their reactions ranged from the prosaic 'an insight into drama translation which I have never had before' and 'relevant theory' to the evocative 'opening the magical door of the translation world'. Students found that the collaborative translation was 'an efficient and effective work model' and that the final version was 'much better than a single person's work'. They said that they had learned about word choice, sentence structure and also about new ways of thinking. Not all were happy with two important decisions made by majority vote: the decision to domesticate the names of the characters (for example, Xitian became 'Tim', Lanhong became 'Linda', etc.) and the reversal of the decision to stage a performance rather than a rehearsed reading of the play. Most of the group were concerned about imminent exams and came to realise through the Christmas vacation, that a performance was not feasible, and that a rehearsed reading would still enable them to test out the notions of performability and speakability, which had been hotly debated throughout the translation process. By the time we reached the staging, the dialogue was so familiar that the readers were, in fact, acting, rather than reading. Staff members, delivering the module, editing the translation and seeing the play through to its public reading, also learned very valuable lessons – not least the idea that democracy is not always popular, and that authority must occasionally be exercised!

A number of interpreting students joined the module and found the experience fruitful: like the translation students, they felt that they had benefited from an intensive honing of judgement with regard to spoken language, and the performance skills they had practised would enhance their interpreting delivery.

The fact that the project received funding enabled us to work towards a more sophisticated staging, in which all the translators were involved as directors, producers, actors, understudies, or dealing with lighting and sound effects, publicity, photography or front of house. The increase in audience interest was commensurate with the increased effort we put into the production. In total 36 of the audience of 70 returned a questionnaire, and these were 100 per cent positive and supportive. All those who responded said that they would come to see another Chinese play performed in translation.

In the words of Edney, 'the translator is not only a writer but also a theatre person, working with other theatre practitioners ... to create a stage piece' (1996: 229). In the case study presented here, this was what we aimed to achieve, and the evidence of our surveys indicates that it was achieved. We have no doubt that our next foray into the world of drama translation will not yield a perfect product, but we are convinced that it will be a rich, formative experience for students and teachers alike.

Practical 8.1 Staging a translated play

Take an exciting, interesting play in a foreign language. Add a suitable number of student translator-actors who translate the play. Stir in some directorial and production talent. Sprinkle with back-stage and technical skills. Allow to ferment for several weeks. The result may not be perfect, but it will be delicious and intoxicating.

9 Translating films

Subtitle translation, usually discussed today in the field of audiovisual translation, has a much shorter history than translation in other fields. Subtitle translation did not appear until the early 1900s when motion pictures started to flourish, or, more accurately, not until globalisation of films started to gain momentum and audiences needed translation to help them understand a film made in a language foreign to them. Since subtitle translation has come with films, filmic codes of meaning inevitably play a role in it. Chaume (2004: 13) argues:

> ... for the analysis of audiovisual texts from a translational perspective at least, the theoretical contributions of Translation Studies and those of Film Studies are necessary. Both disciplines are crucial in the exegesis of audiovisual texts and become necessary in order to understand the interlaced web of meaning in these texts.

As films today are published in different forms – thanks to the advances of technology, especially subtitling software – each of them may have different conditions to consider. For instance, subtitles on films made for video games may not follow the limitations of word counts per line as in cinema. Discussion in this chapter will mainly focus on subtitle translation for cinema.

Since the discovery of persistence vision in the nineteenth century, cinema has been developing fast from simple, silent motion pictures to become a sophisticated, audiovisual, multi-form medium that can capture and inspire our imagination and be used for a variety of purposes. It was christened in the early 1900s by Ricciotto Canudo as 'the Seventh art', possessing both the spatial elements of painting, architecture and sculpture and the temporal, successive elements of music, dance and poetry (Vacche 2002: 17). In the silent era of cinema, to help the audience understand a film, printed texts were used as on-screen captions to help link action and provide narrative explanation (Díaz Cintas and Remael 2007). Such texts, called intertitles, are usually regarded as the predecessors of subtitles (ibid.). Later, when subtitling techniques matured, subtitles started to appear concurrently with oral dialogues and usually at the bottom of the screen. Today subtitles have become an important tool for filmmakers to gain a global reach for their films through translation.

As distinct from translation for other genres of art, where the translator can use textual devices such as paratext and metatext to help explain and interpret the original source text, subtitles are constrained by cinematic, semiotic, spatial and temporal limitations and hence have little room for the use of textual devices. Once a dialogue is uttered and the subtitle for it has been screened, there is no way of going back unless the film or video is played in situations or formats where rewinding is possible. These limitations and others present challenges to subtitle translators. Sometimes linguistic skills can be employed to meet such challenges, and sometimes, a translator's decision-making ability is required to find an optimal rendition, especially when not all the meaning expressed in the film can be conveyed through subtitles. Gutt points out that when no translation considered can capture 'all' that the original seems to express, the solution 'requires a non-trivial decision on the translator's part' (2000: 8).

Such a decision, or perhaps all translation-related decisions, cannot be easily made. Both components within (aural and visual elements, shot changes, narration, auteurism, etc.) and factors surrounding audiovisual material – from historical to philosophical, social, political, commercial, and even technological perspectives, – have to be analysed and considered in order to decide, for instance, whether the components unable to be retained in target-language subtitles have been expressed through other semiotic channels.

Historic, political and social contexts

To make decisions on subtitle translation, it seems appropriate to first ask a question: why are films translated and for whom? According to Nord (1988/ 1991, 1997), translation is a purposeful activity, and any translation is at best one version of the source text, depending on how the functional relationship between the source text and the target text is defined. So, when we come to translating Chinese films, the question can be more specifically rephrased as: what is the purpose of providing English subtitles for Chinese films? In the early days of the development of Chinese films, especially before 1949, Chinese cinema was greatly influenced by Western films, more specifically by Hollywood (Cheng et al. 1980; Lee 2005). Chinese cinemas were flooded with American films. Chinese films – we use the term in a broad sense, referring to films made mainly in Mandarin – had little impact internationally (Cheng et al. 1980; Lee 2005), and tapped into the international film circle mainly through prominent films targeted at international film festivals. The first Chinese film to win an international award was the silent film *Song of the Fishermen* (漁光曲), which was awarded the Medal of Honor at the 1935 Moscow Film Festival (Cheng et al. 1980).

Since the 1950s and 1960s, Chinese films have been made in a variety of genres, and differences in the development and features of Chinese films can be seen among the three major production hubs of Chinese films: China, Taiwan and Hong Kong. Before the Cultural Revolution started in 1966, various genres of film were produced in China, such as the Wan brothers' inspirational cartoon *Princess Iron Fan* (鐵扇公主) (1941) and Shi Hui's realist film *This Life of Mine* (我这一辈子) (1950) (Cheng et al. 1980; China Culture 2013; Sun and Lee 2006). After 1949, films were sometimes used as propaganda tools for China to achieve political purposes, such as Wang Ping's musical epic *The East is Red* (东方红) (1964) (Sun and Lee 2006). Since the end of the Cultural Revolution, China has seen great improvement in film quality and started to gain momentum in both domestic and international markets with the success of films such as Zhang Yimou's *Hero* (英雄) (2002).

Taiwan's film industry started in the early 1900s but was under the influence of Japan as it had been colonised by Japan since 1895, following the First Sino-Japanese War. During the Japanese colonial era, films produced in Taiwan were mainly used as tools for political propaganda. After World War II, which ended Japan's rule of Taiwan, films made in Taiwan continued to be used for political purposes (Lee 2001). In the 1960s, feature films started to gain momentum but it was not until the 1980s that Chinese films made in Taiwan started to win more international recognition with films such as Hou Hsiao-Hsien's historical and realistic *A City of Sadness* (悲情城市) (1989) and Ang Lee's *The Wedding Banquet* (囍宴) (1993). Unlike China and Taiwan, Hong Kong was first known for its commercial action films, including kung fu (功夫) films, which tapped into the global cinema market relatively early. This was perhaps because Hong Kong was a British colony until 1997 and may have had a political and economic advantage over China and Taiwan in terms of film-making.

All these historical developments have had an influence on Chinese films and subtitle translation. For instance, expressions stemming from the Japanese occupation period or from the times when political ideology was emphasised may present challenges to subtitle translators. In other words, if translators are not aware of such roots, some translation may be done inappropriately and insufficiently.

In addition to historical and political contexts, characteristics of individual films need to be taken into consideration. Each film has its own 'personality' and usually carries a strong sense of auteurism. Films are made with a purpose or intention, and may belong to a certain cinematic movement, such as socialist realism, expressionism and New Wave (*Nouvelle Vague*). All these are essential factors to be considered when making linguistic decisions for subtitles. Imagine a film director trying to create a sense of crisis through a rapid exchange of dialogues along with strong rhythmic background music: if the subtitles are long, bland and even desynchronised with the music and images, the artistic and aesthetic value of the film can be compromised.

Although translators enjoy the power of making decisions on their subtitle translation, such decisions can be conditioned by other agents involved in the making and publication of a film. Subtitle translation done for Chinese films targeted at film festivals or commercial markets is usually done by professional subtitle translators commissioned by filmmakers, sponsors or even film festivals. Translators tend to get detailed instructions and guidelines for translation, including technical limitations (see pages 158–9 for examples). The quality of translation usually undergoes a close scrutiny by filmmakers and translation editors to ensure the translation meets their needs and abides by technical guidelines.

Along with the commercialisation of Chinese films, including TV series, and the subsequent demand for subtitle translation to be done under severe time constraints, the quality of subtitle translation is often compromised. The effect of such subtitle translation is controversial, for example, the Chinglish subtitle translation of some Hong Kong films, especially those made in the early days, or those not destined for the silver screens. On the one hand, such subtitle translation may add to the humorous effect of the film if it is a slapstick comedy, but on the other hand, such subtitles may cause confusion to foreign viewers if the relevant meaning in the film cannot be conveyed. In these cases, translation judgements are not solely linguistic but also cinematic and related to viewer reception. Chaume (2004: 12) concludes, ' ... the linguistic code, despite its predominant role, is but one more code at play in the construction and later transfer of meaning in audiovisual texts'.

With the growing accessibility of subtitling software and the internet, we also see Chinese films being fansubbed, that is, translated by fansubbers, amateurs who translate and subtitle a film because of their fondness for the film and because they wish to share it with other fans or audience who do not speak the source language. Fansubbers' translation is sometimes more creative, shows a sense of individualism and does not have to abide by any technical guidelines except those due to the spatial and temporal nature of subtitling (Díaz Cintas 2005; Díaz Cintas and Remael 2007). Now, more English-language films than Chinese films are being translated by fansubbers, often in the name of language learning. Such activities do contribute to cultural exchange and language learning, but their legal and economic implications for the film market and professional translation markets are yet to be understood and evaluated.

Dubbing and subtitling

Whether to dub or to subtitle a film has great implications for subtitle translators due to, at least, the difference between spoken and written languages. Subtitling is the practice of inserting written texts, which can be dialogues or narration of a film or their translation in another language, on the screen to assist viewers' understanding of the film (Díaz Cintas and Remael 2007). Subtitling is differentiated from dubbing (配音) and voice-over (画外音 or 旁白). Dubbing is the re-recording of sound and dialogue, which can take place intralingually, such as when re-recording the audio elements of an old film, or interlingually. When done interlingually, language transfer, i.e., translation, needs to take place prior to dubbing. Voice-over is spoken narrative used by filmmakers to explain story, narration or background or to complement dramatic effects, such as that used in flashback (Parkinson 2012). When a film is screened in a foreign country, its voice-over contents are usually translated and then dubbed and/or subtitled.

Preference for dubbing or subtitling varies among countries for different reasons. In some countries, such as Germany and Spain, dubbing is the preferred practice. This may have historical roots in nationalism, which prompts in viewers a desire to watch films dubbed in their national languages (Gottlieb 1995; Parkinson 2012). This may also be due to a desire to avoid being distracted from the visual images of the film by on-screen subtitles (China Culture 2013; Gottlieb 1995). In the Greater China region, preference for dubbing or subtitling differs geographically. Dubbing has been a common practice in the Greater China region for non-Chinese films, especially in mainland China, while subtitled films without dubbing are more commonly seen in Taiwan. However, in terms of Chinese films screened in cinema and viewed by non-Chinese-speaking viewers, subtitling seems to be more common than dubbing. Nonetheless, the preference may change, especially with advances in technology. For instance, today, most films distributed on DVD are both dubbed and subtitled in multiple languages (Díaz Cintas 2005). This provides viewers with multiple language output options. With the increase in popularity of Chinese films, we have seen the TV series *Princess Pearl* or *My Fair Princess* (还珠格格) subtitled and dubbed in English for American viewers.

From the perspective of the integrity of a film, whether subtitling or dubbing retains more cinematic components of a film is a question still under debate. On the one hand, subtitles, which cover part of a screen, are criticised for causing loss of visual and audio information and destroying the graphic design of a film (Díaz Cintas and Remael 2007; Díaz Cintas 2005; Parkinson 2012). On the other hand, subtitling is regarded as preserving the 'artistic integrity' of a film by 'retaining the original language and vocal performance' (Parkinson 2012: 99) while dubbing may change audiences' perception of characters in a film (Bosseaux 2008). For economic reasons, subtitling is more cost-effective than dubbing. Subtitling does not require a cast of voice actors and the production time is shorter due to fewer post-production processes (Gottlieb 1995; Parkinson 2012).

In terms of translation techniques, whether a film is to be subtitled or dubbed makes a great difference. Colloquial registers are generally adopted for dubbing, while registers can vary for subtitles, depending on genres of films. Below are examples that illustrate the importance and difficulty of lip sync:

ST: 你好
TT (subtitling): *How are you?*
TT (dubbing): *Yo!* or *Hi!*

ST: 我不想去
TT (subtitling): *I don't want to go*
TT (dubbing): *I don't wanna go*

If lip sync is to be considered for dubbing, then syllables need to be counted, at least for short dialogues, to match the mouth shape:

ST: 你好嗎? (Ni-hao-ma, 3 syllables)
TT (dubbing): How are you? (3 syllables)
ST: 不准說! (bu-zhun-shuo, 3 syllables)
TT (dubbing): Not a word! (3 syllables)

When dialogues are long, it is usually difficult to consider lip sync. This is because when Chinese dialogues are translated into English, the number of syllables tends to increase. For instance, the term 發展 has only two syllables. When it is translated as *development*, there will be four syllables. This is why word-for-word translation would not work and translation usually needs to be adjusted at higher linguistic levels than that of lexis.

To translate, or not to translate?

Meaning in, and of, a film is conveyed through various semiotic channels. When meaning is completely represented through verbal signs, such as dialogues, narration, text inserts, forewords and finales, interlingual subtitles are indispensable, or the audience from the target culture will not be able to understand the film. When translating such verbal contents, discussion about meaning from different perspectives, such as semantics, dynamic equivalence, pragmatism, functionalism and systemic approaches, is especially helpful (Baker 1992; Nida 1964; Nord 1988/1991; Toury 1995; Williams and Chesterman 2002). Insights from these and other perspectives have left imprints – some deeper, and some shallower – on the practice of subtitle translation. For instance, it is a concept well established today that translating subtitles simply from a linguistic point of view is insufficient, and the target audience and culture must be taken into consideration.

However, meaning in a film is not only represented through verbal signs. It can also be through audio elements, like sound tracks, and visual images, such as graphics or any physical objects present in the film. When meaning is fully expressed through these semiotic signs, there is no need for subtitles, and their existence may even spoil the scene. One can imagine how it might change our emotional response if there were lines of subtitles explaining what happened during the first 20 minutes of *Saving Private Ryan* (1998), which realistically depicts the Normandy landings. Sometimes meaning is constructed through cinematography, like the classic match cut in *2001: A Space Odyssey* (1968), which uses a shift from a prehistoric bone to a nuclear satellite to symbolise human's technological advancement.

Sometimes meaning is construed and constructed along with the unfolding of the storyline of a film. One may say that the leading actress's crying for more than six minutes at the end of the award-winning *Vive L'Amour* (愛情萬歲) (1994) comes from an overwhelming sense of vanity, loneliness and suppression in her life. The unfolding storyline explains why Yu Jiaolong, played by Zhang Ziyi (章子怡), jumps off a cliff at the end of *Crouching Tiger, Hidden Dragon* (卧虎藏龙) (2000). No matter whether the film is in English or Chinese or any other language, meaning is for individual viewers to construe and construct based on their understanding of the film's plot and also their own past experience. The meaning they construct with the unfolding of the plot can help subtitle translators to decide what to translate and what not to. If the meaning can be universally understood and constructed through unfolding of the film's plot, there is no need to translate it. Then, the translator can focus on meaning that is difficult to get across without subtitles. The case study of this chapter will explain how this works.

Difficulties in subtitle translation usually arise when there is incongruity between meaning represented through different semiotic channels. Take the famous Chinese tragic love story, the butterfly lovers, also depicted in the 2008 Hong Kong film *The Butterfly Lovers* (武俠梁祝), as an example. The two lovers, Liang Shanbo (梁山泊) and Zhu Yingtai (祝英台), are well-known figures in Chinese culture. When encountering the two names, subtitle translators may consider whether to translate them as 'Romeo and Juliet', who are also lovers from a tragic love story and are also well known to the target English audience. In certain situations, especially when no visual image is involved, it might not cause problems if 梁山泊 and 祝英台 are translated as 'Romeo and Juliet'. However, this might result in incongruity between meaning construed and constructed through, for instance, the visual channel and the linguistic channel. The visual images in the film, including the Chinese characters, film properties and settings, bring the viewers to an oriental – or, more specifically, Chinese – cultural context while the English words (i.e. Romeo and Juliet) place them in an occidental one. To avoid such semiotic incongruity, it might be preferable to translate the two Chinese names phonetically rather than translate them as similar English names.

Sometimes when a message exists in the visual elements, such as an object or graphic in the film, but not in the acoustic elements, subtitle translators should consider whether they actually need to translate. Take one scene from *Once upon a Time in Kinmen* (巨獸) (2011) as an example. The film is about the psychological battles across the Taiwan Strait between Taiwan and China in 1964. During these battles, leaflets and loudspeakers were used as propaganda tools. Leaflets and loudspeakers are essential objects in the film and also in the plot. Therefore, the written texts on leaflets and the noises made by the loudspeaker should be translated so as to better deliver the meaning of the film and also to help the audience contextualise scenes. So, for example, the words 沒有共產黨就沒有新中國 printed on a leaflet, which is visible in the scene, were translated as: 'No Communist Party means no new China.'

The music or soundtrack of a film provides another example. When the meaning of a song intended to be perceived by viewers exists in other semiotic channels than the acoustic one, there will be a need to translate it. An example is the song 'You are on the front line' (君在前哨) sung by Teresa Teng (鄧麗君) and used as the finale of the film *Once upon a Time in Kinmen*. Songs are seldom translated in Chinese films, partly because music itself is a source of sensibility to the audience. When listening to music, one can 'sense' what it tries to convey. However, when subtitling a film, if a soundtrack contributes to helping the audience understand the film, the translator needs to consider whether to translate the music or provide some information about it. The song 'You are on the front line' (君在前哨) is meaningful because it is part of the psychological battle:

今天我把懷念送給你   Today I send my yearnings to you
謝謝你把溫暖送給我   Thank you for sending me your warmth
我有了你在前哨保護我   You protect me from the front line
為了你，我會珍惜我   Because of you, I treasure myself
有時我也問白雲   Sometimes I ask the white clouds
有時我也託藍天   Sometimes I ask the blue sky
向你，問候   To send my greetings to you

(Translated by Dariush Robertson)

The lyrics also express a sense of warmth and welcome with a purpose of enticing soldiers of Mainland China to come to Taiwan. They have a healing power for the soldiers of Taiwan as they express greetings and also gratitude for the soldiers' devotion to protecting Taiwan.

The constraints of subtitling

The success of subtitles is conditioned by technical limitations. No matter how beautifully a line is translated, the translation is doomed to fail if it cannot be subtitled for reasons such as insufficient time or space on screen. In other words, although they are endowed with freedom of choice of word and expression while translating, subtitle translators have to abide by pre-set limitations. In addition to technical limitations, subtitle translation is subject to requirements by, for instance, filmmakers. Below are the instructions provided to the translator, Dariush Robertson, for the English subtitles of *Once upon a Time in Kinmen*:

1 39 characters per line, only one line allowed on screen. (Space for 1 character = 1 letter = 1 punctuation mark).
2 The whole script needs to be translated, including the foreword and text inserts, the translation of which should be placed in parentheses.
3 Scurrilities can be translated faithfully.
4 It is hoped that the translation prioritizes conveyance of meaning and feelings (希望譯稿能以達意且傳情為理想).

The first instruction stipulates technical limitations and the second decides which visual written texts are to be translated. The third instruction is related to social norms, censorship and classification. Strong language and vulgarities are regarded in Chinese culture and Chinese cinema markets as taboo and have to pass censors and/or be classified before they can be screened in cinemas. Since *Once upon a Time in Kinmen* was targeted at film festivals rather than commercial English cinema markets where film classification rules might apply, what meant more to the filmmakers was the artistic integrity of the film and the delivery of meaning and feelings (i.e. the fourth instruction). In the official English subtitles of the film therefore, strong language was translated faithfully. It is not uncommon, especially in the commercial movie markets that, in order to pass censors and be screened in cinemas in target countries, filmmakers have to compromise their film integrity. For instance, China's censorship requires that immoral and culturally controversial scenes and contents have to be edited out and Chinese subtitles have to be changed or at least toned down from the original English source, before release in China, as in the case of the Bond film *Skyfall* (2012).

When we are translating subtitles from Chinese into English, compliance with limitation on word count per line is usually challenging. This is because, when translating from Chinese into English, the space required tends to expand. For instance, 動機 occupies the space of four characters while its English translation 'motivation' occupies the space of ten characters. Translators therefore need to apply their language skills, using shorter synonyms or expressions, to generate shorter subtitles. This strategy also applies to temporal limitations. On average, viewers need two to three seconds to read one line comfortably and four to six seconds for two lines. Shorter subtitles and hence less reading time allow viewers more time to assimilate other semiotic information and to appreciate the film.

Another important skill that is often used in subtitle translation is segmentation, which is defined by Díaz Cintas and Remael as 'the division of the ST dialogue, narration etc. into sections or segments – subtitles – that the viewers can understand at a glance' (2007: 172). Segmentation needs to be used in accordance with temporal and spatial limitations. Take, for example, the propagandist words, 唯有全體青年都能自由發揮聰明、才智，國家的未來才會有充滿光明和希望, broadcast by Teresa Teng in *Once upon a Time in Kinmen*. A linguistically complete rendition can be:

Only when all the youth can play their full potential of talent can the country's future be full of brightness and hope. (120)

The number in the parentheses is the total character count per line, including punctuation marks and spaces. If these words are to be dubbed and not subtitled in English, this rendition is perhaps workable. However, if it is to be subtitled, with the technical limitations for *Once upon a Time in Kinmen* in mind, it has to be segmented into four lines and each line has to be no more than 39 characters, as follows:

> Only when all the youth can play their (38)
> full potential of talents will the (34)
> country's future be full of brightness (38)
> and hope. (9)

The possible subtitles above are correct in meaning and have a word count within the technical limitation, but they are not viewer-friendly. All of the four lines start or stop at an inappropriate place of the sentence. This is why segmentation needs to be applied in order to 'reinforce coherence and cohesion in subtitling' (Díaz Cintas and Remael 2007: 172) and facilitate readability. The above subtitles could be segmented as follows:

> Only when all the youth can (27)
> play their full potential of talents (36)
> will the country's future be full of (36)
> brightness and hope. (20)

Since subtitles are sometimes criticised for covering too much screen space and distracting the audience, rendition using fewer words can be considered. Since 光明 and 希望 are, in this case, tantamount to synonyms, as they both convey the meaning of 'bright', 'hopeful' and 'promising', there is no need to translate them as two separate English words and thus the word count and number of lines can be reduced:

> Only when the youth can (23)
> bring their talents into full play (34)
> will the country have a bright future. (38)

This does not necessarily mean that fewer words and lines are better. Sometimes when a subtitle is much shorter than its source dialogue, resulting in a lengthy stay on screen, the audience may feel bored and distracted.

The extract below is part of a video interview with director Fan Jian (范俭) about his film, *The Next Life* (2011). The subtitle translation of director Fan's interview was a collaborative student project done for the Beijing Independent Film Festival – Newcastle Tour in 2012, and was supervised by the authors.

When translating this extract, only verbal information needs to be considered. However, translating repeats (the underlined parts) does not increase our understanding of the interview, so there is no need to translate them. Moreover, at first hearing, the three phrases in boxes, 即将生育 (about to give birth to), 已经生育 (already gave birth to) and 正在生育 (is giving birth to), refer to three different stages of pregnancy and labour. In the context of the film, these phrases actually emphasise that the families who lost their children in the earthquake were trying to have new babies. Therefore, it does not make sense if they are translated literally. The '//' sign indicates line breaks.

导演范俭谈纪录片《活着》

在时隔一年之后，也就是09年的4、5月间，我重新再去到四川，从北川一直走到都江堰。那么在我走到都江堰的时候呢，我就先是认识了一些从事心理援助的志愿者团队。那么我发现他们从事心理援助的主要对象就是失去孩子的家庭。那么这个失去孩子的家庭，其实在都江堰有很多很多。都江堰这个地方可能是不同于其他的一些受灾的县市，特点就在于在那里遇难的孩子特别的多。这个我想很多人已经了解到了。那么对于这些家庭，我接触了不少之后，我就发现，他们当中绝大多数都是处在这样一个生命状态里，就是要么是即将生育，要么是已经生育，要么是正在生育。那么这个行为，就是这个生育行为，一下子就引起了我的注意。不仅仅在于它的数量很庞大，有几千个家庭在重新生育小孩，更重要的在于他们这种生育动机，和复杂的生育心理。

Director Fan Jian on his documentary//*The Next Life*
In April and May 2009,//one year after the earthquake,
I went to Sichuan again,//travelling from Beichuan to Dujiangyan.
There I met some volunteer teams//offering psychological support,
mainly to families//who had lost their children.
There were many such families//in Dujiangyan.
Dujiangyan is different from other cities//suffering from the disaster.
Many children lost their lives there,
This is already well known.
After contacting a few families,
I found most of them were//in this situation:
women were pregnant or had new babies.
This childbearing phenomenon//caught my eye at once.
Besides the huge number,//thousands of families were bearing babies,
more important was their motivation//and complex feelings about having
    babies.

Today, with rapid developments in subtitling software and audiovisual media, temporal and spatial limitations are constantly changing. For instance, the relative distance between film viewers and screen has changed. We have already seen some subtitles for video games displayed in ways that disregard conventional word count per line. Below is a dubbed, two-line subtitle from a game action scene in *Starcraft II: Wings of Liberty* (the version in traditional Chinese characters).

Upper line: 弗米利恩： … 另外今天的其他新聞是，阿克圖洛斯‧蒙斯克大帝舉行了一個記者招待會，紀念四年前結束的「怒火燎原」戰役，我們的凱特‧羅克韋

Lower line: 爾也在現場。

In this example, the upper line contains 65 full-width characters, including punctuation marks, rather than 12–16 Chinese characters per line, which is usually the norm for Chinese subtitles. The word count of the upper line is obviously much more than what is traditionally adopted. Therefore, the font is relatively small. This is perhaps only feasible because the distance between the viewer – that is, the PC game player – and the computer screen is much shorter than that between moviegoers and the big screen. In addition, advanced technology can give viewers more control of their own device, such as PC and DVD players, so that they can pause the game action at any time and/or rewind if they cannot finish reading the subtitles on screen.

In addition to word count, the position, font and colour of subtitles can also be different from what is traditionally adopted. In the subtitle above, '弗米利恩', the Chinese name of the speaking character, is in yellow rather than in white in order to differentiate it from words spoken by other characters in the game. Both lines are left-aligned rather than centre-aligned. Much research needs to be done to find out how technology has been influencing the way subtitles are created, presented and received.

As many fewer video games are translated from Chinese into English than from English into Chinese, how video games originally developed in Chinese will be translated and subtitled in English is yet to be observed and evaluated.

A case study – This Life of Mine

As noted previously, when we are translating Chinese films, there are several layers of meaning that need our attention. Sometimes, these layers of meaning exist coincidentally but are delivered through different semiotic channels, and sometimes they connote auteurist meaning. Therefore, before we start to translate a film, it is necessary to first analyse and understand meanings implicitly and explicitly expressed in and through the film. In the following sections, we will use an award-winning film, *This Life of Mine* (1950), as a case study to demonstrate how a Chinese film can be analysed and translated from the perspective of subtitling.

This Life of Mine, adapted from Lao She's (老舍) novel of the same title and directed by Shi Hui (石挥 1915–57), was produced in black and white in 1950 by Wenhua Film Company (文华影片公司) in China. Shi was a versatile artist. He was a prominent stage actor, writer and film director (Shu 2003). He was the leading actor and also the narrator of the film *This Life of Mine*. Through realistically depicting the life of a patrol policeman (the 'I' first person narrator), the film reflects what China had been through over a period of more than 40 years, from the late Qing dynasty to the Warlord era, the Sino-Japanese War and up to the eve of the establishment of the People's Republic of China (Sun and Lee 2006; Yuan 2008). Shi brought an astonishing depth to this film by integrating historical incidents and personal tragedies and, at the same time, allowed the audience to feel the conflicting ideologies of this time period and the struggles of ordinary people's lives. The film is rich in historical incidents as well as culture-specific items. It uses both dialogue and first-person voice-over narration to tell the story. The register used in the film is easy to understand and not archaic, though the film was made more than 60 years ago and contains many terms relating to culture-specific items.

This Life of Mine, which can be accessed on the website of Internet Archive (http://archive.org/details/this_life_of_mine), already has English subtitles, which are used below merely for the sake of discussion. It is not clear what the style guides for the subtitle translators were, but it appears that two-liners are allowed and the maximum number of characters per line is 36–39, including punctuation marks and spaces.

A balance among aural, visual, linguistic and cultural meaning

All four images from *This Life of Mine* in Figures 9.1a–d contain culture-specific items and/or terms as their visual elements, have aural messages (i.e. the narration) accompanying the image, and form an integral part of the storyline of the film. Their subtitles share the same limitations of technical styles (such as two-liners allowed), space (the same screen size and word font), and duration of time (two to three seconds).

When translating the narration accompanying these images, different layers of meaning should be considered. Figure 9.1a is perhaps the simplest in terms

Figures 9.1a–d Four images from *This Life of Mine*.

of subtitling. The audience can see four Chinese characters, 正大光明, which are exactly what the first-person narrator says in the film, so that the aural meaning matches the visual meaning perfectly. The four characters are inscribed on the tablet in the Palace of Heavenly Purity (or Qianqing Palace, 乾清宮), which is located in the Forbidden City in Beijing and was where the Qing emperors lived and received audience (Chiculture 2013). The phrase 正大光明 means justice and righteousness or honour. In this film, it is an ironic contrast to the real life of the common people: corruption is often cited as one reason why the Qing dynasty collapsed and people desired a revolution. In the story of the film, the first-person narrator suffers a lot from injustice and sometimes struggles to maintain his own righteousness. Therefore, the rendition of 正大光明 as 'justice and righteousness', or 'justice and honour', as provided in the film, is consistent with its linguistic, aural and visual meaning in Chinese and also meets the needs of the storyline of the film. As the rendition is quite short, it can be read easily within the temporal and spatial limitations.

There are more things to consider when subtitling the image in Figure 9.1b. The first-person narrator says, '昆明湖、十七孔橋，多好的風景啊！'. The literal translation is 'Kunming Lake, the 17-arched bridge. What a beautiful view!' In the visual image, one can see the lake and the bridge, and the scene is beautiful. Therefore, there is no difference or contradiction between the visual message and the narration. What the translator needs to consider is perhaps only the spatial and temporal limitation. Since the view refers to the lake and the bridge, it is justifiable to use the adjective 'beautiful' to describe the lake and the bridge and change the translation to 'Beautiful Kunming Lake and the 17-Arched Bridge'.

However, if we look at the role this image plays in the story of the film, the translation above may lose the sense of irony. The beauty presented in the image is in reality a sharp contrast to the 'poor' life of the common people. The exclamation '多好的風景啊！' implies ironically how poor the people are. The richer the imperial family, the poorer the people. Reducing the exclamation weakens the sense of irony. Nonetheless, since the effect of this contrast can be made up for by the subsequent visual images of the poor people, the reduction in the translation at the linguistic level can be justified.

At the cultural level, there is a different story. The translation of '17-Arched Bridge' matches linguistically the name of the bridge and also visually the appearance of its 17 arches but it does not explain the meaning of 十七. Numbers are important in Chinese and bear cultural significance. The bridge has 17 arches and, if counted from both ends, the central arch will be the 9th one, and 9 (九) is phonetically identical to 久, meaning a long time or long life: the name of the bridge actually means 'long live the emperor' (Chiculture 2013). This, again, conveys a sense of irony as, in the film, the Qing dynasty collapsed shortly after. There is obviously no space or time here for the subtitle to explain all these cultural messages and since this knowledge about numbers may not be known even to some Chinese, it is perhaps justifiable to simply reduce these messages. If in a printed publication, such texts, which have an intention to convey a sense of irony and contain diverse cultural meaning, might be deliverable in their full meaning with the support of paratexts and metatexts.

Figure 9.1c requires, again, different analysis. The narration that goes along with this image is '崇禎皇帝吊死在煤山上'. This can be translated as 'The Ming Emperor Chongzhen hung himself on Coal Hill', as translated in the film. Due to spatial limitation, this translation needs to be divided into two lines. From a linguistic point of view, a better point of segmentation should be after the word 'Chongzhen' since it is the name of the emperor. However, in order to cover as little as possible of the image (Díaz Cintas 2005), it is better to have a shorter upper line and a longer lower line.

The visual message in the image is slightly different from the aural message. The item that stands out from the image is apparently the stone stele, inscribed with the words 明思宗殉國處, the literal translation of which is 'the place where the Emperor Chongzhen sacrificed his life for his country'. The stele marks the place where, according to legends, Chongzhen hanged himself. If judging only from the aural message, a viewer might think this is Coal Hill, which is right, and this stele is the tombstone of Chongzhen's grave. However, the stele is not exactly a tombstone (墓碑) but more like a memorial stone (紀念碑). The death of Chongzhen marked the end of the Ming dynasty and the start of the Qing dynasty, a historical time period of great upheaval in China. As the story of the film unfolds, it becomes clear, through the eye of the first-person narrator, that change of dynasty does not necessarily improve the life of the people, and there is always injustice and corruption. For the translator, what needs to be considered is whether the discrepancy between the aural and visual messages and the cultural meaning contained in the film needs to be translated or whether related information needs to be provided. Since the discrepancy is not important and the cultural messages could be obtained from the rest of the film, it is perhaps not necessary to provide information in addition to translation of the aural message, i.e., the narration.

In comparison, Figure 9.1d is more complex in terms of subtitling. The major visual message in the image is 達志橋東口, a literal translation of which is 'the east entrance of Dazhi Bridge'. The narration accompanying this image is '達志橋, 還說什麼呢', which can be literally translated as 'Dazhi Bridge, what is there to say about it now?' The English translation provided in the film is 'Dazhi Bridge! That's all in the past now'. But one might wonder what is going on here? What is in the past? Why is there nothing to say about it now?

'達志橋東口' actually refers to Dazhi Bridge Hutong, or Lane (达志桥胡同). 达志桥 was the homonym of 鞑子桥, which was once used as military quarters of the Mongolian troops and also of the Manchu bannermen (旗兵) of the Qing dynasty (Huaxia 2013; Oldbeijing 2013). As 鞑子 was used by Han Chinese to refer to the northern nomads of China and carried pejorative connotations, the bridge name was later changed to 达志 (達志), the literal meaning of which is 'to achieve one's ambition' or 'to fulfil one's aspiration'. Dazhi Bridge is also famous because it is where Songyun An (松筠庵) was located. Songyun An is regarded by historians as the landmark building of the Gongche Shangshu (公车上书) movement, led mainly by Kang Youwei (康有为 1858–1927) and Liang Qichao (梁启超 1873–1929) to protest the signing of the Treaty of Shimonoseki (马关条约), which was the treaty in which Taiwan was ceded to Japan. In the end, the aspiration of the Gongche Shangshu movement was not achieved but the incident symbolised the patriotism of the intellectual class. All the historical meaning presented above, and more, is what the first-person narrator refers to as having been lost in the past. This also foreshadows the treacherous behaviour depicted later in the film.

From the perspective of subtitling, cultural loss is perhaps unavoidable as it is impossible to include and convey the various meanings, delivered linguistically, visually, aurally and culturally, in two to three seconds. Unlike the situation in Figures 9.1a, b and c, where, for instance, the sense of irony can be perceived through visual messages or as the story unfolds, the discrepancy in the messages coming from different channels in Figure 9.1d cannot be easily resolved. In this case, the best strategy for subtitling may be to focus on the linguistic, aural and visual messages as they have direct influence on the audience's real-time perception of the film.

Like the video interview with director Fan, above, this historic film of the 1950s illustrates the technical and linguistic challenges of subtitle translation. Both the professional subtitler and the fansubber work with prescriptions and limitations, particularly in cases where there is linguistic difference and cultural complexity. The key to successful subtitles is the application of creativity within the tight constraints.

Appendix

Chapter 1

Practical 1.1 Talking about art

大千先生实为大师也。 他的山水、人物、花鸟、要工就工，要写就写，要泼就泼，要大就大，要小就小；花鸟画也就花鸟画吧，还特擅画那出污泥而不染的荷花，凡工凡写凡泼均极尽荷花之净、之致、之意、之情、之态。读也、看也、观止也、有人评他之画荷曰："兼取古今各家画荷之长，于石涛取 '气'，与八大取 '毅'，于宋人得体察物情之理，乃集古今画荷之大成。居士画荷，无论工笔、没骨、写意、设色、水墨皆精绝当世，更创泼墨泼彩法为之，气势撼人，不但超越了花卉的属性，更将文人花卉的笔墨范围，拓展至另一境地。"

(Chen 2003: 164)

Suggested translation:

Zhang Qian was a true master of landscape painting, people, and 'bird and flower' paintings. He was equally at home with meticulous realism, impressionistic free style, or ink-splash technique, big or small. His 'bird and flower' paintings revealed the essence of birds and flowers, and he was unsurpassed in his depictions of the unsullied lotus that emerges from the mud. He plumbed the depths of realism, free style and ink-splash to reveal the purity, the delicacy, the meaningfulness, the passion and the elegance of the lotus, from every aspect. He has been judged to have absorbed the excellence of every school of lotus painting, bringing ancient and modern qualities together. He has taken inspiration from the energy of Shi Tao and the determination of Ba Da Shan Ren, and has learned the observation of the nature of things from the painters of the Song dynasty. As a lay Buddhist, no matter whether he paints realistically, 'boneless' style, impressionistic free style, or colour block, his painting of lotuses is as perfect as any. His ink-splash technique is beyond compare in its ability to move the onlooker. Not only has he surpassed the ideals of flower painting, he has also taken 'Literary School' painting to new heights.

(Authors' translation)

Chapter 2

Practical 2.2 Avoiding subjectivity in translation

漢字方方正正，橫平豎直，上下左右力求對稱，很像男性敦厚的體形、穩重的風格。女書修長輕盈，舒展秀麗，不拘一格，像少女苗條的體形、飄逸的品格．女性一般比男性富於幻想、更有浪漫氣質，因此，女書的形體佈局不像漢字那樣莊嚴、規範，而是根據筆畫走向，不太嚴格地組成單體、上下、左右、雙合、夾心、包圍等各種組合，其中隱含著一種對稱，如右上與左下均衡，雖傾斜卻不失中心，給人一種特殊的美感。

(Gong 1991: 34)

Suggested translation:

Conventional Chinese characters stand four-square and upright, corresponding from top to bottom and left to right in perfect symmetry, masculine, solid and stable. Women's writing is long and light, loose and elegant. It is willowy, graceful and infinitely variable, like a young woman. Women are more imaginative and romantic than men, and this may be why the form and layout of women's writing is less robust and regular than standard Chinese characters. All the compositional elements of the characters go with the flow of the strokes: monomers, vertical and horizontal components, outer symmetrical components and their central components, and enclosures, none ever too rigid. There is a kind of symmetry, in that upper right corresponds to lower left, and even though the character slants, it does not lose its balance. It has its own particular aesthetic.

(Authors' translation)

Practical 2.3 Aesthetic description

古人說：　'一成一字之規'，意思是筆一落到紙上便是點，其他筆劃都是這一點的延伸，筆鋒向右運行，　是橫，向下運行，是豎。　'亮點'就是根據這個論點創作的　，撇和提的起筆　處可以明顯地看到點的形狀；左豎則一點來造型，像日、品、內、國等字；　豎勾頓挫出鋒後留下點的痕跡，橫劃輕入重出，從中能體會到速度與重量的有機結合；豎的起筆輕捷委婉，一帶而過，　平添了幾分輕鬆和靈動；點劃間顧盼呼應，使字生動活潑，結構端莊均勻。字體貼近人，閱讀就感到親切。

(Liao 2009: 71)

Suggested translation:

There is an old saying: 'one rule to make one character'. It means that the first stroke the brush makes on the paper is the 'dian', the dot, and the other strokes are all extensions of that stroke. The tip of the brush travelling right creates a horizontal, and when it travels downwards, it creates a vertical. I created 'Bright Spot' on this principle, and when you look at the points at which the brush is lifted to sweep left, and 'raise', you can see clearly the form of the dot. The left vertical is made from one dot, as in the case of the characters for 'sun' 日, 'to taste' 品, 'inner' 内, and 'nation' 國. As the brush pauses imperceptibly, emerging at the hook of the vertical, a trace of the dot is left behind. With the horizontal stroke, the brush goes in lightly, and comes out heavily, and you can see the organic integration of speed and weight. To make a vertical, the brush should start nimbly and delicately, in a single sweep, a little relaxed and dexterous; look for an echo between dots and strokes that makes the characters come alive, and make the structure of the characters even and dignified. Characters have an affinity with human beings – when you read them you should feel close to them.

(Authors' translation)

Chapter 4

Practical 4.1 Applying semantic fields

《清明上河图》是北宋张择端的名画，它从一个侧面极其生动地反映了当时汴京繁荣兴旺的景象。画面人物有数百人，百行百业、农工士商、各色人物无不具备。

画面中，凡是体力劳动者担夫、小贩、农民、船家等，都有一个共同的特点，那就是上衣都很短，大多是短襦或短衫，不超过膝盖，或者刚刚超过膝盖。他们头戴巾帕，头巾也是比较随便的，甚至还有的没有戴头巾，直接露出发髻。这类人的脚下一般穿麻鞋或者草鞋。

官吏、商贾、文人、有钱的市民则穿交领长袍或圆领襕衫，头戴巾子或幞头，下身穿长裤足蹬靴履。他们的衣袖虽宽窄不一却比较适中，没有太宽的，也没有太窄的，但衣身都比较宽松。

从画面看，宋代平民的服饰，不论是颜色、配饰、衣料还是式样，都是受到严格的限制的，各行各业的服饰式样也有详细规定，不可以随便地改变和逾越。所以，在宋代，从穿戴上不但可看出等级差别，还可辨认出每个人的职业是什么：披肩子，戴帽子的是卖香人；穿长衫，束牛角带，不戴帽子的是当铺的管事；穿白色短衫，系青花手巾是卖干果的小孩.

(Gao 2005: 123)

Suggested translation:

Qing Ming Festival on the River is a well-known painting by Zhang Zeduan, which reflects the richness and exuberance of life in Kaifeng during the Northern Song dynasty. Several hundred figures from all walks of life are depicted in the painting: peasants, artisans, scholar-officials and merchants are all there. The painting brings to life the coolies bearing their shoulder poles, the pedlars, the peasants and boat people. They have one thing in common: their outer garments are all short, mainly short jackets, or robes, which are knee-length or shorter. The head cloths or head wraps that they wear do not conform to one style, and some have no head covering at all, leaving their topknots visible. These people all wear sandals made of hemp or grass. The officials, merchants and scholars and the more affluent townspeople wear long gowns with a cross-over lapel, or round collar scholar's gown. They wear a head wrap or cowl, and long trousers with boots. There are wide sleeves and narrow sleeves, but the favourite is of medium width, and the clothes are all loose and comfortable.

The painting shows how the clothing of the ordinary people of the Song dynasty was subject to restrictions, in terms of colour, decoration, fabric and style. There were detailed rules on the style of clothing for every profession, which could not be changed or overstepped at will. So we can see the differences in rank which pertained during the Song dynasty. We can distinguish every trade or profession: those with shawls and wearing hats are incense merchants; those who wear long gowns with horn belts and no hat are pawnbrokers; those with short white shirts and blue patterned kerchiefs are children peddling dried fruit …

(Authors' translation)

Practical 4.2 Construction and manipulation of a garment

商周及后来的冠，一般只有一个冠圈，　　在冠圈上装一条不太宽的冠梁，　带上冠以后冠圈与冠梁将头发束住。为了防止冠从头上掉落，在冠圈两边设有丝绳做的冠缨，用冠缨在下巴下面打个结系紧。

(Gao 2005: 48)

Suggested translation:

From the Shang and Zhou dynasty on, the hat usually consisted of a circular crown, with a fairly narrow cross-piece. Once the hat was put on, the hair was secured by means of the cross-piece. To prevent the head-dress falling off, it was secured at each side of the crown with tassels made of silk yarn tied tightly under the chin.

(Authors' translation)

Practical 4.3 Garment care labelling

i

成份含量: 麻100%;
洗涤说明: 可以水洗; 不可氯漂;低温熨烫; 悬挂晾干

Suggested translation:

Fabric 100% hemp
Washing instructions: cold wash, do not bleach; drip dry; cool iron.

ii

标准: 81007 – 2003
面料: 涤纶 66%; 锦纶 34%;
里料:涤纶 100%
洗涤说明: 中温整烫; 只可用手洗;不可漂白;普通干洗;洗后脱水凉干;
   不可曝晒;不可扭干.

Suggested translation:

Standard 81007–2003
Outer fabric 66% polyester; 34% polyamide fibre
Lining: 100% polyester
Washing instructions: dry clean or wash by hand; do not bleach; do not
   wring; do not dry in full sun; squeeze out excess water and dry in
   shade; warm iron.

Chapter 5

Practical 5.1 Rites of passage for girls

蝴蝶儿穿花裙
十三岁做新人,
十四岁拖儿胞女上爹门,
长竹竿晒红裙,
短竹竿打媒人,
不是媒人故,
是爹娘做错了人。

(Ma 1996: 93)

Suggested translation:

Butterfly in your floral gown
At thirteen years you'll be a bride
At fourteen back to your parents' town
With a clinging baby at your side.
On a long bamboo cane you'll air your wedding skirt
With a short bamboo pole you'll beat her till it hurts,
That go-between, but she's not the reason
Your parents decided on the wrong person.

(Authors' translation)

Practical 5.2

送奶奶
好八连，八连好，
开荒种地上西郊。
上西郊，脚步齐，
来回要走几十里。
几十里，走得快，
回来遇见老奶奶。
老奶奶，走亲家，
肩上挑的大南瓜。
大南瓜，重又重，
奶奶累得走不动。
走不动，汗水淌。
八连叔叔来帮忙。
来帮忙，送到家，
好像儿子送媽媽。

(*A Selection of New Children's Songs and Nursery Rhymes* 1964)

Suggested translation:

Escorting Granny
Company Eight good, Company Eight tops,
Opening up wasteland, planting crops,
Out to the West, marching in time,
There and back, ten miles plus nine.
Ten miles plus nine, their march is brisk,
As they meet a Granny whose load's at risk.
She's off to see her family and friends
With pumpkins loaded on the shoulder pole ends.
Great big pumpkins, heavy as can be,
She can scarcely move, it is plain to see.
Scarcely moving, pouring with sweat,
Uncles of Company Eight will help her yet.
Carrying her load, they see her home,
Just as a son would not leave his mum alone.

(Author's translation)

Notes for parents:

1 Company Eight (八连) was a famous unit of the People's Liberation Army that had great success in resistance against Japan, the Korean War, and border disputes with Vietnam. At the same time they are a model of the notion that the army and the people are close and interdependent, like 'fish and water' (鱼水).

2 'Granny' (奶奶) (father's mother) is a polite term of address for an elderly woman.
3 'Uncle' (叔叔) is a polite term of address for a mature or older man.

Chapter 7

Practical 7.2 Translating for blog readers

记得我曾一度为约会总得花钱而感到无奈，尤其是有一回在绿茵阁咖啡厅点了个所谓的"浪漫情侣套餐"更是搞笑到雷人，每上一道菜服务员都要大声报一遍"浪漫情侣套餐"，当真是有些尴尬，加上当时我和他都没什么钱，彼此暗中算计着要不要点果汁，哪还有半点浪漫。

Suggested translation:

I well remember unavoidably shelling out on various dates. There was one occasion in a certain café when we ordered the 'Romantic Lovers' Special'. We almost split our sides laughing as the waiter brought dish after dish of romantic food, yelling loudly each time 'Romantic Lover's meal coming up!' What could be less romantic, added to the embarrassment of being broke, and eyeing each other doubtfully as we assessed our ability to pay for the final course of fruit.

(Authors' translation)

Bibliography

English language references

Ai Weiwei (2012) 'China's art world does not exist', *The Guardian g2*, 11 September 2012: 10–11.

Aitchison, J. (1994) *Words in the Mind: An Introduction to the Mental Lexicon*, Oxford: Blackwell.

Anderman, G. (1996) 'Classical you win, modern you lose', in D. Johnston (ed.) *Stages of Translation,* Bath: Absolute Classics.

——(ed.) (2007) *Voices in Translation: Bridging Cultural Divides*, Clevedon: Multilingual Matters.

Ash, R. (1999) *The Sapir-Whorf Hypothesis*, available HTTP: <http://www.angelfire.com/journal/worldtour99/sapirwhorf.html> (accessed 30 November 2011).

Ashmore, R. (2007) 'Recent-style *shi* poetry: heptasyllabic regulated verse (*qiyan lushi*)', in Z. Q. Cai (ed.) *How to Read Chinese Poetry: A Guided Anthology*, New York: Columbia University Press.

Austin, J. L., (1971) *How to do Things with Words,* Oxford: OUP.

Baker, M. (1992) *In Other Words: A Coursebook on Translation*, London/New York: Routledge.

Baker, M. and Saldanha, G. (eds) (1998) *The Routledge Encyclopedia of Translation Studies*, London and New York: Routledge.

Barras, G. S. (2002) *The Art of Calligraphy in Modern China*, London: The British Museum Press.

Bartlett, N. (1996) 'Interview: a different night out in the theatre', in D. Johnston (ed.) *Stages of Translation*, Bath: Absolute Classics.

Bassnett, S. (1980/2002) *Translation Studies*, London: Routledge.

——(1991) 'Translating for the theatre: the case against performability', *Traduction, Terminologie, Redaction*, IV.1: 99–111.

Bellos, A. (2010) *Alex's Adventures in Numberland*, London: Bloomsbury.

Belsey, C. and Moore, J. (eds) (1991) *The Feminist Reader: Essays in the Politics of Literary Criticism*, Basingstoke: Macmillan.

Billig, M. (2005), *Laughter and Ridicule: Towards a Social Critique of Humour*, London: Sage.

Boase-Beier, J and Holman, M. (eds) (1999) *The Practices of Literary Translation: Constraints and Creativity*, Manchester: St Jerome.

Bosseaux, C. (2008) 'Buffy the Vampire Slayer: characterization in the musical episode of the TV series', *The Translator:* Vol. 14, No. 2: Special Issue. Translation and Music: 343–72.

Bowman, M. (2000) 'Scottish horses and Montreal trains: the translation of vernacular to vernacular', in C. Upton (ed.) *Moving Target: Theatre Translation and Cultural Relocation*, Manchester: St Jerome.

Bradley, A. and DuBois, A. (2010) *The Anthology of Rap*, Newhaven: Yale University Press.

Branigan, T. 'Chinese sex fair serves up porn for a prudish society', *The Guardian*, 9 October 2012.

Brodie, G. (2012) 'Theatre translation for performance: conflict of interests, conflict of cultures', in R. Wilson and B. Maher (eds) *Words, Images and Performances in Translation*, London: Continuum.

Burgess, A. (1972) *A Clockwork Orange*, Harmondsworth: Penguin.

Buruma, I. and Margalit, A. (2005) *Occidentalism: A Short History of Anti-Westernism*, London: Atlantic Books.

Cai, Z. Q. (2007a) 'Recent-style *shi* poetry: pentasyllabic regulated verse (*wuyan lushi*)', in Z. Q. Cai (ed.) *How to Read Chinese Poetry: A Guided Anthology*, New York: Columbia University Press.

——(2007b) *How to Read Chinese Poetry: A Guided Anthology*, New York: Columbia University Press.

Cameron, D. (2000) 'Tradaptation: cultural exchange and black British theatre', in C. Upton (ed.) *Moving Target: Theatre Translation and Cultural Relocation*, Manchester: St Jerome.

Carroll, J. B. (ed.) (1956) *Language, Thought, and Reality: Selected Writings of Benjamin Lee Whorf*, Cambridge, MA: Technology Press of Massachusetts Institute of Technology.

Carroll, P. (2003) 'Refashioning Suzhou: dress, commodification and modernity', in T. M. Chen and P. Zamperini (eds) *Positions East Asia Cultures Critique: Special Issue Fabrications,* Vol. 11, No. 2, Fall: 443–78.

Chan, H. C. (1973) *Chinese Literature, Popular Fiction and Drama*, Edinburgh: Edinburgh University Press.

Chan, L. (1998) 'Liberal versions: late Qing approaches to translating Aesop's fables', in D. Pollard (ed.) *Translation and Creation: Readings of Western Literature in Early Modern China*, Amsterdam: Benjamins.

Chan, L.-T.-H. (2010) *Readers, Reading and Reception of Translated Fiction in Chinese*, Manchester: St Jerome.

Chan, S. and Pollard, D. E. (eds) (1995) *An Encyclopaedia of Translation*, Hong Kong: The Chinese University Press.

Chao, Y. R. (1968) *A Grammar of Spoken Chinese*, Berkeley: University of California Press.

Chaume, F. (2004) 'Film studies and translation studies: two disciplines at stake in audiovisual translation', *Meta: Translators' Journal*, Vol. 49, No. 1, April: 12–24.

Chen, T. M. (2003) 'Proletarian white and working bodies in Mao's China', in T. M. Chen and P. Zamperini (eds) *Positions East Asia Cultures Critique: Special Issue Fabrications*, Vol. 11, No. 2, Fall: 361–93.

Chen, T. M. and Zamperini, P. (eds) (2003) *Positions East Asia Cultures Critique: Special Issue Fabrications*, Vol. 11, No. 2, Fall.

Chen, X. (1995/2002) *Occidentalism: A Theory of Counter-Discourse in Post-Mao China*, Oxford: Rowman & Littlefield Publishers Inc.

Cheung, M. P. Y. (ed.) (2009) *Chinese Discourses on Translation: Positions and Perspectives*, Manchester: St Jerome.

Cheung, M. P. Y. and Lai, J. C. C. (eds) (1997) *An Oxford Anthology of Contemporary Chinese Drama*, Oxford: Oxford University Press.

Chiang Yee (1937/2004) *The Silent Traveller in Lakeland*, Edinburgh: Mercat Press.

——(1938/1973) *Chinese Calligraphy: An Introduction to its Aesthetic and Technique*, Cambridge, MA: Harvard University Press.

Chiculture (2013) Online. Available HTTP <http://www.chiculture.net/> (accessed 24 April 2013).

Cody, E. (2004) 'A language by women, for women', *Guardian Weekly*, 4–10 March 2004: 29.

Coelsch-Foisner, S. and Klein, H. (2004) *Drama Translation and Theatre Practice*, Frankfurt am Main: Peter Lang.

Conceison, C. (2004) *Significant Other: Staging the American in China*, Honolulu: University of Hawai'i Press.

Curran, B. (2008) *Theatre Translation Theory and Performance in Contemporary Japan: Native Voices, Foreign Bodies*, Manchester: St Jerome.

Dahl, R. (1982) *Revolting Rhymes*, London: Jonathan Cape.

Dale, L. and Gilbert, H. (1993) 'Looking the same: a preliminary (post-colonial) discussion of orientalism and occidentalism in Australia and Japan', *Yearbook of Comparative and General Literature Studies*, Vol. 41: 35–50.

de Francis, J. (1984) *The Chinese Language: Fact and Fantasy*, Honolulu: University of Hawai'i Press.

Delabatista, D. (ed.) (1997) *Traductio: Essays on Punning and Translation*, Manchester: St Jerome.

de Lotbiniere-Harwood, S. (1995) 'Geographies of why', in S. Simon (ed.) *Culture in Transit: Translating the Literature of Quebec*, Montreal: Vehicule Press.

Díaz Cintas, J. (2005) 'Back to the Future in Subtitling', in H. Gerzymisch-Arbogast and S. Nauert (eds) *MuTra 2005 – Challenges of Multidimensional Translation: Conference Proceedings*, Saarbrücken: Saarland University. Online. Available HTTP: <http://www.euroconferences.info/proceedings/2005_Proceedings/2005_DiazCintas_Jorge.pdf > (accessed 25 February 2013).

Díaz Cintas, J. and Remael, A. (2007) *Audiovisual Translation: Subtitling*, Manchester: St Jerome.

Edney, D. (1996) 'Translating (and not translating) in a Canadian context', in D. Johnston (ed.) *Stages of Translation*, Bath: Absolute Classics.

Espasa, E. (2000) 'Performability in translation: Speakability? Playability? Or just saleability?' in C. Upton, (ed.) *Moving Target: Theatre Translation and Cultural Relocation*, Manchester: St Jerome.

Evans, H. (1997) *Women and Sexuality in China*, Cambridge: Polity Press.

Federici, F. M. (2012) 'Silenced images: the case of Viva Zapatero!', in R. Wilson, and B. Maher (eds) *Words, Images and Performances in Translation*, London and New York: Continuum.

Fenton, J. (2012) *The Orphan of Zhao*, London: Faber and Faber.

Finnane, A. (2007) *Changing Clothes in China: Fashion, History, Nation*, London: Hurst.

Garfield, S. (2011) *Just My Type: A Book about Fonts*, London: Profile Books.

Garrett, V. M. (1987) *Traditional Chinese Clothing in Hong Kong and South China*, Oxford: Oxford University Press.

——(1994) *Chinese Clothing*, Oxford: Oxford University Press.

Genette, G. (1997) *Paratexts: Thresholds of Interpretation*, tr. Jane E. Lewin, Cambridge: Cambridge University Press.

Gernet, J. (1972/1999) *A History of Chinese Civilization*, Cambridge: Cambridge University Press.

Gil-Bardaji, A., Orero, P. and Rovira-Esteva, S. (eds) (2012) *Translation Peripheries: Paratextual Elements in Translation*, Bern: Peter Lang.

Gombrich, E. H. (1993) *The Story of Art*, London: Phaidon.

Gopinathan, G. (2006) 'Translation, transcreation and culture: theories of translation in Indian languages', in T. Hermans (ed.) *Translating Others Volume 1*, Manchester: St Jerome.

Gottlieb, H. (1995) 'Subtitling', in S. Chan and D. E. Pollard (eds) *An Encyclopaedia of Translation*, Hong Kong: The Chinese University Press.

——(1997) 'You got the picture? On the polysemiotics of subtitling wordplay', in D. Delabatista (ed.) *Traductio: Essays on Punning and Translation*, Manchester: St Jerome.

Grosenick, U. and Schübbe, C. H. (2007) *China Artbook*, Koln: DuMont Buchverlag.

Gunn, E. M. (1983) *Twentieth-Century Chinese Drama: An Anthology*, Bloomington: Indiana University Press.

Guo, Y. (2009) 'Theorizing the politics of translation in a global era: a Chinese perspective', in M. P. Y. Cheung (ed.) *Chinese Discourses on Translation: Positions and Perspectives,* Manchester: St Jerome.

Gutt, E. (1991) *Translation and Relevance: Cognition and Context*, Oxford: Blackwell.

——(2000) *Translation and Relevance: Cognition and Context*, Manchester: St Jerome.

Hale, T. and Upton, C. (2000) 'Introduction' in C. Upton, (ed.) *Moving Target: Theatre Translation and Cultural Relocation,* Manchester: St Jerome.

Harrison, H. (2003) 'Clothing and power on the periphery of empire: the costumes of the indigenous people of Taiwan', in T. M. Chen and P. Zamperini (eds) *Positions East Asia Cultures Critique: Special Issue Fabrications*, Vol. 11, No. 2, Fall: 331–60.

Headland, I. T. (1900) *Chinese Mother Goose Rhymes*, New York: Fleming H. Revell Company.

Hejzlar, J. (1980) *Chinese Watercolours*, London: Cathay Books.

Herdan, Innes (1972) *300 Tang Poems*, Taipei: Far East Book Company.

Hermans, T. (2003) 'Cross-cultural translation studies as thick translation', *Bulletin of the School of Oriental and African Studies*, Vol. 66, No. 3: 380–89.

——(ed.) (2006) *Translating Others Volume 1*, Manchester: St Jerome.

——(2007) *The Conference of the Tongues*, Manchester: St Jerome.

Holmes, J. S. (1994) *Translated! Papers on Literary Translation and Translation Studies*, Amsterdam: Rodopi.

Holton, B. (2010) 'Du Fu in Autumn: a poem and a provocation', in *Renditions,* Autumn, Hong Kong: Chinese University of Hong Kong Press.

Hong, J. (2011) 'The Manchu woman from head to toe: an overview of Qing dynasty fashion', in *Epoch Times* 8 November. Online. Available HTTP: <http://www.theepochtimes.com/n2/china-news/the-manchu-woman-from-head-to-toe-136694.html> (accessed 20 December 2012).

Hughes, R. (1991) *The Shock of the New: Art and the Century of Change*, London: Thames and Hudson.

Hung, E. and Pollard, D. (1998) 'The Chinese tradition', in M. Baker and G. Saldanha (eds) *The Routledge Encyclopedia of Translation Studies*, London and New York: Routledge.

Jin Di (1989) 'The great sage in literary translation: transformations for equivalent effect', *Babel*, Vol. 35, No. 3: 156–74.

Johnson, K. (1971) *Folksongs and Children's Songs from Peiping*, Taipei: publisher unknown.

Johnston, D. (ed.) (1996) *Stages of Translation*, Bath: Absolute Classics.

——(2000) 'Valle-Inclán: the meaning of form', in C. Upton (ed.) *Moving Target: Theatre Translation and Cultural Relocation*, Manchester: St Jerome.

——(2007) 'The cultural engagements of stage translation: Federico Garcia Lorca in performance', in G. Anderman (ed.) *Voices in Translation: Bridging Cultural Divides*, Clevedon: Multilingual Matters.

Jones, A. E. (2003) 'A Chronicle of Changing Clothes by Eileen Chang', translator's Introduction, in T. M. Chen and P. Zamperini (eds) *Positions East Asia Cultures Critique: Special Issue Fabrications*, Vol. 11, No. 2, Fall.

Jones, F. R. (2007) 'Unlocking the black box: researching poetry translation processes', in E. Loffredo and Perteghella M. (eds) *Translation and Creativity: Perspectives on Creative Writing and Translation Studies,* London: Continuum.

Joyce, J. (1972) *Ulysses*, Harmondsworth: Penguin.

Kingsolver, B. (1999/2007) *The Poisonwood Bible*, London: Faber and Faber.

Lakoff, G. and Johnson, M. (1980) *Metaphors We Live by*, Chicago: Chicago University Press.

Lefevere, A. (1975) *Translating Poetry: Seven Strategies and a Blueprint*, Amsterdam: Van Gorcum.

——(1992) *Translation, Rewriting and the Manipulation of Literary Fame*, London: Routledge.

——(1996) 'Translation and canon formation: nine decades of drama in the United States', in R. Alvarez, and M. Carmen-Africa Vidal (eds) *Translation, Power, Subversion*, Clevedon: Multilingual Matters.

Leppihalme, R. (1997) *Culture Bumps: An Empirical Approach to the Translation of Allusions*, Clevedon: Multilingual Matters.

Levy, D. J. (1988) *Chinese Narrative Poetry: The Late Han through T'ang Dynasties*, Durham and London, Duke University Press.

Li, W. H. (Rosanna Li) (2007) *Woman to Love – Man to Quit*, Hong Kong: MCCM Creations. (漫漫地尋雌雌地等)

Link, P. (2012) 'Does this writer deserve the prize?' *New York Review of Books*, reprinted in *The Guardian*, 17 November 2012.

Loffredo, E. and Perteghella, M. (2006) *Translation and Creativity: Perspectives on Creative Writing and Translation Studies*, London: Continuum.

Lu Xun (1927/1980) *Selected Works*, Vol. 2, tr. Yang Xianyi and Gladys Yang, Beijing: Foreign Languages Press.

Lyons, J. (1981) *Language and Linguistics*, Cambridge: Cambridge University Press.

Mao, S. (2009) 'Translating the other: discursive contradictions and new orientalism in contemporary advertising in China', in M. P. Y. Cheung (ed.) *Chinese Discourses on Translation: Positions and Perspectives*, Manchester: St Jerome.

Matthews, P. H. (1997) *Oxford Concise Dictionary of Linguistics*, Oxford: Oxford University Press.

Mayer Thurman, C. C. (2000) Introduction to *Clothed to Rule the Universe: Ming and Qing Dynasty Textiles at the Art Institute of Chicago*, Chicago: The Art Institute of Chicago.

McRae, E. (2012) 'The role of translators' prefaces to contemporary literary translations into English: an empirical study', in A. Gil-Bardaji, P. Orero, and S. Rovira-Esteva (eds) *Translation Peripheries: Paratextual Elements in Translation*, Bern: Peter Lang.

Meech, A. (2000) 'The irrepressible in pursuit of the impossible: translating the theatre of the GDR', in C. Upton, (ed.) *Moving Target: Theatre Translation and Cultural Relocation,* Manchester: St Jerome.

Munday, J. (2001) *Introducing Translation Studies,* Abingdon: Routledge.

Nida, E. A. (1964) *Toward a Science of Translating,* Leiden: Koninklijke Brill NV.

Nida, E. A. and Taber, C. R. (1969) *The Theory and Practice of Translation,* Leiden: Brill.

Nord, C. (1997/2001) *Translating as a Purposeful Activity: Functionalist Approaches Explained,* Manchester: St Jerome.

——(1988/1991) *Text Analysis in Translation: Theory, Methodology and Didactic Application of a Model for Translation-oriented Text Analysis,* tr. C. Nord and P. Sparrow, Amsterdam: Rodopi.

——(1991) 'Text analysis in translation training', in C. Dollerup, and A. Loddegaard (eds) (1992) *Teaching Translation and Interpreting: Training, Talent and Experience,* Papers from the first language international conference, Elsinore, Denmark, 1991, Amsterdam and Philadelphia: John Benjamins.

——(2000) 'Loyalty revisited: Bible translation as a case in point', *The Translator,* Vol. 7, No. 2: 195–202.

Opie, I. and Opie, P. (eds) (1951/1997) *The Oxford Dictionary of Nursery Rhymes,* Oxford: Oxford University Press.

Parkinson, D. (2012) *100 Ideas that Changed Film,* London: Laurence King Publishing.

Pellatt, V. (2007) *Chinese Numbers: the Social Substratum of the Development of Mathematical Thinking,* Lampeter: Mellen.

——(2010) 'How numbers in the discourse of Chinese nursery rhymes, though they are now romanticised in the meta-discourse, represent attitudes of social and sexual pressure on children, especially girls', paper presented at the Conference of the European Association of Chinese Studies, University of Latvia, July 2010.

Pellatt, V. and Liu, E. T. (2010) *Thinking Chinese Translation,* Abingdon: Routledge.

Pelsmaekers, K. and Van Besien, F. (2002) 'Subtitling irony: "Blackadder in Dutch"', in J. Vandaele (ed.) *The Translator: Studies in Intercultural Communication,* Vol. 8, No. 2: *Translating Humour,* Manchester: St Jerome.

Perteghella, M. (2004) 'A Descriptive-anthropological model of theatre translation', in S. Coelsch-Foisner and H. Klein (eds) *Drama Translation and Theatre Practice,* Frankfurt am Main: Peter Lang.

Pickowicz, P. G. (2007) 'Acting like revolutionaries: Shi Hui, the Wenhua Studio, and private-sector filmmaking, 1949–52', in J. Brown and P. G. Pickowicz (eds), *Dilemmas of Victory: The Early Years of the People's Republic of China,* Cambridge, MA: Harvard University Press.

Pinker, S. (1998) *How the Mind Works,* Harmondsworth: Allen Lane.

Pollard, D. (ed.) (1998) *Translation and Creation: Readings of Western Literature in Early Modern China,* Amsterdam: Benjamins.

Pul'ka (2010) *Peach Blossom Spring Rap,* unpublished.

Qu, L. L., (2004) *Chinese Calligraphy: Standard Script for Beginners,* London: The British Museum Press.

Rayner, K. and Pollatsek, A. (1989) *The Psychology of Reading,* Hillsdale NJ: Lawrence Erlbaum Associates.

Reischauer, J. K., Fairbank, E. O. and Craig, A. M., (1965) *East Asia: The Modern Transformation,* London: George Allen and Unwin.

Reiss, K. (1981/2000) 'Type, kind and individuality of text: decision making in translation', tr. S. Kitron, in L. Venuti (ed.) (2000) *The Translation Studies Reader*, London and New York: Routledge.

Reiss, K. and Vermeer, H. J. (1984/1991) *Grundlegung einer Allgemeinen Translationstheorie*, Linguistische Arbeiten 147, 2nd edn, Tübingen: Niemeyer.

Robinson, G. W. (1973) *Poems of Wang Wei*, Harmondsworth: Penguin Classics.

Rohsenow, J. S. (2002) *ABC Dictionary of Chinese Proverbs*, Honolulu: University of Hawai'i Press.

Rossabi, M. (1997) 'The silk trade in China and Central Asia', in J. C. Y. Watt and A. E. Wardell (eds) *When Silk was Gold: Central Asian and Chinese Textiles*, New York: Metropolitan Museum of Art.

Roy, Arundhati (2011) BBC Radio 4, *Bookclub*, 2 October.

Rozhin, S. K. (2000) 'Translating the untranslatable: Edward Redlinski's *Cud No Greenpoincie [Greenpoint Miracle]* in English', in C. Upton (ed.) *Moving Target: Theatre Translation and Cultural Relocation*, Manchester: St Jerome.

Said, E. W. (1978/2003) *Orientalism*, Harmondsworth: Penguin.

See, L. (2006) *Snow Flower and the Secret Fan*, London: Bloomsbury Publishers Plc.

Siddons, T. (2011) 'Flyte Club', *Scottish Field*, May.

Sieghart, W. (2011) *The Verb*, BBC Radio 3, 4 March.

Simon, S. (1996) *Gender in Translation*, London: Routledge.

Simon, W. (1944/67) *How to Study and Write Chinese Characters*, London: Lund Humphries.

Song, B. (1999) 'May Fourth Movement and the formation of modern Chinese drama', in B. Tian (ed.) *Modern Chinese Drama*, Beijing: Culture and Art Publishing House.

Spence, J. (1990) *The Search for Modern China*, London: Hutchinson.

Sperber, D. and Wilson, D. (1986) *Relevance: Communication and Cognition*, Oxford: Blackwell.

Stalling, J. (2011) *Yingelishi: Sinophonic English Poetry and Poetics*, Denver: Counterpath.

Stibbe, M. (November 30, 2009) *Translation vs. Transcreation*. Online. Available HTTP: <http://www.badlanguage.net/translation-vs-transcreation> (accessed 16 March 2010).

Tan, Z. (2009) 'The "Chineseness" vs. "non-Chineseness" of Chinese translation theory: an ethnoconvergent perspective', in M. P. Y. Cheung (ed.) *Chinese Discourses on Translation: Positions and Perspectives*, Manchester: St Jerome.

Taylor, I. and Taylor, M. M. (1995) *Writing and Literacy in Chinese, Korean and Japanese*, Amsterdam: Benjamins.

This is Money.co.uk (11 July 2007). Online. Available HTTP: <http://www.thisismoney.co.uk/money/markets/article-1611920/China-trade-barriers-cost-Europe-13bn.html> (accessed 9 December 2011).

Thorpe, A. (2011) 'A vast puzzle', *The Guardian Review*, 22 November.

Tian, B. (1999) (ed.) *Modern Chinese Drama*, Beijing: Culture and Art Publishing House.

Tophat (n.d.) Online. Available HTTP: <http://www.goldtophat.com/eculture.asp> (accessed 17 July 2011).

Toury, G. (1995) *Descriptive Translation Studies – and Beyond*, Amsterdam and Philadelphia: John Benjamins

Travel China Guide (n.d.) Online. Available HTTP: <http://www.travelchinaguide.com/attraction/shaanxi/xian/stone_stele/> (accessed 23 November 2012).

Turton, M. (2008) Online. Available HTTP: <http://michaelturton.blogspot.com/2008/12/ma-government-seeks-world-heritage.html> (accessed 5 August 2012).

Tymoczko, M. (2007) *Enlarging Translation: Empowering Translators*, Manchester: St Jerome.

Tzeng, O. J. L. and Hung, D. L. (eds) (1981) *Perception of Print: Reading Research in Experimental Psychology*, Hillsdale, NJ: Lawrence Erlbaum Associates.

UNESCO (2003) *Text of the Convention for the Safeguarding of Intangible Cultural Heritage*. Online. Available HTTP: <http://www.unesco.org/culture/ich/index.php?pg=00006> (accessed 5 August 2012).

Upton, C. (ed.) (2000) *Moving Target: Theatre Translation and Cultural Relocation*, Manchester: St Jerome.

Vacche, A. D. (ed.) (2002) *The Visual Turn: Classical Film Theory and Art History*, New Brunswick, NJ: Rutgers University Press.

Vandaele, J. (ed.) (2002) *The Translator: Studies in Intercultural Communication* Vol. 8, No. 2: *Translating Humour*, Manchester: St Jerome.

Venuti, L. (1995) *The Translator's Invisibility: A History of Translation*, London: Routledge.

——(ed.) (2000) *The Translation Studies Reader*, London and New York: Routledge.

Vermeer, H. J. (1989) 'Skopos and commission in translational action', in L. Venuti (ed.) (2000) *The Translation Studies Reader*, London and New York: Routledge.

Von Spee, C. (2012) *Modern Chinese Ink Paintings*, London: British Museum Press.

Waley, A. (1961) *Chinese Poems*, London: Unwin Books.

Watt, J. C. Y. and Wardell, A. E. (eds) (1997) *When Silk was Gold: Central Asian and Chinese Textiles*, New York: Metropolitan Museum of Art.

Weinberger, E. (1987) *Nineteen Ways of Looking at Wang Wei*, Wakefield: Moyer Bell.

Williams, J. and Chesterman, A. (2002) *The Map: A Beginner's Guide to Doing Research in Translation Studies*, Manchester: St Jerome.

Wilson, R. and Maher, B. (eds) (2012) *Words, Images and Performances in Translation*, London: Continuum.

Wilson, V. (2001) *Chinese Dress*, London: Victoria and Albert Museum.

Wu, Y. (1990) *The Techniques of Chinese Painting*, London: The Herbert Press.

——(1996) *The Techniques of Chinese Painting*, London: The Herbert Press.

Xing, J. Z. (2006) *Teaching and Learning Chinese as a Foreign Language: a Pedagogical Grammar*, Hong Kong: Hong Kong University Press.

Xinran (2008) *China Witness*, tr. Julia Lovell, London: Random House.

Xu, Y., Loh, B. and Wu, J. (eds) (1987/1992) *300 Tang Poems: a New Translation*, Taipei: Bookman Books

Yang, L. (2005) *Concentric Circles*, tr. B. Holton, and A. H.-C. Chan, High Green: Bloodaxe.

Yen, Y. (2005) *Calligraphy and Power in Contemporary China*, Abingdon: Routledge.

Yu, P. (1980) *The Poetry of Wang Wei: New Translations and Commentary*, Bloomington: Indiana University Press.

Zamperini, P. (2003) 'In their dress they wore a body: fashion and identity in late Qing Shanghai', in T. M. Chen and P. Zamperini (eds) *Positions East Asia Cultures Critique: Special Issue Fabrications*, Vol. 11, No. 2, Fall: 301–33.

Zheng, D. (2004) 'Foreword', in Chiang Yee (1937/2004) *The Silent Traveller in Lakeland*, Edinburgh: Mercat Press.

Chinese language references

Baidu 韦诞 Wei Dan (2013) Online. Available HTTP: <http://baike.baidu.com/view/231535.htm> (accessed 14 February 2013).

Baidu (n.d.) 'Women's writing' (Nüshu 女书), available HTTP: <http://baike.baidu.com/view/32675.htm#1> (accessed 26 October 2012).

曹禺，《经典戏剧选集》，北京，新华出版社 2010 年. Cao Yu (2010) *Selected Drama Classics*, Beijing: Xinhua Publishing House.

陈萱，《失落的价值》，Chen, X. (2010) 'Lost Values', Online. Available HTTP: <http://blog.sina.com.cn/s/blog_49b2fed20100w3s7.html> (accessed 1 October 2012).

陈洙龙，(2003)　《张大千》北京，中国人民大学出版社，Chen, Z. (2003) *Zhang Daqian*, Beijing: Chinese People's University Publishing House.

程季华、邢祖文、李少白编着 (1980)，中国电影发展史，北京：中国电影出版社。Cheng J., Xing, Z. and Lee, S. (1980) *History of Chinese Movies*, Beijing: China Film Press.

高格《细说中国服饰》，北京，光明日报 2005 年. Gao, G. (2005) *A Detailed Discussion of Chinese Costume*, Beijing: Guangming Daily.

宫哲兵，（编）(2001) 女書，台北，婦女新知基金會出版部. Gong, Z. (ed.) (2001) *Women's Writing*, Taipei: Awakening Foundation Publications.

何懷碩, (2001)《序》齊白石——中國傳統繪畫最後的高峰，齊白石，白石老人自述。He Huaishuo, 'Qi Baishi – the Last High Point of Chinese Traditional Painting', Preface to Qi Baishi 2001/2003.

Hong Kong Museum of History (2010)《歷久常新：旗袍的變奏》*The Evergreen Classic: Transformation of the Qipao*, exhibition brochure.

心培和尚　（編）《歡喜抄經》，台北，香海文化出版事業有限公司 2008 年. Monk Hsin Pei (ed.) (2008) *How to Copy Sutras and Enjoy it*, tr. Shi Man-He, Yvonne Tan, Chi Gong-Sheng (Jason Chi), Taipei: Xianghua Publishing Company.

华梅《中国服饰》，于红，张蕾译，北京：五洲传播出版 2004 年. Hua, M. (2004) *Chinese Clothing*, tr. Yu and Zhang, Bejing: China Intercontinental Press.

黄耀樞 （編）《柳公權書法入門：寫字練習冊》，九龍，匯豐圖書公司. Huang, Y. (n.d.) (ed.) *Liu Gongquan's Calligraphy Style: Getting Started*, Hong Kong: Hui Feng Company Ltd.

Huaxia (2013) 華夏經緯, Online. Available HTTP: <http://big5.huaxia.com/ly/fsdl/00265806.html> (accessed 31 May 2013).

互动百科，牛李党争. Hudong (n.d.) 'The Niu-Li factional struggles', Online. Available HTTP: <http://www.hudong.com/wiki/%E7%89%9B%E6%9D%8E%E5%85%9A%E4%BA%89> (accessed 28 August 2012).

鳳凰網《铁凝王蒙等百名文艺家手抄毛泽东延安文艺座谈会讲话》Ifeng (2012) 100 authors and artists including Tie Ning and Wang Meng copy Mao Zedong's talks at the Yanan Forum on Literature and Art. Online. Available HTTP: <http://news.ifeng.com/mainland/detail_2012_05/28/14869452_0.shtml> (accessed 23 November 2012).

老舍 (1947) 我這一輩子，上海：惠群出版社. Lao, S. (1947) *This Life of Mine*, Shanghai: Huichun Publishing.

李今 (2005)，海派小說論，台灣：秀威資訊科技. Lee, J. (2005) *On Shanghai-Style Novels*, Taipei: Showwe Information.

李道明 (2001)，驀然回首－台灣電影一百年，歷史月刊158刊3)，41–51。Lee, T. (2001) 'A Hundred Years of Taiwan Cinema', *Historical Monthly*, no. 158 (3): 41–51.

雷僑雲，《中國兒童文學教育理論與輔導教學》，高雄，高雄復文圖書出版社 2002 年. Lei, R.-Y. (2002) *Chinese Children's Literary Education Theory and Tutorial Pedagogy*, Kaohsiung: Kaohsiung Fuwen Books Publishing Company.

李静，以奥运之名，《世界时装之苑》，2008 三月号. Li Jing (2008) 'In the Name of Olympic' in *Elle*, Chinese edition, March 2008, 74.

廖潔連《一九四九年後中國字體設計人》香港 2009 年. MCCM Creations: Liao, J. (2009) *Chinese Font Designers after 1949*, Hong Kong: MCCM Creations.

劉經菴，歌謠與婦女，《歌謠周刊》1925 年. Liu, J. (1925) 'Songs, rhymes and women', in *Songs and Rhymes Weekly*, cited in Zhu (1977).

鲁迅《经典作品选》，北京，当代世界出版社 2002 年. Lu Xun (2002) *Selected Works*, Beijing: Contemporary World Publishers.

马六明：男男女女裸体艺术不尴尬 http://www.sina.com.cn 2011年 01 月 09 日 11:20 四川新闻网-成都商报. Ma, L. (9 January 2011) 'Men and women artists are not embarrassed by naked bodies', Sichuan Newsnet, Chengdu Report. Online. Available HTTP: <http://www.sina.com.cn> (accessed 12 October 2012).

马祖培培 (1996) 中国儿谣，北京，中国妇女出版社。Ma, Zupei (ed.) (1996) *Chinese Children's Rhymes*, Beijing: Chinese Women's Publishing House.

Max (2009), 馬英九推「識正書簡」中國大陸已先實施. 'Ma Yingjiu promotes reading traditional and writing simplified and mainland China have already implemented it', Online. Available HTTP: <http://max.oos.tw/?p=108> (accessed 5 August 2012).

《怎樣寫新魏書》上海，上海书局出版社 1974 年. *How to Write in the New Wei Style*, (1974) Shanghai: Shanghai Book Publishers.

Oldbeijing (2013) 老北京网 Online. Available HTTP: <http://cn.obj.cc/article-11462-1.html> (accessed 31 May 2013).

鳳凰衛視，台推動繁體字列世界文化遺產 稱可爭取兩岸合作 Phoenixtv (2012) 'Taiwan proposes traditional Chinese characters as World Cultural Heritage; co-operation on both sides of the Strait', http://news.sina.com 2008 年 12 月30 日 00:22, Online. Available HTTP: <http://news.sina.com/tw/phoenixtv/101-102-101-103/2008-12-30/00223529079.html> (accessed 5 August 2012).

齊白石 《白石老人自述》，臺北，城邦 2001 年. Qi, Baishi (2001) *Old Baishi's Autobiography*, Taipei: Cite.

新儿歌童谣选，选 (1964) 上海，少 儿童出版社. *A Selection of New Children's Songs and Nursery Rhymes* (1964) Shanghai: Children's Publishing House.

邵亦：識正絕不書簡 台灣就愛正體字. 本文轉自第 127 期《新紀元週刊》Shao, Y. (2009) 'Read traditional, but don't write simplified: Taiwan loves traditional characters', *Epoch Times* 127, 3 July 2009. Online. Available HTTP: <http://www.epochtimes.com/b5/9/7/31/n2608415.htm> (accessed 16 November 2012).

圣野、吴少山，《儿歌三百首》，杭州，浙江少年儿童出版发行 1999 年. Sheng, Y. and Wu, S. (eds) (1999) *300 Children's Rhymes*, Hangzhou: Zhejiang Youth and Children's Publishing Company.

舒晓鸣 (2003 中国艺术史上的一大损失 – 沈寂谈石挥，北京电影学院学报，2003，3)，74–78，北京：北京电影学院. Shu, X. (2003) 'A great loss in the Chinese art history – Shen Ji's view on Shi Hui', *Journal of Beijing Film Academy*, (3), 74–78. Beijing: Beijing Film Academy.

宋强／乔边 等，《中国可以说不：冷战后时代的政治与情感抉择》，北京，中华工商联合出版社 1996 年. Song, Q. and Qiao, B. (1996) *China Can Say No: Political and Emotional Choices in the Post-Cold War Era*, Beijing: The China Industrial and Commercial Joint Publishing House.

孙献韬、李多钰主编 (2006) 中国电影百年，北京：中国广播电视出版社. Sun, X. and Lee, D. (2006) *100 Years of Chinese Film*, Beijing: China Radio & Television Publishing House.

陶方宣，《霓裳. 张爱玲》香港三联书店有限公司 2009 年. Tao, F. (2009) *Clothes and Zhang Ailing*, Hong Kong: Sanlian Bookshop Ltd.

王蒙，买买提处长轶事—维吾尔人的 "黑色幽默"，《王蒙小说报告文学选》，北京出版社 1981 年. Wang Meng (1981) 'The story of Section Chief Maimaiti: the black humour of the Uighur People', in *Wang Meng Selected Fiction*, Beijing: Beijing Publishers.

道是平淡，却见浓艳 – 吴冠中访谈录文稿. Wu Guanzhong (2007) *The Plain Way to Rich Colours*, transcript of interview. Online. Available HTTP: <http://mrmdm.blog.ifeng.com/article/666794.html> (accessed 15 June 2012).

阎连科《为人民服务》香港文化艺术出版社，2005 年. Yan Lianke (2007) *Serve the People*, tr. Julia Lovell, Melbourne: The Text Publishing Company.

阎连科《风雅颂》南京江苏人民出版社 2008 年. Yan Lianke (2008) *The Ode to Elegance*, Nanjing: Jiangsu People's Publishing House.

尹世霖（编）(2007) 名家儿歌，乌鲁木齐，新疆青少年出版社。Yin S. (ed.) (2007) *Children's Rhymes by Well-known Writers*, Urumchi: Xinjiang Children's and Young People's Publishing House.

袁洲 (2008) 主流意识形态下的平民史诗 – 浅析石挥电影《我这一辈子》，电影评介，2008，16)，南京：南京师范大学.Yuan, Z. (2008) 'Civilian epics under the influence of mainstreaming ideology – on Shi Hui's film "This Life of Mine"', *Film Review* 2008(16). Nanjing: Nanjing Normal University.

張羽羽 (2007) 台湾都市文学与海派文学，台湾研究集刊 (2007, 1)，厦门：厦门大学台湾研究院台灣研究集刊編委會. Zhang, Y. (2007) 'On urban literature and Shanghai-style literature of Taiwan', *Taiwan Research Quarterly*, 2007(1): 2–8.

中国文化网 (2013)，国庆六十周年——铭记共和国的文化足迹 (1949–2009)，新中国电影的对外交流，北京：中华人民共和国文化部外联局. Wen Yi (文一) (ed.) Online. Available HTTP: http://www.chinaculture.org/focus/2009-09/01/content_345671.htm China Culture (2013), 'New China's film exchanges with the outside world, the 60th anniversary of the People's Republic of China (1949–2009)', Beijing: Ministry of Culture, P.R.C., http://www.chinaculture.org/focus/2009-09/16/content_349223.htm (accessed 01 March 2013).

鄭至慧 出版緣起 (1990)《女書結下好情意，萬里如花來公園》，宮哲兵，女書. Zheng Zhihui (1990) The Origin of the Publication: Women's Writing is developing goodwill: blossoming near and far in the public eye. Introduction to Gong 2001.

朱介凡 （编）(1977) 中國兒歌，臺北，純文學出版社有限公司. Zhu, J. F. (ed.) (1977) *Chinese Children's Rhymes*, Taipei: Pure Literature Publishing Ltd.

Films

《我這一輩子》 (This Life of Mine) (1950), 石挥 (Shi Hui), 中國. Online. Available HTTP: http://archive.org/details/this_life_of_mine (accessed 25 February, 2013).

《巨獸》(Once upon a Time in Kinmen) (2011), 施君涵 (Chun-Han Shih), 台灣, DVD.

《英雄》 (Hero) (2002), 张艺谋 (Zhang Yimou), 中國, DVD.

《东方红》 (The East is Red) (1964), 王苹 (Wang Ping) Online. Available HTTP: http://archive.org/details/The_East_is_Red, (accessed 25 February, 2013).

《鐵扇公主》 (Princess Iron Fan) (1941), 万籁鸣 (Wan Laiming) 和万古蟾 (Wan Guchan), 中國, Online. Available HTTP: http://archive.org/details/Princess_Iron _Fan_1941_divx5_denoised, (accessed 25 February, 2013).

《海角七號》 (Cape No. 7) (2008), 魏德聖 (Wei Te-She), 台灣, DVD.

徐童的紀錄片拍攝介紹 (A Film Narrative about Xu Tong), Beijing Independent Film Festival Newcastle Tour, 2012.

导演范俭谈纪录片《活着》(Director Fan Jian on his documentary The Next Life), Beijing Independent Film Festival Newcastle Tour, 2012.

《悲情城市》 (A City of Sadness) (1989), 侯孝賢 (Hou Hsiao-Hsien), 台灣, DVD.

《囍宴》 (The Wedding Banquet) (1993), 李安 (Lee Ang), 台灣, DVD.

Index